P9-DBY-252

the food

processor

bible

norene gilletz

whitecap

Copyright © 2002 by Norene Gilletz
Copyright © 1994 by Norene Gilletz
Copyright © 1979 by Norene Gilletz
This revised edition is printed by arrangement with Norene Gilletz. Portions of this book have previously been published under the titles *The Pleasures of Your Food Processor* and *The Pleasures of Your Processor.*

This special edition printed in 2004.

All rights reserved. No part of this publication may be reproduced, stored in a retrieval system, or transmitted in any form or by any means, electronic, mechanical, photocopying, recording or otherwise, without prior written consent of the publisher.

The information contained in this book is not intended to replace your food processor manual or the manufacturer's recommendations. The author and publisher disclaim any and all liability incurred in connection with the use of information and recipes in *The Food Processor Bible*. For additional information, please contact Whitecap Books Ltd. 351 Lynn Avenue, North Vancouver, British Columbia, Canada, V7J 2C4.

www.whitecap.ca

Edited by Alison Maclean
Copy edited by Elaine Jones
Proofread by Lesley Cameron
Cover design by Tanya Lloyd
Front cover photograph courtesy of Cuisinart
Back cover photograph by Lawrence Clemen Photography
Interior design by Tanya Lloyd and Jacqui Thomas
Printed and bound in Canada

NATIONAL LIBRARY OF CANADA CATALOGUING IN PUBLICATION DATA
Gilletz, Norene.
    The food processor bible

    Previously published as: The pleasures of your food processor.
    Includes index.
    ISBN 1-55285-211-3

    1. Food processor cookery. I. Gilletz, Norene. Pleasures of your food processor. II. Title
    TX840.F6G57 2001   641.5'89   C2001-910985-7

The publisher acknowledges the support of the Canada Council and the Cultural Services Branch of the Government of British Columbia in making this publication possible. We acknowledge the financial support of the Government of Canada through the Book Publishing Industry Development Program for our publishing activities.

contents

This book is dedicated with love to my dear friend and assistant Elaine Kaplan, for there would be no book without her dedication, commitment and nagging!

using your food processor

No matter which brand or model of food processor you own, this cookbook will help you make the most of this indispensable kitchen appliance and give you the power to be a processor-pro!

Food processors come in a variety of sizes, shapes and colors. Your little "kitchen magician" takes up less than a square foot of counter space, but it can replace many appliances and utensils: an electric mixer, blender, bread machine, meat grinder, grater, garlic press, parsley chopper, chef's knife, cheese mill, pastry blender, whisk, food mill, peanut butter maker and nut chopper. The food processor requires almost no maintenance. Blades can be changed in a snap and they stay sharp indefinitely.

The speed at which different foods are chopped, minced, puréed, blended or kneaded can vary from model to model because of differences in horse-power and blades.

Read your manual thoroughly to become familiar with your machine, its basic and optional parts, as well as its particular strengths and weaknesses. The hints and tips in this book are not intended to replace your manual.

basic processor parts

The following components are found on most brands of food processors:

Base: The motor is housed inside the base. Some models have stronger motors than others. Better-quality machines have an automatic temperature-controlled circuit breaker in their motor to protect against burnout when processing heavy batters or doughs. Some models feature built-in cord storage. The controls to turn your processor on and off are usually located on the base.

On/Off Controls: The first food processors were turned on by twisting the cover in one direction, then turned off by twisting in the opposite direction. Subsequent models from different manufacturers came with levers, buttons or dials to operate the machine. The pulse control was added to help prevent overprocessing. Some models have multiple speeds. The newest generation of food processors features an electronic touchpad as well as a heavy-duty dough cycle (e.g., Cuisinart DLC-2014).

Work Bowl: The most popular models have a capacity of 7, 11 or 14 cups. There are smaller and larger models available, ranging from 22 ounces up to 20 cups. The majority of recipes in this book can be made in a standard (7 cup) food processor, but a larger bowl is definitely an advantage. The work bowl on better quality models is shatter-resistant and heat-resistant. It should not be used in the microwave oven.

Cover/Feed Tube: The cover has a vertical feed tube which is located either in the front or the back. Food is put through the feed tube when slicing or grating, or when adding ingredients while the machine is running.

The original food processors were made with a standard feed tube. This type of feed tube is still available on many models (e.g., Kitchen Aid) and is very simple to use. However, food must be cut or trimmed to fit the feed tube, which has a capacity of about 1 cup.

The expanded feed tube came next, eliminating much of the trimming needed when slicing or grating whole fruits and vegetables. The pusher of the expanded feed tube houses a small feed tube for smaller fruits and vegetables (e.g., carrots, strawberries) or to add ingredients while the machine is running (e.g., garlic, liquid).

The newest generation of food processors features a wide mouth/expanded feed tube. It has been completely redesigned and is 2½ times the size of the standard feed tube. You can process batch after batch of food easily and quickly, shortening preparation time. I love the new design and find it simple to operate. It is a terrific time-saver when slicing or grating large quantities. Don't fill the feed tube above the maximum fill-line or the machine will not start.

An optional **compact cover** is available on some models. It is used with the **Steel Blade** for chopping and baking. It cannot be used when slicing or grating. The compact cover is very easy to clean.

Pusher/Pusher Assembly: This guides food through the feed tube. It also prevents splashing when working with liquids.

The standard feed tube comes with a one-piece pusher. On some models, there are measurements marked on the pusher (1 cup capacity).

The expanded feed tube has a two-piece pusher assembly.

- A large oval pusher fits into the expanded feed tube. The pusher comes in contact with an activating rod in the center of the handle, causing the motor to start.
- A small pusher fits into a center-located small feed tube. It is used for narrow fruits and vegetables and for adding ingredients. Although the pusher-assembly sounds complicated, it is very easy to use!

Steel Blade: This is the most useful blade of all. It is often referred to as the multi-purpose blade and performs about 95% of the tasks (see p. 10). Some models come with a **Plastic Mixing Blade** or **Plastic Dough Blade.** The new **Metal Dough Blade** works with the Dough Cycle to knead bread dough without overheating.

Slicer, Grater/Shredder: Other basic blades include a medium **Slicer** (p. 11) and a medium **Grater/Shredder** (p. 11). There are optional blades available to make thinner or thicker slices and shreds. Some models come with detachable stem(s) for compact storage. Some blades are reversible.

Mini Machines: Some models come with a chute attachment which allows you to continually slice and grate large quantities, even though the bowl capacity is only 3 cups. There is also a new mini-prep processor that can grind and chop. It can grind hard foods like spices, coffee beans, nuts and seeds. It can also chop onions, mince garlic and herbs, make baby food, dips and sauces. However, this powerful, compact processor doesn't slice or shred foods.

Mini-Bowl/Mini-Blade: In addition to the regular work bowl, some models feature a mini-bowl and mini-blade (e.g., Kitchen Aid). The mini-bowl is used for small chopping or mixing tasks (e.g., chopping fresh herbs, mincing garlic, blending salad dressings). The mini-bowl can process up to 1 cup of liquid or ½ cup solids.

Maxi-Machines: These come with a heavy-duty motor and a work bowl with a capacity of 20 cups. They are very powerful and are ideal for catering and restaurant use.

safety tips

Read your manual thoroughly and follow the manufacturer's safety recommendations.

The blades are very sharp, so store them in a safe place, preferably in a blade holder or storage container. Keep them out of the reach of children. Don't store blades in a drawer where you may reach in blindly and cut yourself. Handle blades with care, especially if you are rushed or distracted. Hold the **Steel Blade** by the hub, not by the blades.

If the **Slicer** or **Grater** has a detachable stem, place the disc upside-down on a flat surface before connecting the stem. (Refer to your manual for proper assembly instructions.)

Never put the blade on the motor shaft unless the bowl is locked in place. Then push the blade all the way down as far as it will go.

Always insert the **Steel Blade** in the bowl before adding ingredients.

Use the pusher to guide food through the feed tube when slicing or grating. Don't put your fingers or any kitchen utensil in the feed tube while the machine is running.

Wait until the blades stop spinning completely before removing the cover or pusher. Never use your fingers, a spatula or any other kitchen utensil to try and stop the blades.

If a piece of food becomes wedged between the bowl and blade, turn off the machine immediately, unplug it, then carefully remove the blade and trapped food.

Be careful that the **Steel Blade** does not fall out of the bowl when emptying it. Either remove the blade, or hold it in place with your finger or a spatula when you tip the bowl to empty it.

If the motor begins to labor (e.g., when mixing heavy, sticky doughs) turn off the machine immediately to protect the motor. If the motor stops because of overheating, wait for it to cool down before continuing. It usually takes 10 to 15 minutes.

Always make sure the machine has been turned off when you are finished using the processor. Models with electronic touchpad controls have an indicator light that will glow until you touch the OFF button.

Always store the processor with the work bowl and cover in the unlocked position when it is not in use to prevent damage to the spring mechanism.

Don't let the cord touch hot surfaces or hang over the edge of a counter or table where it can be pulled down accidentally.

quick clean-ups

Plan ahead to keep clean-ups to a minimum. Process dry or hard foods first (e.g., nuts, cheese, chocolate), then process wet foods. Use paper towels to wipe out the bowl between steps.

To clean the **Steel Blade** quickly, empty the contents of the bowl. Return the bowl and blade to the base of the machine, replace the cover, then turn on the processor. The blade will spin itself clean in seconds!

To avoid "ring around the counter," turn the cover upside-down before placing it on your counter. Place the blade on top of the inverted cover.

Rinse the bowl, cover and blades immediately after use. A bottle brush or dish brush simplifies clean-up.

Make sure that the bowl, cover and blades are dishwasher-safe—check your manual. Load them away from exposed heating elements in the dishwasher. Be careful not to cut yourself on the sharp blades and discs when loading and unloading the dishwasher or when washing by hand.

Never let the blades soak in soapy water. You can accidentally cut yourself by reaching in blindly. When washing by hand, don't use abrasive cleansers or scouring pads. They can scratch or cloud the bowl and cover. Use a dish brush to clean the bowl and blades. A cotton swab will remove sticky dough or batter from the hole on the underside of the **Steel Blade**, or from the underside of the rim of the slicing or shredding disc.

Wipe up spills on the base or cord quickly with a clean, damp cloth. Never immerse the base in liquid as there is a danger of electric shock. Unplug the processor before cleaning.

To prevent the bowl from developing an odor (especially from strong-smelling foods like onions or garlic), leave the bowl uncovered and exposed to air after washing. Also, don't store the pusher in the feed tube when the machine is not in use.

To prevent food poisoning, any processor parts that come in contact with raw or cooked foods must be sanitized. Experts recommend washing all parts with hot soapy water for at least 20 seconds. You can sanitize the bowl, blades and pusher (even your sponge and dish brush) in the dishwasher. Also clean all preparation areas and utensils thoroughly (e.g., cutting boards, counters, knives). And always wash your hands thoroughly with soap and water before handling food!

blades and how to use them

Steel Blade

This is the "do-almost-everything" blade. If you are not slicing or grating, then you are probably using the **Steel Blade**. See Smart Chart (p. 18) for techniques on processing specific foods.

Use the **Steel Blade** to chop foods, using quick on/off pulses. You can also mince, grind, purée, emulsify, mix, blend, knead and whip by letting the machine run until the desired results are achieved. You can control the exact consistency you want, from coarse to fine, even to a purée.

This multi-purpose blade is used for cake batters, frostings, pastries, crumb crusts, cookies, yeast doughs, muffins and quick breads. It will mix up crêpe batters, salad dressings, dips, mayonnaise, sauces and baby foods. It can grind raw or cooked meat, fish and poultry, make peanut butter, mince garlic, parsley and herbs, grate Parmesan cheese, make bread crumbs, chop, mince or purée raw or cooked fruits and vegetables. What a versatile appliance!

Some manufacturers don't recommend grinding hard spices, grains or coffee beans. Always follow the guidelines in your manual. Potatoes are better when mashed with a potato masher, electric mixer or food mill. Cooked potatoes develop a sticky, gluey texture when processed on the **Steel Blade**. The immersion blender is often easier to use when puréeing soups and sauces. For light, fluffy whipped cream with maximum volume, use an electric mixer. Processor whipped cream is lower in volume, but is perfect for garnishing as it holds its shape. A blender is better for chopping ice and liquefying solid foods.

Food may be added directly to the work bowl or through the feed tube. Food placed directly in the bowl should be evenly distributed around the blade. Small or very hard food (e.g., garlic) should be dropped in through the feed tube while the machine is running. It will be drawn into the centrifuge produced by the whirling blades. The food is then flung outwards once it has been processed. Very hard food (e.g., chocolate, nuts) makes a loud noise at first, so don't be alarmed.

Quick on/off pulses will help you control texture and prevent overprocessing. Practice this basic technique a few times without any food in the bowl until you feel confident. It won't take very long to master this essential technique.

Let your eye be your guide. Times given for processing are only estimates.

Each person counts differently, or turns the machine on and off at a different rate. Times also vary according to texture, temperature and size of food being processed.

Check frequently to prevent overprocessing. There is no harm in starting and stopping the machine several times. For a finer chop, press and release the pulse button until the desired texture is reached. Onions, zucchini, bell peppers and other foods with a high water content will quickly become puréed if overprocessed.

For uniform chopping, cut the foods being processed into chunks that are the same size, 1 to 1½ inches. Instead of using a ruler, here is a quick way to measure. Make a circle with your thumb and index finger. The food should not be larger in diameter than the circle.

When chopping, process in batches for best results (see p. 6, p. 13 and p. 14 for recommended capacity of work bowl). If you take shortcuts and overload the processor bowl, you may end up with mush! When chopping or mincing, make sure the bowl, blade and food are dry.

Mincing takes 6 to 8 seconds, mixing cake batters takes 1½ to 2 minutes and kneading yeast doughs takes less than a minute. You may have to stop the processor once or twice to scrape down the sides of the bowl with a rubber spatula.

For smoother purées, process the solids first, then slowly add liquid through the feed tube while the machine is running. Scrape down the sides of the bowl as needed. Excellent for baby food.

You can "grate" foods on the **Steel Blade** when appearance is not important (e.g., cheese for sauces, vegetables for soups). Parmesan cheese can also be "grated" on the **Steel Blade.**

Grater and Slicer (Medium Shredding Disc, Medium Slicer)

See Smart Chart (p. 18) for techniques on grating and slicing specific foods.

Use the **Grater/Shredding Disc** for grating/shredding firm cheeses, raw vegetables (e.g., potatoes, carrots, zucchini), chocolate or nuts.

Use the **Slicer** for slicing vegetables, fruits, chilled meats or firm cheeses.

Some processors come with a **Detachable Stem** that fits the **Grater** and **Slicer.** Fit the stem onto the desired disc, making sure it is locked into place. (Refer to your manual for assembly instructions.) Place the bowl on the base, then insert the blade. Fit the stem of the blade onto the center post of the processor, pushing it all the way down. Then place the cover on the bowl.

Cut food to fit the feed tube. Cut the bottom ends flat so that food lies stable on the disc. Remove any large hard pits and seeds from fruits before processing; peel if desired.

Food should be as large as possible before placing it in the feed tube. Measure the food against the length and width of the pusher as a convenient guide to size. Cut large foods, such as eggplant or cabbage, into wedges. Some recipes will tell you to cut the food in 1-inch pieces, chunks or halves. Place food in the feed tube (either horizontally or vertically) to within 1 inch from the top. Food should fit the feed tube snugly, but not so snugly that the pusher can't move.

Use the pusher to guide food through the feed tube. Adjust pressure according to the texture of the food being processed. Use light pressure for soft foods (e.g., bananas and mushrooms). Use medium pressure for most foods (e.g., apples, potatoes, zucchini). Use firm pressure for harder foods (e.g., turnips, sweet potatoes, partially frozen meats or poultry). Never process any food that is so hard or firmly frozen that it can't be pierced with the point of a sharp knife.

For maximum control, keep the palm of your hand flat on the top of the pusher. Empty the work bowl as often as needed.

For small round slices or short shreds (e.g., carrots, zucchini), cut food to fit feed tube vertically.

For long slices or shreds (e.g., potatoes), cut food to fit feed tube horizontally.

For very thin slices or fine shreds, let foods "self-feed" (i.e., use almost no pressure on the pusher). When slicing or grating hard foods, use either light, medium or firm pressure, depending on the texture desired. Be careful when processing soft or delicate foods (e.g., kiwis) to avoid crushing them.

For diagonal slices, use the standard or small feed tube. Place one or two pieces of food on an angle in the feed tube. Slice, using medium pressure. Ideal for stir-fries (e.g., celery, zucchini).

Combine foods if you don't have enough of one, making a tighter fit (e.g., pack green onions in the indentation of celery stalks). The small feed tube is handy for small quantities.

If foods are narrow at one end (e.g., carrots), pack them in pairs, alternating one narrow end up, one wide end up.

Small quantities of long, narrow foods (e.g., 2 carrots) can be packed into a standard feed tube more securely if you cut them in half to make 4 shorter pieces.

To slice leafy vegetables (e.g., spinach), pile the leaves in a stack, then roll them up into a cylinder. Insert the cylinder upright in the feed tube and slice, using light pressure.

The expanded feed tube on the new generation of food processors has been redesigned for greater ease when slicing or grating. It's very easy to process consecutive batches of food in minutes. Reload the feed tube with one hand and press down on the pusher with your other hand. When processing several batches, select the ON button. If you want more control, use the PULSE button; the machine will stop instantly when you lift your finger off the button. Refer to your manual for further information.

optional blades

Some machines come with additional blades. The **Thin Slicer** is ideal for slicing cabbage for coleslaw. (If you don't have this blade, use the **Medium Slicer** and let food "self-feed" for thinner slices.) The **Thick Slicer** makes ¼-inch-thick slices. There is also a **Fine Grater** and a **Julienne Blade**.

The **French Fry Blade** makes matchsticks (i.e., curved sticks about 2 inches long and ¼ inch wide). Use firm pressure to process potatoes, eggplant, zucchini, cucumber and beets.

Plastic Blade: Some models come with a plastic mixing blade. It can be used for light mixing and blending of foods, usually where a change of texture is not desired (e.g., dips, spreads). Use it to coarsely chop mushrooms, nuts or cookie crumbs. When processing thin liquids, there is more chance of leakage.

Some models come with a **Plastic Dough Blade,** which is used to mix and knead yeast doughs. It creates less friction than the **Steel Blade**, reducing chances of overheating. Follow manufacturer's guidelines for use.

how much food can I process at a time?

The bowl of a large processor (14 cups) can handle double the amount of a standard processor (7 cups). A medium processor holds 11 cups. Follow guidelines in your manual for recommended capacities.

Quantities vary according to the food being processed and the task you are performing. The bowl holds more when slicing or shredding than when chopping or mincing.

When chopping and puréeing fruits or vegetables, don't fill the bowl more than ⅓ to ½ full. For larger quantities, process food in batches.

The thicker the liquid, the more you can process in one batch. If liquid leaks out between the bowl and cover when the machine is running, you've added too much liquid. Some models have a maximum fill-line on the bowl, which indicates the maximum amount of liquid that can be processed.

The following guide is the recommended capacity for a standard (7-cup) processor. A medium or large processor can process 1½ to twice the amounts listed below.

- Sliced or grated vegetables or cheese: 7 cups.
- Chopped fruits, vegetables or nuts: 1½ cups.
- Chopped meat, poultry or fish: 1 lb. (2 cups).
- Thin mixtures: 1½ cups (e.g., 1 milkshake).
- Thick mixtures: 3 cups. (For thick soups, strain vegetables from liquid and purée the solids in batches.)
- Breads: 1 loaf (3 to 3¼ cups of flour).
- Pastry: one 2-crust pie (2 cups of flour).
- Cakes: Recipes generally not exceeding 2 to 2½ cups flour. (See cake chapter for more information.)

tips, tricks and techniques

- Most of your favorite recipes can be adapted easily to the food processor. Use the appropriate blade to slice, grate, chop, mince or mix. Read the recipe completely, then organize the processing tasks for maximum efficiency and minimal clean-up.
- Assemble and measure the ingredients. Cut food to fit the feed tube if slicing or grating. Cut food into chunks if chopping or mincing.
- For uniform results when chopping, all the pieces should be about the same size. When mincing, it's not as important. Do not process larger quantities than recommended in one batch.
- Process hard or dry ingredients first, then soft or wet ingredients. (e.g., chop onions, then add eggs and mayonnaise for egg salad).
- Combine ingredients of the same texture. If foods have different textures, process them separately.
- Never process foods that are too hard to cut with a knife. You could damage the blade or the machine.
- Check often to avoid overprocessing.

- Wait for the blades to stop spinning before removing the cover. If the cover does not move or fit easily, rub a little cooking oil around the rim of the cover and bowl.
- When slicing or grating, if food doesn't fit through the top of the feed tube, try inserting it through the bottom, which is slightly larger.
- If appearance is important, pack the feed tube carefully. Otherwise, don't fuss.
- To slice small items such as mushrooms, strawberries or radishes, trim the bottom ends flat. Place a few pieces cut-side down directly on the **Slicer.** (If you have an expanded feed tube, place food directly in the feed tube.) Stack the remaining pieces in the feed tube. The bottom layer will produce perfect slices for garnishing.
- When slicing small items (e.g., strawberries, mushrooms) in the expanded feed tube, keep the small pusher inside the feed tube. Otherwise, the food will ride up inside the small feed tube and won't slice properly.
- To avoid slanted slices when slicing small amounts, place the food to be sliced in an upright position on the right side of the feed tube if blade spins counter-clockwise, and on the left side if blade spins clockwise.
- For julienne strips or matchsticks, you need to slice twice! Place food horizontally in the feed tube and slice, using steady pressure. You will get long slices. Re-stack the slices and place them vertically in the feed tube, wedging them in snugly. Slice once again, making long julienne strips. Ideal for potatoes, turnips and zucchini.
- **Cheater Chop:** This timesaving technique eliminates emptying the bowl when chopping a large quantity of vegetables (e.g., onions, bell peppers). Place 1-inch chunks of food in the feed tube. Process on the **Slicer** or **French-Fry Blade,** using almost no pressure.
- It is normal for sliced or grated food to pile up on one side of the bowl. Empty bowl as necessary. Don't let food press up against the bottom of the slicing or grating disc.
- Sometimes a small amount of food will not pass through the **Slicer** or **Grater.** Usually, the next item being sliced or shredded will force it through. Otherwise, this tidbit is a snack for the cook. (But no raw chicken, please!)
- The processor can process hot or cold foods. The bowl goes in the refrigerator or freezer (but not in the microwave oven), unless otherwise directed in your manual.

- Butter and cream cheese can be processed directly from the refrigerator—no need to soften them first.
- When adding flour to cakes, etc., blend in with on/off pulses, just until it disappears. Overprocessing results in poor volume or heavy cakes. Refer to cake chapter for more information.
- Remove the bowl and **Steel Blade** from the base as soon as you are finished processing. When they are removed together, the blade drops down around the central opening, forming a seal.
- Here's how to hold the **Steel Blade** in place when emptying the work bowl. Make sure your hands are dry. Insert your middle finger through the hole in the bottom of the bowl, securing the **Steel Blade** so it doesn't slip. Grip the outside edge of the bowl with your thumb. Tip the bowl to empty it, scraping out the contents with a spatula.
- Another method is to hold the blade in place with a rubber spatula while emptying the bowl. Be careful not to drop the blade into the food—or onto your foot!
- Put a potholder, towel or small mat underneath the base of your processor. It will be easier to move the machine around on the counter.
- Be prepared! To save time and clean-up, process more food than you need (e.g., grated chocolate, cheese, nuts, crumbs, parsley, onions). Refrigerate or freeze extras for future use.
- First things first! Process nuts, chocolate and streusel mixtures for coffee cakes first, while the processor bowl is dry, to avoid extra washing of the bowl and blade.
- Paper towels are handy to wipe out the processor bowl for easy clean-ups between steps.
- **Baby Food:** It's quick, easy and economical to make your own, and there is no need to add sugar, salt or preservatives! Steam or cook fruits or vegetables until very soft. Purée solids on the **Steel Blade** until very smooth. Cooked Fruits: Apples, apricots, peaches or pears. Cooked Vegetables: Beans, beets, carrots, peas, sweet potatoes, squash or zucchini. You can also purée ripe bananas, cottage cheese, cooked chicken or meat.
- To make junior baby food or "senior" food (for people of all ages), purée family meals (e.g., macaroni and cheese, spaghetti, chicken, vegetable soup with noodles or rice). Puréed meals are ideal for people on a soft diet, those with chewing, swallowing, digestive or dental difficulties.

- **Cube Food:** Prepare extra baby food and freeze in ice cube trays; wrap well. One cube equals about 2 Tbsp.
- Leftover cooked vegetables will thicken gravies, sauces and soups with minimal calories. Purée on the **Steel Blade** until smooth.
- **Instant Fruit Sauce:** Defrost a 10-oz. package of frozen unsweetened raspberries or strawberries (or use 2 cups cut-up fresh berries, peaches or mangoes). Purée on the **Steel Blade** until smooth. For each cup of fruit, add 1 to 2 Tbsp. sugar (to taste), 1 tsp. orange liqueur and a squeeze of lemon juice. Perfect over ice cream or fruit!

smart chart

Important!
- Peel, core and/or remove any pits or seeds if necessary.
- **To use the Slicer or Grater,** cut food in the largest possible size to fit the feed tube. Adjust the pressure according to the texture of the food being processed.
- **To use the Steel Blade,** cut food in even-sized chunks (1 to 1½ inches). Fill the bowl no more than ⅓ to ½ full. Process in batches if necessary. Use quick on/off pulses to chop; let the machine run to mince, grind or purée.
- Equivalents given for each food are approximate and are only provided as a guideline. Final yields may vary, depending on trimming, method of preparation and processing techniques.
- If a food you wish to process is not on this list, follow directions for a food that is similar in shape and/or texture.

Food & Blade	Comments
Apples	(1 lb. yields 3 cups; 1 medium yields ¾ cup sliced.)
Slicer or Grater	Medium pressure.
Steel Blade	On/off pulses to chop, let machine run to mince. Sprinkle with lemon juice to prevent discoloration.
Applesauce	
Steel Blade	Peel and core apples; cook until tender. Process in batches with quick on/offs for chunky texture, let machine run for puréed texture. (A food mill does a better job on unpeeled apples.)
Apricots	*See* **Fruits.** *Also see* **Peaches.**
Avocados	(1 medium yields 1 cup purée.)
Steel Blade	Peel, pit and cut in chunks. Quick on/off pulses to chop; let machine run to mince or purée. Sprinkle with lemon juice to prevent discoloration.

Baby Food
Steel Blade

To avoid pesticides, use organic produce. Wash thoroughly to avoid chemical residue. Cook or steam until very tender. Purée very well for infants, coarser for older babies. For smoother texture, process solids first, then add liquids. Combine two fruits or vegetables for variety. Refrigerate or freeze in ice cube trays. One cube equals 2 Tbsp.

Bananas
Slicer

(3 medium yield 1 cup purée.)

Use firm bananas. Light pressure. Use small feed tube for 1 or 2 bananas. Sprinkle with lemon juice to prevent discoloration.

Steel Blade

The riper the better! Let machine run until puréed. Extras can be frozen for future use.

Beans
Slicer

Green or Wax (1 lb. yields 3 cups; 1 cup yields ½ cup purée.)

French Style: Trim and cut beans in half to fit feed tube **crosswise**. Cook in boiling salted water for 1 minute, then plunge into ice water. Drain, dry and slice. Medium pressure.

Steel Blade

Process cooked beans with quick on/offs to chop, let machine run to mince or purée. Use in soups, spreads or latkes (pancakes).

Beef

See **Meat and Poultry.**

Beets
Slicer or Grater

(1 medium yields ½ to ¾ cup.)

Raw: Peel and trim. Firm pressure, with bouncing motion on pusher.
Cooked: Parboil with skins on to retain color. Peel and trim. Light pressure.

Steel Blade

On/off pulses to chop, let machine run to mince or purée.

Bread Crumbs
Steel Blade

Dry or Toasted (1 slice yields ¼ cup crumbs.)

Store scraps of bread or rolls in freezer. To dry, place on a baking sheet; dry at 300°F for 1 hour. Process chunks until fine. Store at room temperature.

Italian Seasoned Crumbs: To each cup of crumbs, add ½ tsp. salt, dash pepper, oregano, basil and ¼ cup grated Parmesan cheese (optional). Process a few seconds to combine.

Bread Crumbs
Steel Blade

Soft (1 slice yields ½ cup crumbs.)

Tear fresh bread or rolls in chunks. Process up to 4 slices at a time. For larger quantities, add additional chunks through feed tube while machine is running. Process to make fine crumbs. Store in freezer or crumbs will get moldy.

Buttered Crumbs: Blend 1 to 2 Tbsp. butter or oil into crumbs with on/off pulses.

Crumb Topping: Blend in 1 to 2 Tbsp. oil, salt, pepper and your favorite herbs.

Broccoli
Slicer or Grater

Steel Blade

(1 lb. yields 2 cups chopped [raw] or 1 cup purée [cooked].)

Peel and trim raw broccoli stems. Medium pressure. (Reserve florets for stir-fries; they will crumble if sliced.)

Cut raw or cooked broccoli in chunks. On/off pulses to chop; let machine run to mince or purée.

Butter
Slicer
Steel Blade

(¼ lb. [1 stick] yields ½ cup.)

Butter must be cold, but not frozen. Medium to firm pressure.

Pies: Use frozen butter. Cut in chunks with a knife.

Baking: Use directly from refrigerator.

Flavored Butters: Chop garlic or herbs first.

Homemade Butter: *See* **Whipping Cream.**

Lighter Butter: Process 1 cup soft butter or margarine until smooth. Gradually add ½ cup cold water through feed tube while machine is running. Process 2 to 3 minutes, scraping down bowl as needed. Contains half the calories of regular butter or margarine!

Cabbage
Slicer

Grater
Steel Blade

(1 medium cabbage [about 2 lbs.] yields 8 cups.)

Use **Slicer** to "grate." Young cabbages are best. Cut in wedges to fit feed tube; remove core. Light pressure.

For coleslaw, let cabbage self-feed, with almost no pressure.

Roll soft, outer leaves into a cylinder. Light pressure.

Medium pressure. Ideal for egg rolls, extra-fine coleslaw.

On/off pulses to chop; let machine run to mince.

Cake Mixes
Steel Blade | Place dry mixture in work bowl. Add eggs and liquid while machine is running; process for 1 minute, scraping down sides of bowl as needed.

Candy
Steel Blade | **Hard** (Peppermint sticks, cinnamon candy)
Drop chunks through feed tube while machine is running, keeping your hand on top to prevent pieces from flying out. Process until fine.

Carrots
(1 lb. [6 medium] yields 3 cups; 2 medium yield $\frac{1}{2}$ cup purée. Substitute 3 or 4 baby carrots for 1 medium carrot.)

Slicer or Grater | Medium to firm pressure. If grating, use bouncing motion with pusher. For small round slices or short shreds, pack upright in feed tube. For long slices or shreds, pack horizontally in feed tube. To slice 1 or 2 carrots, use small feed tube.

Steel Blade | Quick on/off pulses to chop. For raw or cooked carrots, let machine run to mince or purée.

Cauliflower
(1 lb. yields 2 cups chopped [raw] or 1 cup purée [cooked].)

Steel Blade | Cut raw or cooked cauliflower in chunks. On/off pulses to chop; let machine run to mince or purée. (Crumbles if sliced.)

Celery
(2 medium stalks yield $\frac{1}{2}$ cup.)

Slicer | Peel; pat dry. Medium pressure. For diagonal slices, place on an angle in feed tube.

Steel Blade | On/off pulses to chop; let machine run to mince. See **Cheater Chop** (p. 15).

Celery Root
($1\frac{1}{2}$ lbs. yield 4 cups grated.)

Grater or Julienne | Peel; cut to fit feed tube. Remove spongy flesh in center. Parboil 3 minutes. Plunge into ice water. When cool, drain and dry. Medium pressure.

Cheeses
Steel Blade | **Hard** (Parmesan) ($\frac{1}{4}$ lb. yields 1 cup grated.)
Parmesan cheese should be at room temperature. Break into small chunks with a blunt knife or chisel. Process no more than 1 cup at a time. Drop pieces through feed tube while machine is running; let machine run until finely grated, 20 to 30 seconds. Refrigerate or freeze extras.

Cheeses	**Semi-Hard or Soft** (Cheddar, Swiss or Mozzarella) (¼ lb. yields 1 cup grated.)
Grater	Chill thoroughly for best results (especially Mozzarella). If not cold enough, freeze for 15 to 20 minutes before grating. Light pressure produces fine shreds, medium pressure produces coarser shreds. Grate extra to use in salads, casseroles or pizzas and refrigerate or freeze.
Slicer	Don't slice soft cheese (e.g., Mozzarella) or hard cheese (e.g., Parmesan). You may damage the blade! Cut cheese to fit feed tube. Place in freezer until partially frozen; you should be able to pierce it with the tip of a sharp knife. Light to medium pressure.
Steel Blade	On/off pulses to chop. Use when appearance is not important (e.g., sauces, casseroles).

Cheeses	**Soft** (Cream, Cottage, Ricotta) (½ lb. yields 1 cup.)
Steel Blade	May be used directly from refrigerator.
	Cream Cheese: Cut in chunks; process until smooth. Scrape down bowl as necessary.
	Cottage Cheese: Process until very smooth and lump free, scraping down bowl as necessary. Dry cottage cheese may require addition of a little milk.
	Crêpe or Blintz Filling: Use less eggs in cheese mixture; processor makes cheese very creamy.

Chicken	*See* **Meat and Poultry.**

Chocolate	(1-oz. square yields ¼ cup grated; 6-oz. pkg. chocolate chips yields 1 cup.)
Grater	Chill chocolate. Medium to firm pressure. (Processor will be extremely noisy!) Grate extras and refrigerate or freeze. Ideal for garnishing. If recipe calls for melted chocolate, use ¼ cup grated. It will melt in moments!
Steel Blade	Use chocolate chips or cut chocolate squares in half. On/off pulses to start, then let machine run until desired degree of fineness is reached (10 to 15 seconds for coarsely chopped, 20 to 30 seconds for finely chopped). Texture will be more "pebbly" than grated, but is fine where appearance is not important (e.g., cake batters).

Coconut	(1 medium yields 4 cups grated.)
Steel Blade	Pierce the eyes with a nail; drain out liquid from coconut. Place in a 400°F oven for about 20 minutes. Remove from oven and crack shell with a hammer. Peel off inner brown skin with a potato peeler. Rinse, pat dry and cut in chunks. Process 1 cup at a time. On/off pulses, then let machine run until minced. Refrigerate for 3 days or freeze.

Coffee	
Steel Blade	Some manufacturers do not recommend grinding coffee beans. Refer to your manual.
	Caffé Latte: Heat milk until steaming. Process for 20 to 30 seconds, until foamy. Fill cups half full with hot espresso, then top with foamy milk. Sprinkle with ground cinnamon and/or grated chocolate.

Coriander/Cilantro	
	Process as for **Parsley.**

Crumbs	**(Cookies, Crackers, Corn Flakes)**
	For 1 cup crumbs use:
	• 18 chocolate wafers
	• 22 to 26 vanilla wafers
	• 12 to 14 single graham wafers
	• 15 ginger snaps
	• 28 soda crackers
	• 4 cups corn flakes
Steel Blade	Break cookies or crackers in chunks. Place in bowl or drop through feed tube while machine is running. Process until fine.

Cucumbers	**English Cucumbers** (1 medium yields 1$\frac{1}{2}$ cups.)
Slicer or Grater	Long, slim, firm cucumbers are best and have fewer seeds. Medium pressure. Pat dry before using. Use small feed tube for small quantities. (Remove seeds if grating.)
	Crescents: Cut in half lengthwise; scoop out seeds with a spoon. Cut to fit feed tube. Slice, using medium pressure. Pretty for salads!
Steel Blade	Remove seeds. On/off pulses to chop. Do not overprocess because of high water content. Drain or pat dry.

23

Dates	*See* **Fruits.**

Eggplant — (1 lb. yields 3½ cups chopped [raw] or 1½ cups purée [cooked].)

Slicer — Cut in wedges to fit feed tube. Medium pressure. Makes thin slices. Use expanded feed tube for large slices. See **Cheater Chop** (p. 15).

Steel Blade — Cut in chunks; process in batches if necessary. Quick on/off pulses to chop raw eggplant. Do not overprocess cooked eggplant.

Eggs — (1 large yields ¼ cup.)

Grater — **Hard-Cooked:** Light pressure. **Steel Blade** "grates" better. For slices, slice by hand for best results.

Steel Blade — **Hard-Cooked:** Cut in half. On/off pulses. For egg salad, chop or mince vegetables first, then add eggs, mayonnaise and seasonings. (Up to 1 dozen eggs at a time.)

Raw: Process for 2 or 3 seconds, until blended. For omelettes or frittatas, the processor is faster than a fork!

Egg Whites — (1 egg white yields 2 Tbsp.; 8 egg whites equal 1 cup.)

Steel Blade — (An electric mixer or whisk produces firmer whites and greater volume.) To process, use at least 3 egg whites, or up to 6. For each egg white, add 1 tsp. lemon juice or vinegar. Bowl and blade must be absolutely clean and grease-free. Process until firm, 1½ to 2 minutes.

Fish — **Raw** (1 lb. fillets yields 2 cups.)

Steel Blade — Remove skin and bones; cut in chunks. Grind in batches (2 cups at a time). Let machine run until smooth, about 20 seconds.

Fish — **Cooked or Canned** (6- to 7-oz. can yields ½ to ⅔ cup drained.)

Steel Blade — 2 or 3 quick on/off pulses. Maximum 2 cups at a time. Chop or mince vegetables first, then add fish, mayonnaise and seasonings. If over-processed, flaked tuna will have a gritty texture.

Flax Seed

Steel Blade — Process until finely ground, 2 to 3 minutes. Store in freezer to prevent rancidity. (Some manufacturers do not recommend grinding seeds, spices or grains. Check your manual.)

Fruits Steel Blade	**Dried or Candied** (Apricots, Dates, Prunes, Raisins) (1 lb. yields 2½ cups.) Freeze sticky fruit for 10 minutes. Check pitted prunes carefully to make sure all pits have been removed. To prevent sticking, add about ¼ cup flour if called for in recipe. Quick on/off pulses to chop candied or dried fruits. To grind or purée dried fruits, let machine run until fine.
Garlic Steel Blade	(1 head contains 12 to 15 cloves; 1 medium clove yields ½ tsp.) Not necessary to peel if bowl and blade are dry. Drop through feed tube while machine is running; process until minced, 8 to 10 seconds. Discard peel. (Pieces are easy to pick out if bowl is dry.) Don't bother if garlic is to be cooked; peel disintegrates during cooking.
Ginger Steel Blade	(1-inch piece yields 1 Tbsp.) Peel; cut in pieces. Drop through feed tube while machine is running; process until minced. Process extra ginger, place in a glass jar, adding sherry to cover. Refrigerate up to 3 months. (Sherry can be used in cooking.)
Herbs, Fresh	*See* **Parsley.** (1 Tbsp. fresh chopped herbs equals 1 tsp. dried.)
Ice	Not recommended by most manufacturers as ice can dull or damage blades. A blender does a better job of chopping ice because rotation speed of blades is much faster and action of blades is more effective.
Jicama Slicer or Grater	Peel just before using; cut to fit feed tube. Firm pressure.
Kiwis Slicer	(2 kiwis yield ¾ cup.) Chill before slicing. Use firm fruit; peel. Fill feed tube snugly or use small feed tube. Light pressure to prevent crushing.
Lamb	*See* **Meat and Poultry.**

Leeks	*Also* **Green Onions** (Scallions) (1 lb. leeks yields 2 cups; 1 or 2 green onions yields $1/4$ cup. For 1 leek, substitute 6 green onions.)
Slicer	Trim off most of green portion from leeks and green onions; cut to fit feed tube. Wash very well, especially leeks. Pack upright in feed tube or use small feed tube. If slicing small quantities, combine with other foods (e.g., pack green onions in the hollow of celery stalks). Medium pressure. Some slivering will occur.
Steel Blade	On/off pulses to chop; let machine run to mince. Some slivering will occur.
Lemons	*Also* **Limes, Oranges** (1 medium lemon yields 2 tsp. zest and 3 Tbsp. juice. 1 medium lime yields 1 tsp. zest and 1 to 2 Tbsp. juice. 1 medium orange yields 2 Tbsp. zest and $1/3$ to $1/2$ cup juice.)
Slicer	Do not peel; scrub well. Cut ends flat. Medium pressure. Use expanded feed tube for whole oranges, or cut to fit feed tube.
Steel Blade	Cut in quarters; remove any seeds. Process until fine, just a few seconds for peeled fruits, 20 to 30 seconds for unpeeled fruits. **Zest (Rind):** Use peeler to remove colored rind from fruit. Add part of sugar called for in recipe. Start with on/off pulses, then let machine run until finely minced, 30 to 60 seconds. Refrigerate or freeze extra zest. (When recipe calls for zest and juice, remove rind first, then squeeze out juice.)
Lettuce	(1 lb. yields 6 cups.)
Slicer	Light pressure. Good for layered salads, sandwiches, tacos. For tossed salads, tear by hand into pieces.
Mangoes	(1 medium yields $3/4$ to 1 cup.)
Steel Blade	On/off pulses to chop, let machine run to purée. Sprinkle with a few drops of lemon or lime juice.
Margarine	($1/2$ lb. yields 1 cup.)
Steel Blade	Cut in chunks. No need to soften first. Process until smooth. For spreads, add herbs or garlic. (*Also see* **Butter.**)
Matzo Meal	(3 matzos or 2 cups matzo farfel yield 1 cup.)
Steel Blade	Break matzos into chunks. Process matzos or farfel until fine, 45 to 60 seconds.

Meat and Poultry	**Cooked** (Beef, Lamb, Veal, Chicken, Turkey) (1 lb. yields 2 cups.)
Slicer	Chill first. The firmer the meat, the better it will slice. Trim fat, gristle and bones. Cut to fit feed tube. Cut ends flat. Firm pressure.
	Roasts/Brisket: Slices will be narrow. You may prefer to slice by hand.
	Boneless Chicken Breasts: Chilled breasts slice well for sandwiches or salads.
	Salami or Pepperoni: Cut to fit feed tube or use small feed tube. If soft, freeze until partially frozen, following directions for raw meat. You should be able to insert the point of a knife.
	Julienne Strips: Roll up sliced deli meat into a cylinder. Fill feed tube snugly. Ideal for salads.
Steel Blade	Trim fat, gristle and bones from meat. Remove and discard skin from poultry. Cut in chunks. Process in batches. Fill bowl ⅓ full. On/off pulses to chop coarsely, or let machine run 8 to 10 seconds, until finely chopped. Blend in additional ingredients with quick on/off pulses.
Meat and Poultry	**Raw** (1 lb. boneless yields 2 cups.)
Slicer	(**Slicer** must be **serrated** to slice raw meat or poultry. Refer to your manual.) Remove skin, bones and excess fat. Cut pieces as large as possible to fit feed tube. Freeze 30 to 60 minutes, or until semi-frozen. (Time will vary, depending on thickness.) Food is ready to slice when easily pierced with the tip of a sharp knife. For maximum tenderness, slice across the grain. Firm pressure. (If not firm enough, food won't slice well. If too firm, partially thaw until you can do the knife test.) Ideal for stir-fries.
Steel Blade	**Grind Your Own:** Remove bones, excess fat and gristle from meat. Remove skin and bones from poultry. Cut in 1-inch chunks. Should be very cold but not frozen. Process in batches. Fill work bowl ¼ to ⅓ full. To grind, use on/off pulses, until desired texture is reached. Scrape down sides of bowl as needed. Do not overprocess.
Milkshakes	*Also* **Smoothies**
Steel Blade	Not more than one milkshake at a time to prevent leakage. Process until blended. Make smoothies with cold milk (skim or soy), orange juice and frozen berries or cut-up fruit (e.g., bananas, mangoes). Some manufacturers do not recommend processing ice cubes.

Mushrooms	(½ lb. yields 2 to 2½ cups.)
Slicer	The firmer the better. Light pressure. If appearance is not important, stack feed tube at random. Use small feed tube for small amounts.
	Hammerhead Slices: Trim ends. Stack mushrooms on their sides, alternating direction of caps (one facing right, the next facing left).
	Round Slices: Remove stems; place mushrooms rounded-side down.
Grater	Medium pressure.
Steel Blade	Quick on/off pulses to chop; let machine run to mince. If overprocessed, make Duxelles (p. 114) or quiche.

Nectarines	*See* **Peaches.**

Nuts	(¼ lb. yields 1 cup.)
Grater or Slicer	Medium pressure. **Grater** produces fine texture. **Slicer** produces coarser texture.
Steel Blade	Timing depends on hardness of nuts used and degree of fineness desired. Do not overprocess or you will get nut butter! Process in batches (up to 1½ cups in a standard processor, 3 cups in a large processor). If recipe calls for flour or sugar, add some to nuts before chopping so you can chop them as fine as you want without making nut butter.
	Coarsely Chopped: 6 to 8 on/off pulses, or let machine run 6 to 8 seconds.
	Finely Ground: On/off pulses to start, then process 20 to 30 seconds, until desired texture is reached. Freeze or refrigerate extras.
	Peanut Butter: Process 2 cups salted peanuts for approximately 2½ minutes, stopping several times to scrape down sides of bowl. For a smoother texture, add 2 to 3 Tbsp. oil. (Use any nuts except dry-roasted peanuts.)
	Chocolate Peanut Butter: Process 1½ cups peanuts and ½ cup chocolate chips for about 2½ minutes, scraping down sides of bowl as needed.

Olives	*See* **Pickles.**

Onions (1 lb. yields 4 medium; 1 medium yields $^1/_2$ to $^3/_4$ cup.)

Slicer For round rings, onions must be small or processor must have expanded feed tube. Light to medium pressure. For "diced" onions, cut onions in 1-inch chunks. Slice, using light pressure. For "grated" onions, **Steel Blade** is better as some catching may take place with **Grater**. (For milder flavor, soak onions in ice-cold water for 15 minutes after slicing.)

Steel Blade Cut small onions in half, larger onions in quarters or chunks. On/off pulses to chop (1 onion takes 2 to 3 quick on/off pulses, 2 onions take 3 to 4 pulses). To mince or grate, let machine run 8 to 10 seconds. Overprocessing onions produces a purée. Also see **Cheater Chop** (p. 15).

Oranges *See* **Lemons.**

Parsley *Also* **Coriander/Cilantro, Fresh Herbs** (1 cup loosely packed sprigs yields $^1/_3$ cup minced.)

Steel Blade Discard tough stems. Herbs, bowl and blade should be clean and dry. For best results, chop or mince at least ½ cup (or up to a whole bowlful at a time). On/off pulses, then let machine run until minced. For small quantities, drop through feed tube while machine is running; process until minced. Wrap in paper towels and store in an airtight bag in refrigerator for up to a week.

Herb Cubes: Process 3 cups fresh herbs with 2 cups water for 30 to 45 seconds. Mixture will look like thick slush. Freeze in ice cube trays. Transfer to freezer bags. One cube equals 2 Tbsp. fresh or 2 tsp. dried herbs. Best used in cooked dishes.

Parsnips (1 lb. (4 medium) yields 2 to $2^1/_2$ cups.)

Process as for **Carrots.**

Peaches *Also* **Pears, Plums, Apricots, Nectarines** (1 lb. yields 2 to $2^1/_2$ cups.)

Slicer Remove pits or core. Peel if desired. Light pressure.

Steel Blade On/off pulses to chop, let machine run to mince or purée. Sprinkle with lemon juice to prevent discoloration.

Peppers, Sweet (1 medium yields ³/₄ to 1 cup.)

Slicer
Remove stems and seeds; cut stem end flat. Do not cut bottom end flat when cutting pepper into rings. Medium pressure.

Long Slices: Cut in half or in widest width to fit feed tube.

Narrow Slices: Arrange long, narrow strips upright in feed tube or use small feed tube.

Pepper Rings: Use expanded feed tube for large peppers. For standard feed tube, use small peppers that fit through bottom of feed tube. If too big, cut down one side; roll up to fit snugly in feed tube. Medium to firm pressure.

Steel Blade
Quick on/off pulses; do not overprocess. Pat dry. Let machine run to mince or grate. Also see **Cheater Chop** (p. 15).

Roasted Peppers: 2 or 3 quick on/off pulses to chop, let machine run to mince or purée.

Hot Peppers: Remove ribs and seeds before processing. Caution—don't rub your eyes (or any sensitive body parts) after handling hot peppers!

Pickles

Also **Olives, Water Chestnuts**

Slicer
Pickles: Choose firm pickles. Arrange either upright or horizontally in feed tube. Medium pressure.

Olives: Arrange with flat ends down in feed tube. Medium pressure. (Hand-slicing may be easier.)

Water Chestnuts: Peel fresh water chestnuts just before using. Firm pressure.

Steel Blade
Quick on/off pulses to chop; let machine run to mince.

Pineapple (1 medium yields 4 cups.)

Slicer
Peel; remove eyes with point of sharp knife. Cut in wedges to fit feed tube. Cut flat ends. Medium to firm pressure. Makes thin slices.

Steel Blade
Cut in chunks; process in batches. Fill bowl ¼ to ⅓ full. On/off pulses to chop. (If recipe calls for canned crushed pineapple but you only have slices or chunks, drain well and process 6 to 8 seconds, until crushed.)

Potatoes	*Also* **Sweet Potatoes, Yams** (1 lb. yields 3½ to 4 cups.)
Slicer	Cut in largest possible size to fit feed tube. Medium pressure for raw potatoes, firm pressure for sweet potatoes or yams. (Cooked potatoes crumble somewhat when sliced.)
Grater	Light to medium pressure, depending on texture desired. Makes long shreds. (Store grated or sliced raw potatoes in cold water to prevent discoloration. Dry well before using.)
Steel Blade	Cut in chunks; process in batches. Fill bowl ¼ to ⅓ full. On/off pulses to chop, let machine run to mince or "grate." Processor-mashed potatoes will be glue-like and sticky. (See p. 106).
French Fry Blade	Makes short shoestring fries.

Prunes	*See* **Fruits**. *Also see* **Prune Purée** (p. 155).

Purées	(1 cup cooked vegetables or 1 cup fruit or berries [fresh or frozen] yields about ½ cup purée.)
Steel Blade	Excellent for most cooked or leftover vegetables (except starchy ones like potatoes). Choose ripe fruit; frozen fruit should be thawed first. See individual listings.
	Vegetable Purées: Cook or steam vegetables until tender. Drain, reserving cooking liquid (1 to 2 Tbsp. per cup of vegetables). Process in batches. Fill bowl ⅓ full. Process until smooth, scraping down sides of bowl and adding liquid if needed. Broth can replace cooking liquid. Season with salt, freshly ground black pepper and a little butter or margarine, if desired.
	Puréed Soups: Strain out solids. Process in batches until smooth; scrape down sides of bowl as needed. Add up to ¼ cup liquid for each cup of vegetables.

Radishes	(½ lb. yields 1½ cups sliced.)
Slicer	Trim ends; place cut-side down in feed tube. Firm pressure. Large varieties (e.g., black radish, daikon) should be cut to fit feed tube; grate on **Grater** to use in salads.
Steel Blade	Quick on/off pulses to chop; let machine run to mince.

Rhubarb (1 lb. yields 2 cups chopped and cooked.)

    Slicer   Peel with potato peeler. Discard leaves (they are poisonous). Medium pressure. Makes thin slices.

    Steel Blade   Quick on/off pulses to chop.

Scallions *See* **Leeks.**

Shallots (These are a cross between garlic and onions. Do not confuse with green onions.) (1 yields 1 to 2 Tbsp.)

    Steel Blade   For small quantities, drop through feed tube while machine is running. On/off pulses to chop; let machine run to mince.

Spinach (1 lb. fresh yields about 10 cups raw or 1½ cups cooked and drained. A 10-oz. pkg. frozen yields 1 cup cooked and drained.)

    Steel Blade   Discard tough stalks. On/off pulses to chop; let machine run to mince. Cooked spinach should be squeezed dry before processing.

    Slicer   To shred, stack leaves. Roll up into a cylinder and stand upright in feed tube. Medium pressure.

Squash **(Winter, Summer)**
See **Turnips.** *Also see* **Zucchini.**

Strawberries *Also* **Raspberries, Blueberries** (1 pint fresh yields about 2 cups; a 10-oz. pkg. frozen yields 1½ cups.)

    Slicer   Strawberries should be firm; stack on their sides in feed tube. Light pressure. (Partially thaw frozen strawberries. Medium pressure.)

    Steel Blade   Use fresh or frozen berries, thawed and drained. Let machine run until puréed. Strain to remove seeds, if desired.

Sugar	**Fruit Sugar, Brown Sugar, Icing Sugar** (1 lb. granulated yields 2 cups; 1 lb. brown sugar yields 2¼ cups packed)
Steel Blade	**Fruit (Caster) Sugar:** Process granulated sugar for 1 minute, or until fine. Measure after processing.
	Brown Sugar: To remove lumps, process 15 to 20 seconds. If very hard, soften by placing ½ apple, cut-side up, in bag. Discard apple the next day. Chunks of very hard sugar can be used in cooking (e.g., sweet and sour meatballs).

Swiss Chard	Process as for **Spinach.**

Toffee/Skor Bits	(4 bars [1.4 oz. each] yield 1 cup chopped.)
Steel Blade	Chill before processing. Break into chunks. On/off pulses until desired texture is reached. Use for cookies, coffee cake toppings, desserts.

Tofu, Blended	(10 oz. package yields about ¾ cup.)
Steel Blade	Drain liquid. Process firm or extra-firm tofu until well-blended, about 2 minutes. Scrape down sides of bowl as necessary. Use as a substitute for mayonnaise or to replace eggs in baking. It can also replace uncooked eggs in desserts. Use ¼ cup for each egg. Refrigerate for up to 1 week.

Tomatoes	(1 lb. (3 medium) yields 1½ to 2 cups.)
Slicer	For standard feed tube, cut firm tomatoes in half and cut ends flat. Medium pressure. Whole firm tomatoes can be sliced in expanded feed tube. Cherry tomatoes can be sliced in small feed tube. Drain well after slicing.
Steel Blade	Cut in quarters. Peeling is not necessary if cooking tomatoes, as blade does an excellent job on skins. On/off pulses to chop or mince. If desired, squeeze out seeds and juice before processing. In season, freeze ripe chopped tomatoes to use in sauces.
	Canned Tomatoes: Drain liquid. On/off pulses to chop, let machine run to mince or purée.

Turkey	*See* **Meat and Poultry.**

Turnips	*Also* **Winter Squash** (Acorn, Butternut, Hubbard)
	(1 lb. yields 2 to 2½ cups chopped [raw] or 1 cup purée [cooked].)
Slicer or Grater	Peel and trim. Remove seeds from squash. Cut to fit feed tube. Firm pressure, with bouncing motion on pusher.
Steel Blade	Process in batches if necessary. Fill bowl ¼ to ⅓ full. On/off pulses to chop; let machine run to mince, "grate" or purée.

Veal	*See* **Meat and Poultry.**

Watercress	Process as for **Parsley.**

Whipping Cream	*Also* **Dessert Topping** (1 cup yields 1½ cups when whipped.)
Steel Blade	Will be firmer, but less volume than with an electric mixer. Good for garnishing.
	Method: Chill bowl and blade for 15 minutes. Place a heavy book under back part of base so machine is tipped forward. Do not insert pusher in feed tube. Whip chilled cream until texture of sour cream, 35 to 40 seconds. Add sugar and process 5 to 10 seconds longer, just until firm. Dessert topping takes about 2 minutes.
	Homemade Butter: Process up to 2 cups whipping cream at a time. Let machine run about 2 minutes, until cream separates and forms butter. Add a little salt if desired. Drain liquid; rinse well and pat dry. Refrigerate or freeze. An excellent way to use up leftover whipping cream or to rescue overwhipped cream!

Yeast Doughs	Refer to Bread chapter for full information. Some models are not strong enough to process yeast doughs. Check manual for guidelines.
	Standard (7-cup) Processor: Recommended capacity is 3 cups flour.
	Large (14-cup) Processor: Recommended capacity is 6 cups all-purpose flour or 3½ cups whole-grain flour. If recipe calls for more flour than recommended, mix and knead dough in equal batches.
Steel Blade	For breads made with less than 3 to 3½ cups flour.
Metal Dough Blade	Use with **Dough Cycle** for breads with more than 3½ cups flour. Dough Cycle uses lower speed so dough doesn't heat up.

Zucchini	*Also* **Summer Squash** (1 lb. yields 3 cups.)
Slicer or Grater	Peel if desired. Cut to fit feed tube. Use small feed tube for small quantities. Medium pressure.
Steel Blade	Process in batches if necessary. On/off pulses to chop; let run to mince, "grate" or purée.

freezing tips

- Cooked foods, such as meats, roasts, stews (without potatoes), poultry (without stuffing), fish, pasta, grains, soups, sauces and most baked goods, freeze well. Potatoes may become slightly grainy. Rice may get hard if frozen, unless there is an adequate amount of sauce. Don't freeze cream fillings, puddings, salad greens, mayonnaise or hard-cooked eggs. Refer to specific recipes in this book as to whether a dish freezes well.

- Cool foods quickly to room temperature before freezing by placing the dish in a larger pan of ice water or cold running water; stir occasionally. Then wrap well to prevent freezer burn and loss of flavor.

- Pack it right! Use freezer-safe containers, heavy-duty freezer bags or double-wrap with heavy-duty foil. Remove as much air as possible and seal tightly. More food can be packaged in square or oblong containers than in round or cylindrical shapes. To save on clean-up, use ovenproof or microwavable dishes to freeze cooked casseroles. Avoid surprises—mark packages with contents, quantity and date frozen.

- Here's a great trick! Freeze food in a casserole dish that has been lined with heavy-duty foil. When it is completely frozen, remove the foil-wrapped food from the dish. Now your casserole is free for everyday use! To defrost or reheat, unwrap the food and place it back in the original casserole.

- Make double or triple batches of recipes for future meals. Freeze in portions suitable for your family. Pack some single portions for unexpected company or for quick, kid-sized meals. Smaller packages freeze and defrost faster than larger ones.

- Foods can be stored longer in an upright or chest freezer than those stored in the freezer compartment of your refrigerator. Although foods may be safe to eat if frozen beyond the recommended time, taste or texture may be affected.

- If there is a power failure, don't panic. Be sure to keep the freezer door closed to prevent cold air from escaping. If your freezer is fully stocked, the contents will remain frozen for at least 2 days. If it is half-full, the contents will stay frozen at least 1 full day. If the power remains off longer, place dry ice on top of the food.

- Once food has thawed, use it as soon as possible. If there are still some ice crystals, it can be refrozen, but texture may be affected. You can refreeze cookies, cakes and breads even if they have thawed completely. Raw fish, chicken or meat that has defrosted must be cooked before you can freeze it again.

- Defrost foods before reheating unless otherwise indicated. Your microwave oven is ideal for defrosting. Foods can also be thawed overnight in the refrigerator. Do not thaw meat, poultry or fish at room temperature.

- When reheating foods, cover them to prevent them from drying out. Crispy foods should be reheated uncovered to prevent them from becoming soggy. Most casseroles, roasts and poultry should be reheated in a covered casserole at 350°F for about 20 minutes. When reheating in the microwave, allow 1 to 2 minutes on HIGH per cup of food. Two pieces of chicken or a serving of soup will take about 2 minutes to reheat.

- To test if a food is fully heated, insert the blade of a knife into the center. When you remove the knife, it should feel hot when you touch it!

microwave oven tips

- Glass baking dishes are ovenproof and microsafe (i.e. microwavable). Parchment paper makes an excellent cover.

- Do not microwave foods in disposable plastic containers from the supermarket, plastic bags or plastic wrap. When subjected to heat, chemicals can leach and migrate into foods, especially fatty foods.

- Cooking times are based on a 650- to 700-watt microwave oven. (1 cup of water boils in $2\frac{1}{2}$ minutes on HIGH.)

- Always check food shortly before estimated cooking time is completed. Always allow for standing time.

- To double the recipe, allow $\frac{1}{2}$ to $\frac{2}{3}$ more cooking time. To make half the recipe, allow $\frac{1}{3}$ less cooking time.

metric pan equivalents

- To prevent sticking, use a nonstick spray made of canola oil and spray pans lightly.
- When baking in glass or dark baking pans, reduce temperatures by 25°F (10°C).

Pan	Metric Measure	Capacity
8 x 8 x 2-inch square pan	20 x 20 x 5 cm	2 litres (8 cups)
9 x 9 x 2-inch square pan	23 x 23 x 5 cm	2.5 litres (10 cups)
9 x 5 x 3-inch loaf pan	23 x 13 x 6 cm	2 litres (8 cups)
10 x 3½-inch fluted tube pan (Bundt)	25 x 9 cm	3 litres (12 cups)
10 x 4-inch tube pan	25 x 10 cm	4 litres (16 cups)
8 x 2-inch round layer pan	20 x 5 cm	1.5 litres (6 cups)
9 x 2-inch round layer pan	23 x 5 cm	2 litres (8 cups)
7 x 11 x 2-inch glass baking dish	18 x 28 x 5 cm	2 litres (8 cups)
9 x 13 x 2-inch glass baking dish	22 x 33 x 5 cm	3.5 litres (15 cups)
9-inch pie plate	23-cm	1 litre (4 cups)
10 x 15 x 1-inch cookie sheet	25 x 38 x 3 cm	2.5 litres (10 cups)
9-inch springform pan	23 cm	2.5 litres (10 cups)
10-inch springform pan	25 cm	3 litres (12 cups)

metric measurement equivalents

One inch equals 2.5 centimetres (cm). Each 5 cm is 2 inches.

⅛ inch	.3 cm	4 inches	10 cm
¼ inch	.6 cm	6 inches	15 cm
½ inch	1.2 cm	12 inches	30 cm
1 inch	2.5 cm		

metric temperature conversions

To convert from °F to °C: (°F −32) divided by 1.8 = °C.
To convert from °C to °F: (1.8 x °C) plus 32 = °F.

0°F	−18°C	Freezer temperature
32°F	0°C	Water freezes
40°F	4°C	Refrigerator temperature

68°F	20°C	Room temperature
105–115°F	41–46°C	Water temperature to proof yeast
212°F	100°C	Water boils

Oven Temperatures

250°F	120°C	400°F	200°C
275°F	135°C	425°F	220°C
300°F	150°C	450°F	230°C
325°F	160°C	475°F	240°C
350°F	180°C	500°F	260°C
375°F	190°C		

metric measurements for volume and weight
Quick Conversions (Approximate)

To ounces: Drop the last digit from the number of millilitres (mL) or grams (g) and divide by 3. For example, 156 mL is about 5 oz. (15 divided by 3 = 5).

To millilitres or grams: Multiply the number of ounces by 30. For example, 1 ounce is about 30 mL or grams.

approximate metric equivalents (volume)

¼ tsp.	1 mL		⅓ cup	75 mL
½ tsp.	2 mL		½ cup	125 mL
1 tsp.	5 mL		¾ cup	175 mL
1 Tbsp.	15 mL		1 cup	250 mL
2 Tbsp.	25 mL		4 cups	1 L
¼ cup	50 mL			

approximate metric equivalents (weight)

1 oz.	30 g (actual is 28.4 g)		½ lb.	250 g (actual is 227 g)
2 oz.	60 g		¾ lb.	375 g
3 oz.	85 g		1 lb.	500 g (actual is 454 g)
3½ oz.	100 g		2 generous lbs.	1 kg

metric packaging

Common can/bottle sizes

3 oz.	85 mL	14 oz.	398 mL
5½ oz.	156 mL	16 oz.	454 mL
7½ oz.	213 mL	17.6 oz.	500 mL
8 oz.	227 mL	19 oz.	540 mL
8.8 oz.	250 mL	28 oz.	796 mL
10 oz.	284 mL	35.2 oz.	1 L
12 oz.	340 mL	48 oz.	1.36 L

approximate metric equivalents for ingredients

Butter, Margarine

115 g	½ cup	¼ lb.
250 g	1 generous cup	½ lb.

Cheeses, Hard

125 g	1 cup grated	¼ lb./4 oz.
227 to 250 g	2 cups grated	½ lb./8 oz.

Cheeses, Soft (Cottage/Ricotta/Cream Cheese)

125 g	½ cup	¼ lb./4 oz.
227 to 250 g	1 cup	½ lb./8 oz.
454 to 500 g	2 cups	1 lb./16 oz.

Chocolate, Chocolate Chips, Cocoa

30 g	¼ cup grated chocolate	1 oz. (1 square)
175 g	1 cup chocolate chips	6 oz.
110 g	1 cup cocoa	3¾ oz.

Cream, Milk, Sour Cream, Yogurt, Ice Cream

227 to 250 mL/g	1 cup	8 oz.
454 to 500 mL/g	2 cups	16 oz.
1 L	about 4 cups	35.2 oz.

Dried Fruits, Nuts

150 g	1 cup dates, raisins	5¼ oz.
115 g	1 cup chopped walnuts	4 oz.
110 g	1 cup ground almonds	3¾ oz.

Fish/Meat/Poultry, Fruits/Vegetables (Fresh)

227 to 250 g	½ lb.
454 to 500 g	1 lb.
1 kg	2.2 lbs.
1.5 kg	3½ lbs. (an average chicken)
5 kg	11 lbs. (an average turkey)

Fruits and Vegetables (Frozen)

300 g	10 oz. pkg.
454 to 500 g	16 oz. pkg. (1 lb.)
1 kg	2.2 lbs.

Flour, Cornstarch, Crumbs, Cereal

145 g	1 cup all-purpose flour	5 oz.
125 g	1 cup cornstarch	4½ oz.
110 g	1 cup cookie crumbs	3¾ oz.
125 g	1 cup bread crumbs	4½ oz.
90 g	1 cup oats	3¼ oz.

Pasta, Grains, Dried Beans

200 g	1 cup split peas, lentils, rice
250 g	8-oz. pkg.
375 g	12-oz. pkg.
454 to 500 g	16-oz. pkg. (1 lb.)
1 kg	2.2 lbs.

Sugar, Honey

200 g	1 cup sugar	7¾ oz.
170 g	1 cup packed brown sugar	6 oz.
150 g	1 cup icing sugar	5 oz.
340 g	1 cup honey	12 oz.

appetizers

- You can make delicious dips, spreads and hors d'oeuvres in minutes using your processor, making any time party time!
- Refer to the Smart Chart (p. 18) for basic techniques.
- Use the **Slicer** for vegetables to serve with dips. Long vegetables (such as carrots, zucchini, celery) can be cut to fit crosswise in the feed tube rather than upright. Use fairly firm pressure or slices may be too thin. For a decorative effect, pull fork tines down the length of zucchini or cucumber. Cut into pieces slightly shorter than the feed tube; trim both ends flat. Stand the pieces upright in the feed tube. Slice, using medium pressure.
- Some vegetables require hand slicing (e.g., cauliflower or broccoli florets; tomato wedges).
- Add color, flavor and nutrients to dips and spreads with finely chopped carrots, celery, bell peppers, onions and herbs.
- Leftover dips can be thinned with a little milk and used as salad dressings. Chop leftover veggies on the **Steel Blade** and use in soups, sauces, etc.
- Creative containers for dips and spreads can be made from hollowed-out bell peppers, tomatoes, grapefruit, melon or avocado shells. Cut bottoms flat so they won't tip. Pumpernickel bread also makes a great container. Cut 1 inch off the top. Hollow out, leaving half-inch-thick sides. Fill with dip and serve with crudités and the hollowed-out bread, cut into cubes.
- **Pitas, Wraps and Roll-ups:** Fill mini pitas with your favorite spread (e.g., tuna, chicken salad, hummous). Or spread plain or flavored tortillas with your favorite filling. Fold up the bottom of the tortilla about 1 inch, then

roll it around the filling. Refrigerate. For pinwheels, trim off the ends and cut into 1-inch slices.

- Many appetizers may be served as a main dish, or vice versa. A main dish for 4 people will serve 6 to 8 as an appetizer. Bite-sized delights are Zucchini Puffs (p. 115) and Broccoli Cheese Squares (p. 79).
- Make quick pastry canapés with leftover pastry. Roll it out and cut out 2-inch rounds. Bake on an ungreased cookie sheet in a preheated 400°F oven for a few minutes, until golden. Top with grated cheese and veggies, such as mushrooms or bell peppers. Broil for 3 or 4 minutes, until the cheese is melted.

appetizers

roasted red pepper dip

Roasted peppers from a jar should be rinsed well and patted dry to remove the vinegary taste. When peppers are in season, it's cheaper to roast your own.

Yield: About 1 cup. Recipe may be doubled. Do not freeze.

1 clove garlic	$1/2$ cup firm tofu or light cream cheese
2 green onions	2 tsp. olive oil
2 Tbsp. fresh basil	1 tsp. fresh lemon juice
(or 1 tsp. dried basil)	salt and freshly ground black pepper
1 large roasted red bell pepper	to taste
(or $1/2$ cup roasted red bell	pinch sugar
peppers from a jar)	dash cayenne pepper or hot sauce

STEEL BLADE: Drop garlic and green onions through feed tube while machine is running; process until minced. Add basil, red pepper and tofu or cream cheese. Process until very smooth, about 45 seconds, scraping down sides of bowl as needed. Add remaining ingredients and process briefly to blend. Chill well be-fore serving.

roasted red peppers

Preheat broiler or barbecue. Cut bell peppers in half and discard stem, core and seeds. Broil or grill peppers until skin is blackened and blistered. Transfer peppers to a bowl, cover and let cool. Rub with paper towels to remove blackened skin. Freezes well.

sun-dried tomato spread

Great for Salmon Tortilla Pinwheels (p. 46) and delicious with bagels or rolls.

Yield: About $1 1/2$ cups. Do not freeze.

$1/4$ cup oil-packed sun-dried	2 Tbsp. fresh basil (or 1 tsp. dried basil)
tomatoes, well drained	1 cup cream cheese (low-fat or regular)
$1/3$ cup pitted black olives	2 Tbsp. yogurt or sour cream
2 green onions, cut in chunks	(low-fat or regular)

STEEL BLADE: Process sun-dried tomatoes, olives, green onions and basil until finely chopped, about 10 seconds. Add cream cheese and yogurt or sour cream. Process with quick on/off pulses to combine. Do not overprocess. Chill be-fore serving.

chef's tip:
• To use this as a dip, thin it with a little milk.

appetizers

guacamole

Yield: 2 cups.
Do not freeze.

1 small onion, halved

$1/_2$ green bell pepper or chili
   pepper, cored and seeded

1 tomato, quartered

1 avocado, peeled,
   pitted and cut in chunks

$1/_4$ cup mayonnaise (regular or light)

1 Tbsp. lemon juice or vinegar

salt and freshly ground black
   pepper to taste

2 or 3 drops hot sauce

STEEL BLADE: Process onion and pepper until minced, about 6 seconds. Add tomato and process a few seconds longer. Add remaining ingredients and process until smooth, 20 to 30 seconds, scraping down bowl as necessary.

simply salsa

Excellent served with crudités or tortilla chips, or as a topping for fish or chicken.

Yield: About 1$1/_2$ cups.
Keeps for 2 days
in the refrigerator.
Do not freeze.

2 cloves garlic

4 Roma (Italian plum) tomatoes,
   cored and halved

$1/_2$ small onion (or 2 green onions)

$1/_4$ cup fresh basil
   (or 1 tsp. dried basil)

$1/_4$ cup fresh parsley or coriander

1 Tbsp. lemon juice

1 tsp. extra-virgin olive oil

salt and freshly ground black
   pepper to taste

dash of sugar and cayenne pepper to taste

STEEL BLADE: Drop garlic through feed tube while machine is running; process until minced. Add remaining ingredients and process with quick on/off pulses until coarsely chopped. Adjust seasonings to taste.

salmon mousse

appetizers

This delicious mousse is perfect for any festive occasion. Make it in a fish-shaped mold, using a grape for the eye and a red pepper strip for the mouth. Insert a hook, line and sinker into the mouth as the ultimate garnish!

Yield: Serves 16 to 20.
Do not freeze.

1 envelope (1 Tbsp.) unflavored gelatin	$^1/_2$ cup mayonnaise (regular or light)
$^1/_4$ cup cold water	1 cup cream cheese (regular or light)
$^1/_2$ cup boiling water	2 $7^3/_4$-oz. cans salmon, drained and flaked
4 green onions, cut in chunks	1 Tbsp. lemon juice
$^1/_4$ cup fresh dill (or 1 Tbsp. dried dill)	6 drops hot sauce
	$^3/_4$ tsp. salt
	dash freshly ground black pepper

In a measuring cup, sprinkle gelatin over cold water. Let stand for 5 minutes to soften. Add boiling water and stir to dissolve. Cool slightly.

STEEL BLADE: Process green onions and dill until minced. Add mayonnaise and cream cheese; process until smooth. Blend in dissolved gelatin. Add remaining ingredients and blend with on/off pulses, scraping down sides of bowl as needed.

Pour mixture into sprayed 6-cup fish mold. Cover and refrigerate overnight. (Can be made a day or two in advance.)

To unmold, loosen edges with a knife, dip mold ¾ of the way into hot water, count to 3 and invert onto a lettuce-lined platter. Garnish with sliced lemon, dill, cucumbers and olives. Serve with crackers or black bread.

variation:
• Substitute 1½ to 2 cups fresh cooked salmon or canned tuna.

lox and cheese spread

Spread strips of lox with cheese and lox mixture. Roll up jelly-roll style. Stand on end and insert a sprig of parsley in the center of each roll.

Yield: About 1$^1/_4$ cups.
Freezes well.

3 or 4 green onions, cut in 2-inch lengths	1 to 2 Tbsp. milk (if mixture is too thick)
1 cup cream cheese or cottage cheese, cut in chunks	$^1/_4$ lb. lox/smoked salmon

STEEL BLADE: Drop green onions through feed tube while machine is running; process until minced. Add cheese and process until smooth. If necessary, add milk to soften. Add lox and process with 3 or 4 quick on/offs, just until mixed. (Or let machine run to blend thoroughly, making the mixture a pale salmon color.) Chill and serve with bagels, pumpernickel bread, pita or assorted crackers.

salmon tortilla pinwheels

Tortilla pinwheels
are today's version
of party sand-
wiches. Blend
salmon with cream
cheese to make
this creamy filling.
For a dairy-free
version, use tofu
"cream cheese" and
mayonnaise.

Yield: About 32.
These can be frozen if
you omit spinach when
filling the tortillas.

appetizers

2 green onions, cut in chunks
2 Tbsp. fresh dill
1 cup cream cheese
  (regular or light)
2 Tbsp. honey mustard
7³/₄-oz. can salmon, drained

2 Tbsp. sour cream or mayonnaise
  (regular or light)
4 10-inch flour tortillas
¹/₂ 10-oz. pkg. baby spinach leaves
grape tomatoes, for garnish

STEEL BLADE: Process green onions and dill until minced, about 10 seconds. Add cream cheese, mustard, salmon and sour cream or mayonnaise. Process until blended, 15 to 20 seconds longer, scraping down sides of bowl as needed.

Spread mixture evenly on tortillas. Cover with a layer of spinach leaves, leaving ½-inch border around the outside edge of each tortilla so that it will stick together when rolled up. Use any remaining spinach leaves to line serving platter.

Roll tortillas up tightly and wrap in plastic wrap. Refrigerate for at least an hour or overnight.

At serving time, slice each roll on the diagonal into 8 slices. (The ends are for nibbling!) Arrange on a large platter lined with spinach; garnish with grape tomatoes.

variations:

- Replace spinach with red leaf lettuce. Place a narrow band of roasted red bell peppers (from a jar or homemade) along one edge of tortillas before rolling them up. Roasted asparagus spears also make a pretty presentation.
- Try other fillings: Lox & Cheese Spread (p. 45) or Sun-dried Tomato Spread (p. 43). Do not freeze fillings containing mayonnaise.

mango quesadillas

This recipe comes from a great little cookbook called "Let's Eat" by Sheilah Kaufman of Potomac, Maryland. Ideal as appetizers or a main course.

Yield: 2 to 4 servings.
Do not freeze.

8 oz. chilled Monterey Jack cheese (2 cups grated)
7-oz. jar roasted red bell peppers, drained
dash hot sauce

1 large mango, peeled and cut in chunks
4 10-inch flour tortillas
4 Tbsp. pesto (p. 63) (or use store-bought)
2 Tbsp. butter or margarine
salsa and sour cream, for serving

Preheat oven to 375°F.

GRATER: Grate cheese, using medium pressure. Remove from bowl and set aside.

STEEL BLADE: Process red peppers and hot sauce until smooth. Place mixture in small bowl. (This can be done ahead, covered and refrigerated.) Chop mango, using quick on/off pulses.

Place tortillas on work surface and brush 1 Tbsp. pesto over half of each tortilla. Sprinkle ¼ of cheese and mango over pesto. Fold in half. Melt 1 Tbsp. butter or margarine in a large skillet over medium heat. Cook quesadillas until golden brown on each side, adding more butter as needed.

Transfer to large baking sheet and brush tops with red pepper mixture. Bake at 375°F until cheese melts and tortillas are crisp, 5 to 10 minutes. Cut each quesadilla into wedges. Serve with salsa and sour cream.

asparagus cheese rolls

Prepare these in advance and pop them under the broiler when your company arrives. Leftover cheese mixture can be used as a spread.

Yield: About 3 dozen.
Freezes well.

18 slices thinly sliced white or whole wheat bread, crusts removed
8 oz. chilled low-fat Cheddar cheese (2 cups grated)

$1/2$ cup soft butter or light margarine, cut in chunks
1 tsp. Dijon mustard
1 tsp. Worcestershire sauce
18 steamed asparagus spears

Flatten bread slices lightly with a rolling pin.

GRATER: Grate cheese, using medium pressure. Leave cheese in processor bowl.

STEEL BLADE: Insert blade, pushing it all the way down. Add butter or margarine, mustard and Worcestershire sauce. Process until mixed, scraping down bowl as needed. Spread on bread slices.

Place an asparagus spear on each slice of bread, trimming asparagus to fit. Roll up and cut in half. Place seam-side down in a single layer on a cookie sheet. Wrap well; refrigerate or freeze until needed. Broil until golden. Serve hot.

appetizers

bruschetta

This easy, healthy appetizer tastes best when fresh tomatoes are in season. The tomato mixture also makes a terrific topping for grilled fish or chicken.

Yield: 4 to 8 servings.
Do not freeze.

appetizers

1 clove garlic
$1/4$ cup fresh basil leaves
4 firm, ripe tomatoes,
    cored and quartered
salt and freshly ground black
    pepper to taste

2 to 3 Tbsp. extra-virgin olive oil
8 1-inch slices French or
    Italian crusty bread
2 additional cloves garlic,
    cut in half

STEEL BLADE: Process 1 clove garlic with basil until minced. Add tomatoes and process with several quick on/off pulses, until coarsely chopped. Do not over-process. Season with salt, pepper and 1 Tbsp. of the olive oil.

Toast or grill bread slices on both sides until crisp and golden. Rub one side of bread slices with cut garlic. Brush lightly with remaining olive oil. Top with tomato mixture and serve immediately.

variation:

• Top with grated Mozzarella or crumbled feta cheese. You will need ¾ to 1 cup cheese. Broil just until melted.

make-and-bake pizza

Warning: Once you try this recipe, you may never order from the local pizzeria again! Pizzas may be frozen un-baked—just pop into the oven and increase baking time by 5 minutes. Pizzas may also be frozen after baking.

Yield: 2 large or 12 miniature pizzas.
Freezes well.

Dough
1 pkg. dry yeast
$1/4$ cup warm water
    (105°F to 115°F)
$2^3/4$ cups flour (half whole wheat
    flour may be used)
1 Tbsp. sugar
1 tsp. salt
1 Tbsp. olive oil
1 cup lukewarm water

Topping
2 tsp. olive oil
1 cup tomato or pizza sauce
    (bottled or homemade)
dash oregano and basil
1 cup mushrooms
1 green, red and/or yellow bell
    pepper, halved and seeded
8 oz. chilled Mozzarella cheese
    (2 cups grated)

For dough: Sprinkle yeast over ¼ cup warm water and let stand for 8 to 10 minutes. Stir to dissolve.

STEEL BLADE: Process flour, sugar and salt for 6 seconds. Add yeast; process 10 seconds longer. Combine oil and water; drizzle through feed tube while machine is running. Process until dough gathers together and forms a mass around the blades. (Have an additional ¼ cup flour ready in case machine begins to slow down; dump in through feed tube, if necessary.) Process dough 30 to 40 seconds longer. Dough should be somewhat sticky.

Divide dough in half. Knead on a floured surface into smooth balls. Flatten and roll into two 12-inch circles (or make 12 smaller circles). Place on sprayed pizza pans or baking sheets. Turn edges to raise slightly. Let rise 10 to 15 minutes in pans.

For topping: Preheat oven to 425°F. Brush dough with oil. Spread with sauce and sprinkle with seasonings.

SLICER: Slice mushrooms and peppers, using light pressure. Spread over sauce.

GRATER: Grate cheese, using medium pressure. Top pizzas. Bake on lowest rack for 20 minutes.

variations:

• Top pizzas with any of the following toppings: Pesto (p. 63), chopped sun-dried tomatoes, roasted red bell pepper strips, thinly sliced zucchini, tomatoes, onions, marinated artichoke hearts, basil leaves, chopped spinach, thinly sliced smoked salmon, drained and flaked tuna, grated Parmesan cheese, crumbled feta cheese … design your own personal pizza!

sesame cheese straws

Yield: About 7 to 8 dozen. May be frozen either baked or unbaked. It is not necessary to thaw them before baking.

4 oz. chilled Cheddar cheese (about 1 cup grated)	$^1/_3$ cup chilled butter or margarine, cut in 1-inch chunks
1 cup flour	$^1/_2$ tsp. Worcestershire sauce
$^1/_2$ tsp. salt	2 to 3 Tbsp. cold water
$^1/_4$ tsp. paprika	$^1/_4$ cup sesame seeds

Preheat oven to 400°F.

GRATER: Grate cheese, using light pressure. Empty bowl.

STEEL BLADE: Process flour, salt, paprika and butter or margarine for 8 to 10 seconds, until particles are size of small peas. Add cheese, Worcestershire sauce, 2 Tbsp. water and sesame seeds. Process just until dough begins to gather in a ball around the blades, 12 to 15 seconds. Add extra tablespoon of water if dough seems too dry. Do not overprocess.

Divide mixture in half. Roll out each part into 8 x 12-inch rectangle about ⅛ inch thick. Using sharp knife or pastry wheel, cut in strips about ½ inch x 3 inches.

Place on ungreased foil-lined cookie sheets. Bake for 10 to 12 minutes, until golden.

stuffed italian mushrooms

Ideal as an
appetizer or a
side dish.

Yield: 4 servings.
To freeze, bake for
only 10 minutes at
350°F. When cool,
wrap well and freeze
until needed. Bake
frozen mushrooms,
covered, at 350°F for
15 minutes. Uncover
and broil until golden.

1 dozen very large mushrooms
   (or 2 dozen medium)
1 clove garlic
1 Tbsp. olive oil
1 small onion
1 stalk celery, cut in chunks
$1/2$ red bell pepper

$1/3$ cup bread crumbs
salt and freshly ground black
   pepper to taste
pinch of dried oregano and dried basil
   (or 1 Tbsp. fresh oregano and basil)
2 oz. chilled Mozzarella cheese
   ($1/2$ cup grated)

Preheat oven to 350°F.

Wash mushrooms quickly and pat dry with paper towels. Remove stems and set aside.

STEEL BLADE: Drop garlic through feed tube while machine is running; process until minced. Add mushroom stems and process until finely chopped, 6 to 8 seconds. Heat oil in large skillet; add garlic and chopped mushrooms. Process onion, celery and red pepper until minced, 6 to 8 seconds. Add to skillet and sauté about 5 minutes on medium heat. Stir in bread crumbs and seasonings.

Stuff mushroom caps with mixture and arrange in single layer in sprayed baking dish.

GRATER: Grate cheese, using medium pressure. Sprinkle stuffed mushrooms with cheese. (Can be made in advance and refrigerated.)

Bake, uncovered, for 15 to 20 minutes.

variation:

• Omit celery, red bell pepper and Mozzarella cheese. Process ¼ cup almonds on STEEL BLADE for 15 seconds, until coarsely chopped. Add ¼ cup each of sun-dried tomatoes and roasted red bell peppers to almonds. Process with 3 or 4 quick on/offs. Add almond mixture, bread crumbs and seasonings to sautéed mushrooms stems. Stuff mushrooms; sprinkle lightly with grated Parmesan cheese or melted margarine. Bake as directed.

vegetarian egg rolls

To save time, buy
frozen egg roll
wrappers, avail-
able in most
supermarkets.

$2^1/4$ cups flour
$1/2$ tsp. salt
2 eggs
$1/4$ cup warm water
   (approximately)

Egg Roll Filling (p. 51)
1 egg, lightly beaten
oil for deep-frying (about 2 cups)
plum sauce or duck sauce, for dipping

appetizers

Yield: About 30 large
or 60 small egg rolls.
Freezes well.

STEEL BLADE: Process flour, salt, 2 eggs and water until dough forms a ball on the blade and is well kneaded, 25 to 30 seconds. Remove from bowl, cover and let stand for 15 minutes. Prepare filling as directed and let cool.

Divide dough in half. Roll one piece out into a large, thin rectangle. Cut in 4-inch squares for large egg rolls, or into 2 x 4-inch rectangles for miniatures. Brush edges of dough with beaten egg. Place spoonful of filling along lower edge of dough. Roll up and press edges to seal. Repeat with remaining dough and filling.

Heat oil to 375°F in deep-fryer or deep saucepan. Fry egg rolls until golden, about 5 minutes. Drain on paper towels. (May be frozen at this point. Thaw before reheating.)

To reheat: Place in single layer on foil-lined cookie sheet and heat, uncovered, at 350°F until piping hot and crisp, 10 to 15 minutes.

appetizers

egg roll filling

Yield: Filling for 24 to
30 egg rolls or 16 to
20 crêpes.

1 or 2 cloves garlic
1 slice fresh ginger, peeled
   (1 Tbsp.)
2 medium onions, quartered
2 stalks celery, cut in chunks
1 green or red bell pepper,
   cut in chunks

1 cup mushrooms
2 Tbsp. oil
1 lb. fresh bean sprouts
2 Tbsp. soy sauce
1 tsp. toasted sesame oil
dash freshly ground black pepper

STEEL BLADE: Drop garlic and ginger through feed tube while machine is running; process until minced. Process onions with 3 or 4 quick on/off pulses, until coarsely chopped. Empty bowl. Repeat with celery, bell pepper and mushrooms. In large skillet or wok, quickly brown chopped vegetables in hot oil on high heat. Add bean sprouts and stir-fry until mixture is fairly dry, about 2 minutes. Stir in soy sauce, sesame oil and pepper.

variation:

• About ½ a medium cabbage or bok choy may be substituted for bean sprouts. Process on SLICER, using light pressure. Measure approximately 3 cups.

51

falafel

appetizers

Serve this Middle Eastern specialty in warmed pita pockets with garnishes, such as chopped onion, cucumber, hot pepper, pickles, tomatoes, peppers and lettuce. Drizzle with Tahini Dressing (p. 64).

Yield: About 100 balls. May be frozen.

2 cups dried chickpeas
4 to 6 cloves garlic
2 large onions, quartered
$1/2$ cup fresh parsley
$1\,1/2$ tsp. salt (or to taste)
freshly ground black pepper
  to taste

1 tsp. ground cumin (or to taste)
dash cayenne pepper or ground coriander
6 Tbsp. bread crumbs
2 eggs
$1/2$ tsp. baking powder
oil for deep-frying (about 4 cups)

Pick over chickpeas; discard any stones or debris. Soak overnight in cold water. Drain thoroughly. Divide ingredients in half and process in two batches.

STEEL BLADE: Drop garlic through feed tube while machine is running; process until minced. Add onion and parsley; process until minced. Add remaining ingredients and process until finely ground, 20 to 30 seconds, scraping down bowl as necessary. Transfer to mixing bowl and repeat with second batch of ingredients. Form into 1-inch balls.

Heat oil to 375°F in deep-fryer or deep saucepan. Fry falafel in hot oil until crisp and golden, about 5 minutes. They will float to the surface when done. Drain on paper towels.

note:
• If desired, substitute 4 cups drained canned chickpeas for the dried chickpeas. Soaking is not necessary.

hummous

Serve this Middle Eastern spread with pita bread or assorted vegetables.

Yield: About 2 cups. Keeps about a week in refrigerator. Do not freeze.

$1/4$ cup fresh parsley
2 or 3 cloves garlic
19-oz. can chickpeas,
  drained and rinsed
$2/3$ cup olive oil
$1/2$ cup tahini (sesame seed paste)
6 Tbsp. fresh lemon juice

1 tsp. salt (or to taste)
freshly ground black pepper to taste
$1/2$ tsp. ground cumin (or to taste)
additional olive oil, for garnish
paprika and olives, for garnish
  (optional)

STEEL BLADE: Make sure parsley and processor bowl are dry. Process parsley until minced. Set aside. Drop garlic through feed tube while machine is running; process until minced. Add chickpeas, olive oil, tahini, lemon juice, salt, pepper and cumin. Process until smooth.

Spread mixture on large flat serving plate. Drizzle with additional oil and sprinkle with reserved parsley. Garnish with paprika and olives, if desired.

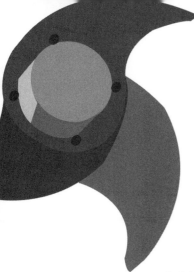

soups, sauces and marinades

- If you don't have homemade broth, use canned soup, instant powdered soup mix, bouillon cubes dissolved in water or the cooking water from vegetables. Add a few parsley stems, green onion tops and 1 or 2 garlic cloves, simmer for a few minutes, then strain. Use immediately, refrigerate or freeze.

- To add extra flavor to broths or soups, save the soaking water from dried mushrooms or sun-dried tomatoes. Freeze in ice cube trays until needed. One cube equals 2 tablespoons.

- Use leftover cooked vegetables to thicken soups. Strain vegetables, then purée on the **Steel Blade** until smooth, about 10 seconds. For thick purées (vegetables only), process 3 to 3½ cups at a time. For thin purées (vegetables and liquid), process 2½ cups at a time. Check your manual for guidelines. Approximately 1 cup of puréed vegetables or legumes will thicken 3 to 4 cups of broth.

- Add meat or chicken bones to soups for a heartier flavor.

- Barley, beans, lentils and split peas add vitamins and fiber to soups.

- Add chopped fresh herbs (e.g., basil, dill) to soups in the last few minutes of cooking. A squeeze of fresh lemon juice also improves the taste.

- Don't throw out those celery tops. Chop with the **Steel Blade** and add them to soups for a fresh flavor.

- When freezing soups, leave 2 inches at the top of the container to allow for expansion. To defrost, place the container in hot water for a few seconds, then transfer the soup to a microwavable bowl. One cup of frozen soup takes 4 minutes on HIGH to defrost, plus 2 to 3 minutes to reheat. Stir often.

- Refrigerate soups and gravies overnight. Discard congealed fat and say goodbye to unwanted calories and cholesterol!
- Thicken sauces and gravies with leftover cooked vegetables (especially potatoes). Purée the vegetables, then add hot broth or pan juices through the feed tube until the desired texture is reached. Season to taste.
- Dump those lumps! Make sauces smooth by processing them for a few seconds on the **Steel Blade**.
- Marinades enhance flavor and increase tenderness. Marinades used for meat, poultry or fish must be boiled for 1 or 2 minutes if you want to serve them as a sauce.

phony minestrone

When my kids were young, they called this spaghetti soup! For a vegetarian version, omit chicken and substitute vegetable broth for water.

Yield: 12 hearty servings.
May be frozen.

2 whole chicken breasts
6 cups cold water
1 Tbsp. salt
3 or 4 cloves garlic
1 large onion, cut in chunks
2 carrots, cut in chunks
2 stalks celery, cut in chunks
$1/2$ cup green split peas
$1/4$ cup barley
$5^1/2$-oz. can tomato paste
28-oz. can tomatoes, drained
   (reserve juice)

2 bay leaves
freshly ground black pepper to taste
$1/2$ tsp. each dried basil and dried oregano
$1/4$ tsp. each dried rosemary
   and dried thyme
1 cup fresh green beans (optional)
2 additional carrots
1 cup canned baked beans
14-oz. can green peas, drained
$1^1/2$ to 2 cups spaghetti, broken
   into 2-inch pieces

Place chicken, cold water and salt in large soup pot. Bring to a boil. Skim.

STEEL BLADE: Drop garlic through feed tube while machine is running; process until minced. Add onion, 2 carrots and celery and process until fine. Add to soup. Add split peas, barley, tomato paste and reserved juice from canned tomatoes to soup.

Process drained tomatoes on STEEL BLADE until puréed, about 6 seconds. Add to soup. Add bay leaves, pepper, basil, oregano, rosemary and thyme. Cover and simmer for 2 hours.

SLICER: Cut green beans to fit crosswise in feed tube. Slice, using firm pressure. Slice additional 2 carrots, using firm pressure. Add all remaining ingredients to soup. Simmer about 25 minutes longer, stirring occasionally. Adjust seasonings.

quick potato soup

An excellent lunch for the kids.

Yield: 4 to 6 servings.
Freezes well.

3 medium potatoes or 2 sweet
   potatoes, peeled
2 Tbsp. fresh dill
1 medium onion
1 large carrot

1 stalk celery
3 cups boiling water
2 tsp. salt
$1/4$ tsp. freshly ground black pepper
$1^1/2$ cups milk or soy milk

STEEL BLADE: Cut potatoes in chunks. Process with dill until minced, 8 to 10 seconds. Transfer to a 3-quart saucepan. Cut onion, carrot and celery in chunks. Process until minced. Add to potatoes along with boiling water, salt and pepper.

Cover and simmer for 15 to 20 minutes, until vegetables are tender. Add milk and heat just to boiling.

variation:

- Prepare Quick Potato Soup as directed. Grate 4 oz. chilled Swiss cheese, using medium pressure (about 1 cup grated). Stir into soup. Adjust seasonings to taste. If too thick, add more water or milk. Serve with crusty fresh rolls. May be frozen, but add cheese when reheating.

parmentier soup

Yield: 6 servings.
Freezes well.

$1/4$ cup fresh parsley
2 large leeks (or a combination of leeks and onions, about 3 cups sliced)
2 Tbsp. margarine or butter
3 Tbsp. flour

6 cups water
4 medium potatoes, peeled and cut in chunks
salt and freshly ground black pepper to taste
2 cups milk
1 Tbsp. additional butter (optional)

STEEL BLADE: Process parsley until minced. Set aside.

SLICER: Wash leeks well. Cut to fit feed tube, discarding most of green part. Slice, using firm pressure.

Melt margarine or butter in heavy saucepan. Add leeks and/or onions, cover pan and cook for 5 minutes over low heat without browning. Blend in flour and cook for 1 minute more without browning. Add water gradually, blending with a whisk.

STEEL BLADE: Chop potatoes in 2 batches with on/off pulses, until coarsely chopped. Add potatoes, salt and pepper to saucepan; bring to a boil, cover and simmer for 30 to 35 minutes. Add milk and additional butter, if desired and garnish with parsley. Adjust seasonings, if necessary.

variations:

- Substitute a 10-oz. package of frozen chopped broccoli (or 3 cups broccoli florets) for the potatoes.
- To make Vichyssoise, prepare as for Parmentier Soup, but strain vegetables through a sieve over another saucepan. Purée half the vegetables at a time on the STEEL BLADE. Return to cooking liquid. Stir in milk plus ½ cup heavy or light cream. Omit additional butter. Cover and refrigerate. Garnish with parsley to serve.

56

carrot and sweet potato soup

This easy, nutritious soup is packed with beta-carotene. You can use a combination of carrots and squash for a tasty variation. Baby carrots save time because they don't need peeling!

Yield: 10 servings. Delicious hot or cold. Freezes well.

2 cloves garlic
1 slice fresh ginger, peeled
  (about 1 Tbsp.)
1 large onion, cut in chunks
1 or 2 stalks celery, cut in chunks
1 Tbsp. olive oil
1 1/2 lbs. carrots, cut in chunks
  (4 cups)
1 medium potato, cut in chunks

2 medium sweet potatoes, cut in chunks
8 cups water or vegetable broth
2 tsp. salt (or to taste)
freshly ground black pepper to taste
2 Tbsp. fresh basil
2 Tbsp. fresh dill
1 to 2 Tbsp. lemon juice (or to taste)
1 to 2 Tbsp. honey (or to taste)

STEEL BLADE: Drop garlic and ginger through feed tube while machine is running; process until minced. Remove from bowl and reserve. Process onion and celery with quick on/off pulses, until coarsely chopped.

Heat oil in large soup pot. Sauté onions and celery for 6 or 7 minutes, until tender, stirring occasionally. Add a little water if vegetables begin to stick.

Process carrots with quick on/off pulses, until coarsely chopped. Add to soup pot along with reserved ginger/garlic; cook 2 minutes longer. Coarsely chop potato and sweet potatoes. Add to soup pot along with water or broth, salt and pepper.

Bring to a boil, reduce heat and simmer partly covered about 30 minutes, until vegetables are tender. Process basil and dill until minced, about 10 seconds.

Because of the quantity, it is easier to use an immersion blender and purée soup directly in the pot. (To purée soup in the processor, place a strainer over a large bowl or saucepan. Strain soup. Purée solids in two batches on the STEEL BLADE until smooth. Stir puréed vegetables into cooking liquid.) Add basil, dill, lemon juice and honey; season with salt and pepper to taste. Add additional water or broth if soup is too thick.

carrot soup

Eliminate sweet potatoes and use 2 lbs. carrots. If desired, eliminate dill and add 1 tsp. ground cumin. For a calcium boost, add approximately 1 cup milk or soy milk to puréed soup. Garnish with chopped chives or green onions.

broccoli lentil soup

This nutritious, low-fat soup is a terrific way to sneak some fiber into your day! One hearty serving contains 168 calories, 3.6 grams of fat and 6 grams of fiber.

Yield: 6 to 8 servings. Reheats and/or freezes well.

2 Tbsp. fresh dill (or 1 tsp. dried dill)
1 large or 2 medium onions, cut in chunks
1 Tbsp. olive or canola oil
2 or 3 carrots, cut in chunks
2 medium potatoes, cut in chunks
1 large bunch broccoli (3 to 4 cups, cut up)
6 cups vegetable or chicken broth
1 tsp. soy sauce
$1/2$ cup red lentils, rinsed and drained
salt and freshly ground black pepper to taste
1 Tbsp. fresh lemon juice (or to taste)

STEEL BLADE: If using fresh dill, process until minced, about 10 seconds. Remove from bowl and set aside.

Process onions with quick on/off pulses, until coarsely chopped. Heat oil in large saucepan and sauté onions on medium-high heat for 5 to 7 minutes, until golden.

Chop carrots and potatoes with quick on/off pulses; add to pan. Chop broccoli with quick on/off pulses. Add to pan along with broth, soy sauce and lentils. Bring to a boil and reduce heat. Simmer, partially covered, for 25 to 30 minutes, stirring occasionally, until lentils soften. Season with salt and pepper.

Purée soup in batches until fairly smooth. If soup is too thick, thin with a little water or broth. Add dill and lemon juice; adjust seasonings to taste.

roasted squash soup

All the cooking for this flavorful, fat-free soup takes place in your oven! It can also be made with a combination of butternut, hubbard and/or acorn squash.

Yield: 6 servings. Reheats and/or freezes well.

$2^1/2$ to 3 lbs. butternut squash
4 or 5 cloves garlic
1 large onion (unpeeled)
2 large, firm apples, unpeeled (e.g., Cortland)
3 cups vegetable broth
1 cup skim or soy milk
salt and freshly ground black pepper to taste
$1/4$ tsp. chili powder
1 tsp. curry powder or ground cumin
$1/2$ tsp. dried basil

Preheat oven to 400°F.

Cut squash in half and scoop out seeds. Place cut-side down on a sprayed foil-lined baking sheet. Wrap garlic cloves in foil. Rinse unpeeled onion and apples, pierce skin in several places with sharp knife and place on baking sheet along with garlic and squash. Roast for 45 minutes, until tender. Don't worry if apples burst open during cooking. Remove pan from oven. When cool enough to handle, discard skins from squash, onions and apples. Discard apple core.

STEEL BLADE: Place squash, garlic, onion and apples in processor bowl. Process until smooth, about 25 to 30 seconds, scraping down sides of bowl as needed. You will have about 4 cups of purée. Transfer mixture to large saucepan or microwavable bowl; stir in broth and milk. Add remaining ingredients and heat until piping hot.

cream of pumpkin soup

A delicious way to use up leftover pumpkin purée from Pumpkin Pie (p. 210). This easy soup can also be made with cooked squash.

Yield: 4 servings. May be frozen. Reheat on low heat; do not boil.

1 medium onion, halved
1 to 2 Tbsp. margarine or butter
$2^{1}/_{4}$ cups boiling water
2 cups canned or fresh
   Pumpkin Purée (below)
2 tsp. instant chicken soup mix

$3/_{4}$ tsp. salt
freshly ground black pepper to taste
1 Tbsp. minced fresh dill
   (or $^{1}/_{2}$ tsp. dried dill)
$1^{1}/_{4}$ cups milk or soy milk
2 tsp. additional margarine or butter

STEEL BLADE: Process onion with 3 or 4 quick on/off pulses, until coarsely chopped. Melt margarine or butter in a saucepan and sauté onion for 3 or 4 minutes on medium heat, until golden. Add water, pumpkin, soup mix, salt, pepper and dill. Cover partially and simmer for 15 to 20 minutes.

Process soup on STEEL BLADE about 30 seconds, until smooth. Return mixture to saucepan. Pour milk into processor and process for a few seconds to remove any purée clinging to bowl. Add milk to saucepan along with 2 tsp. additional margarine or butter. Season to taste. Serve hot or cold.

pumpkin purée

Wash pumpkin and cut in several pieces. Discard stringy portion. Remove seeds and set aside. Place pumpkin in a pan skin-side up, cover with boiling water and bake in a preheated 350°F oven for 1 hour, until tender. Drain well and cool. Scrape out the pulp and process on the STEEL BLADE until smooth. Makes 2 to 3 cups. May be frozen, but drain off any excess liquid when thawed.

roasted pumpkin seeds

For a tasty snack, roast the pumpkin seeds in a preheated 200°F oven until dry and crisp, about 1 hour. If desired, sprinkle lightly with oil during roasting. Sprinkle with salt and cool on paper towels.

onion soup au gratin

soups, sauces and marinades

Place soup bowls on a baking sheet lined with foil to catch any drips.

Yield: 8 servings.
May be frozen.

6 medium onions, halved
3 Tbsp. oil or margarine
1/2 tsp. sugar
2 Tbsp. flour
8 cups hot broth (e.g., vegetable broth or onion soup mix)
1/2 cup red wine or sherry
1 bay leaf

1/4 tsp. dried basil
1/4 tsp. nutmeg
salt and freshly ground black pepper to taste
8 1-inch slices French bread
4 oz. chilled Mozzarella cheese
4 oz. chilled Swiss cheese
1/4 cup grated Parmesan cheese

SLICER: Slice onions, using medium pressure. Heat oil in heavy 4-quart saucepan. Stir in onions. Cook, uncovered, on low heat for 25 to 30 minutes, until deep golden brown, stirring often. Stir in sugar and flour and cook for 2 minutes. Add broth, wine, bay leaf, basil, nutmeg, salt and pepper. Cover and simmer 20 to 25 minutes. (Soup may be prepared to this point and refrigerated or frozen.)

Place bread slices in preheated 325°F oven for about ½ hour to dry. Remove bread. Increase oven temperature to 350°F.

GRATER: Grate Mozzarella and Swiss cheeses, using medium pressure. You should have about 4 cups. Mix lightly.

Ladle soup into individual ovenproof bowls. Top each bowl with a bread slice. Sprinkle with combined Mozzarella and Swiss cheeses. Top with a little Parmesan cheese. Bake at 350°F about 20 minutes, then broil lightly to brown cheeses. (If soup is already hot when you ladle it into bowls, eliminate baking and just broil for 4 to 5 minutes, until bubbly and golden.)

béchamel (white) sauce

This technique makes a creamy, lump-free sauce.

Yield: 1 cup.
May be frozen.

2 Tbsp. butter or margarine
2 Tbsp. flour
1/4 tsp. salt

dash white pepper
1 cup milk (regular or low-fat)

STEEL BLADE: Process butter or margarine with flour, salt and pepper until blended, about 5 seconds. Microwave milk in a 2-cup glass measuring cup on HIGH for 1¾ to 2 minutes, until steaming hot. Pour hot milk through feed tube while machine is running. Process until smooth. Pour sauce back into measuring cup and microwave on HIGH for 30 to 60 seconds, until bubbly and thickened. Stir once or twice.

note:

- Recipe may be doubled. For a thinner sauce, use 1 Tbsp. butter and 1 Tbsp. flour for each cup of milk. For a thicker sauce, use 3 Tbsp. butter and 3 Tbsp. flour for each cup of milk.

variations:

- Substitute chicken stock for milk and use non-dairy (pareve) margarine instead of butter.
- **Cheese Sauce:** Stir 1 cup grated Cheddar or Swiss cheese, ¼ tsp. dry mustard and ½ tsp. Worcestershire sauce into hot Béchamel Sauce. Stir until cheese melts.

mushroom sauce

Yield: About 1³/₄ cups.
May be frozen.

1 cup mushrooms
3 Tbsp. butter or margarine
3 Tbsp. flour
1¹/₂ cups hot milk, soy milk or broth

³/₄ tsp. salt
¹/₄ tsp. white pepper
dash nutmeg

SLICER: Slice mushrooms, using light pressure. Melt 1 Tbsp. of the butter or margarine in a nonstick skillet. Sauté mushrooms until golden. Set aside.

STEEL BLADE: Process remaining 2 Tbsp. butter with flour until blended, about 5 seconds. Pour hot liquid through feed tube while machine is running. Add seasonings. Process until smooth.

Transfer sauce to 4-cup glass measuring cup. Microwave on HIGH for 1 to 2 minutes, until bubbly and thick, stirring once or twice. Stir in mushrooms.

easy barbecue sauce

Use for spare ribs,
London broil,
chicken or tofu.

Yield: About 1¹/₂ cups.
May be frozen.

1 clove garlic
¹/₂ cup brown sugar, packed

¹/₂ cup bottled barbecue sauce
¹/₂ cup applesauce

STEEL BLADE: Drop garlic through feed tube while machine is running; process until minced, about 8 seconds. Scrape down sides of bowl. Add remaining ingredients and process just until blended.

61

quick tomato sauce

A delicious substitute for bottled spaghetti sauce.

Yield: About 4 cups. Keeps about a week in the refrigerator, or may be frozen.

3 or 4 cloves garlic
1 large onion, cut in chunks
28-oz. can tomatoes
5$1/2$-oz. can tomato paste
$1/4$ tsp. each salt, dried basil,
    dried oregano and sugar

freshly ground black pepper to taste
$1/4$ tsp. cayenne pepper or red
    pepper flakes
3 to 4 Tbsp. red wine or water
1 Tbsp. olive oil

STEEL BLADE: Add garlic through feed tube while machine is running; process until minced. Add onion and process until minced, 6 to 8 seconds.

Combine all ingredients in covered microwave casserole or large saucepan. To microwave, cook covered on HIGH for 12 to 15 minutes, stirring once or twice. To cook conventionally, bring to a boil, reduce heat and simmer covered for 25 to 30 minutes, stirring occasionally. Adjust seasonings to taste.

vegetarian spaghetti sauce

This nutritious sauce is great on pasta or spaghetti squash.

Yield: 6 to 8 servings. Freezes well.

2 or 3 cloves garlic
2 medium onions, quartered
1 green or red bell pepper,
    cut in chunks
2 Tbsp. olive oil
1 cup mushrooms
1 eggplant, peeled (about
    1$1/4$ lbs.)
1 medium zucchini, peeled

19-oz. can tomatoes
2 5$1/2$-oz. cans tomato paste
$1/4$ cup dry red wine (optional)
salt and freshly ground black
    pepper to taste
$1/4$ tsp. each dried oregano, dried
    basil and chili powder
1 bay leaf (optional)

STEEL BLADE: Drop garlic through feed tube while machine is running; process until minced. Add onions and bell pepper. Process with 3 or 4 quick on/off pulses, until coarsely chopped. Heat oil in a large pot. Sauté garlic, onions and pepper for 5 minutes on medium heat, until tender.

SLICER: Slice mushrooms, using light pressure. Add to pan and cook 2 minutes longer.

GRATER: Cut eggplant to fit feed tube. Grate, using medium pressure. Repeat with zucchini. Add to pan and cook 5 minutes longer. Stir in remaining ingredients, cover and simmer about 45 minutes, stirring occasionally. Taste and adjust seasonings.

pesto

When basil is expensive, use a combination of basil and fresh spinach leaves. Pesto is perfect with pasta, fish or in salad dressings, soups and casseroles.

Yield: About 1 cup. Pesto keeps 4 or 5 days in the refrigerator or freezes well.

4 cloves garlic
1 cup fresh basil, tightly packed
$1/_4$ cup fresh parsley
$1/_4$ cup pine nuts or almonds
$1/_2$ tsp. salt (or to taste)

freshly ground black pepper to taste
$1/_2$ cup olive oil (preferably extra-virgin)
$1/_3$ to $1/_2$ cup grated Parmesan cheese

STEEL BLADE: Drop garlic through feed tube while machine is running; process until minced. Add basil, parsley, nuts, salt and pepper. Process until finely minced, about 20 seconds. Drizzle oil through feed tube while machine is running and process until blended. Blend in Parmesan cheese. Transfer pesto to a bowl, cover and refrigerate. If you cover it with a thin layer of olive oil, it will keep about a month in the refrigerator.

lighter variation:
• Use ¼ cup olive oil and ¼ cup tomato juice or vegetable broth. Reduce cheese to 3 Tbsp. and nuts to 2 Tbsp.

rina's red pepper sauce

This delicious sauce comes from the personal recipe collection of Rina Perry of Israel. Rina can't imagine life without her food processor! Serve with pasta, meat patties or your favorite fish.

Yield: About 3 cups.

8 large red bell peppers
3 cloves garlic
$1/_2$ cup olive oil

$1/_4$ cup white vinegar
1 tsp. salt
2 tsp. sugar

Broil or grill peppers on all sides until skin is blackened and blistered. Transfer them to a bowl, cover and let cool. Remove the blackened skin. Cut peppers in half; discard the core and seeds.

STEEL BLADE: Drop garlic through feed tube while machine is running; process until minced. Add remaining ingredients and process until you get a smooth sauce, scraping down sides of bowl as necessary. Adjust seasonings to taste. Pour sauce into a glass container, seal the top with additional olive oil and store tightly covered in the refrigerator.

Sauce will keep up to 3 weeks in the refrigerator. If you have extra sauce left and want to keep it longer, bring it to a boil for a minute, let cool, then transfer to a clean glass container. Seal again with olive oil. The oil will harden and form a seal on top of the sauce.

soups, sauces and marinades

mango salsa

This is wonderful with grilled sea bass or boneless chicken breasts. As a variation, substitute fresh pineapple or papaya instead of mango. Ginger adds a wonderful kick!

Yield: About 1 1/2 cups.
Do not freeze.

1 large ripe mango, peeled (about 1 cup)
1 slice fresh ginger, peeled (about 1 Tbsp.)
1/4 cup fresh coriander or parsley
1/2 small red onion (or 2 green onions)
1/2 red bell pepper, cut in chunks

1 jalapeño pepper, cored and seeded
2 Tbsp. fresh basil
1/4 cup fresh lime juice (juice of 2 limes)
2 tsp. extra-virgin olive oil
1 tsp. honey
salt and freshly ground black pepper to taste

Using a sharp knife, cut down one side of the flesh of the mango, feeling for the pit with your knife. Repeat on the other side. You will have 2 large pieces. Cut in chunks.

STEEL BLADE: Process ginger with coriander or parsley until minced. Add mango, onion and peppers. Process with quick on/off pulses, until coarsely chopped. Add remaining ingredients and process with 2 or 3 quick on/offs to combine. May be prepared up to a day in advance and refrigerated. Bring to room temperature before serving.

tahini dressing

Yield: About 3/4 cup.
Keeps about 2 weeks in the fridge.

1 clove garlic
1/2 cup tahini (sesame paste)
1/3 cup water
2 Tbsp. lemon juice

1/2 tsp. salt (or to taste)
freshly ground black pepper to taste
dash ground cumin (optional)

STEEL BLADE: Drop garlic through feed tube while machine is running; process until minced. Add remaining ingredients and process until smooth and creamy, 10 to 15 seconds.

chinese sweet and sour sauce

Delicious with fish or chicken.

Yield: 3 cups.
Keeps about 1 month in the refrigerator.

$^1/_2$ cup ketchup
$^1/_2$ cup vinegar
$^3/_4$ cup cold water
2 Tbsp. lemon juice

$1^1/_4$ cups granulated sugar
$^1/_2$ cup brown sugar, lightly packed
3 Tbsp. cornstarch dissolved
   in $^1/_4$ cup cold water

Combine all ingredients except cornstarch mixture in an 8-cup microwavable bowl and stir well. Microwave uncovered on HIGH for 6 to 7 minutes, until boiling, stirring at half time. Stir cornstarch mixture into sauce. Microwave on HIGH for 2 minutes longer, until bubbling and thickened.

teriyaki marinade

This is a delicious marinade for beef, chicken, turkey, tofu or fish. It also makes an excellent sauce (see below).

Yield: About $^3/_4$ cup.

1 or 2 slices fresh ginger, peeled
   (about 1 to 2 Tbsp.)
3 cloves garlic
$^1/_4$ cup soy sauce

$^1/_4$ cup honey, maple syrup or
   brown sugar
$^1/_4$ cup white wine or water
2 tsp. toasted sesame oil (optional)

STEEL BLADE: Drop ginger and garlic through feed tube while machine is running; process until minced. Add remaining ingredients and process for 8 to 10 seconds to blend.

Marinate meat, poultry or tofu for 1 to 2 hours or up to 24 hours in the refrigerator. Fish only needs to be marinated for 1 to 2 hours.

teriyaki sauce:
- Prepare marinade as directed; heat until boiling. Dissolve 1 Tbsp. cornstarch in 2 Tbsp. cold water or orange juice. Stir into boiling marinade and cook, stirring constantly, until smooth and thickened, about 2 minutes. Serve as a sauce over fish, poultry, meat or tofu.

cantonese marinade

Delicious for spare ribs, chicken, London Broil or tofu.

2 cloves garlic
1 slice fresh ginger, peeled (or 1 tsp. ground ginger)
$1/_4$ cup soy sauce

$1/_4$ cup honey
$1/_4$ cup apricot jam
$3/_4$ cup pineapple or orange juice

Yield: $1^{1}/_2$ cups. Will keep 7 to 10 days in refrigerator.

STEEL BLADE: Drop garlic and fresh ginger through feed tube while machine is running; process until minced. Add remaining ingredients and process a few seconds longer to blend.

chinese marinade

Excellent on chicken, London broil, spare ribs or tofu.

2 cloves garlic
4 green onions
1 Tbsp. ketchup
1 Tbsp. chili sauce

2 Tbsp. soy sauce
2 Tbsp. dry sherry or wine
2 Tbsp. honey or corn syrup
dash salt and freshly ground black pepper

Yield: Enough marinade for 3 lbs. meat or chicken.

STEEL BLADE: Drop garlic and green onions through feed tube while machine is running; process until minced. Scrape down sides of bowl. Add remaining ingredients and process for a few seconds to blend.

honey garlic sparerib sauce

This is delicious as a sauce or marinade for spare ribs, chicken, tofu or brisket.

1 or 2 cloves garlic
$1/_2$ small onion
1 Tbsp. ketchup or chili sauce
1 Tbsp. lemon juice or vinegar
2 Tbsp. soy sauce

$3/_4$ cup honey
$1/_2$ tsp. salt
$1/_4$ tsp. each dry mustard, ground ginger, chili powder and freshly ground black pepper

Yield: 1 cup. Recipe may be doubled. Keeps in the refrigerator for about 1 month.

STEEL BLADE: Drop garlic through feed tube while machine is running; process until minced. Add onion and process until minced. Scrape down sides of bowl. Add remaining ingredients and process for 3 or 4 seconds to blend.

Transfer to 2-cup glass measuring cup and microwave on HIGH for 2 minutes, or until bubbling. Stir well. Microwave 1 minute longer.

fish and dairy dishes

- Calculate 1 lb. per serving when buying a whole fish. One pound of fillets serves 2 to 3.
- Cook fish within 24 hours of purchase, for maximum flavor. Store in the coldest part of your refrigerator.
- Fish can be stored for about 1 month in the freezer section of your refrigerator, or up to 3 months in a deep freezer.
- Defrost fish in the refrigerator, not at room temperature. Calculate 6 hours per pound in the refrigerator. In the microwave, allow 4 to 6 minutes per pound on DEFROST; a few ice crystals should remain. Place in cold water for a few minutes, until ice melts. Cook and serve within a day.
- Cooking times: For fresh fish, allow 10 minutes per inch of thickness at 450°F; for frozen fish, allow 20 minutes per inch of thickness. Measure fish at the thickest point. If baked in sauce, increase cooking time by about 5 minutes per inch of thickness. Cook fish just until it flakes. When done, fish should be opaque and juices on surface will be white.
- Baking, steaming, poaching, broiling, grilling and microwaving are excellent low-fat cooking methods for fish.
- Microwave fish (e.g., salmon, halibut) between wet lettuce leaves to stop it from popping during cooking. Calculate 4 minutes per pound as your microwave cooking time.
- Thin fish fillets don't need to be turned when broiled. Cook about 3 inches from heat on one side only, just until cooked.

- Infants, young children, the elderly and those with weakened immune systems should avoid raw or undercooked eggs. Pasteurized liquid egg product can be substituted—¼ cup equals one egg. For more information on egg safety, proper storage, etc., check out www.aeb.org or www.fightbac.org.

- When making hard-cooked eggs, immediately place them under cold running water to stop the cooking process. Drain; then vigorously shake the pot back and forth to crack the shells. Cover eggs with cold water and let stand for 2 or 3 minutes. Shells will slip off easily! If desired, discard some of the yolks.

- In the Jewish kitchen, cheese and dairy dishes such as blintzes and noodle kugels (puddings) are considered main dishes and not desserts! Team them up with a big bowl of soup and fruit or vegetable salad.

- Dishes that contain dairy ingredients (e.g., cottage or cream cheese, sour cream, yogurt, butter and/or milk) are traditionally served in Jewish homes as part of a dairy meal. Although they can be served as either side or main dishes, they are in this chapter because of their dairy content. For side dishes which can be served with either meat or dairy meals, see the Vegetables and Side Dishes chapter.

- See "Cheese" in the Smart Chart, pp. 21–22, for tips on processing.

- **Flavored Cheese Spreads:** Mince any of the following, using the **Steel Blade:** green onions, carrots, sun-dried tomatoes, roasted peppers, spinach. Add your favorite herbs (e.g., dill, basil), plus cream cheese or cottage cheese. Process until combined.

baked salmon with mango salsa

You'll be hooked
on salmon once
you try this dish.
It tastes fabulous
either hot or cold.
A fillet of salmon
in one piece
makes a beautiful
presentation.

Yield: 6 to
8 servings.

1 lime, ends trimmed	2¹/₂- to 3-lb. salmon fillets (or 6 to 8 fillets)
1 slice fresh ginger, peeled (1 Tbsp.)	salt, freshly ground black pepper and paprika to taste
¹/₄ cup fresh basil	juice of 1 lime (2 Tbsp.)
Mango Salsa (p. 64)	1 to 2 Tbsp. honey

SLICER: Slice lime, using medium pressure. (If you don't have an expanded feed tube, cut lime in half to fit feed tube.) Reserve to use as a garnish.

STEEL BLADE: Process ginger and basil until minced, about 10 seconds. Empty bowl. Prepare salsa as directed.

Line baking sheet with aluminum foil; spray with nonstick spray. Place salmon on baking sheet and sprinkle with salt, pepper and paprika. Rub with lime juice and honey; sprinkle with basil and ginger. (Can be prepared up to 2 hours in advance and refrigerated.)

Bake uncovered in preheated 450°F oven about 15 minutes, or until fish flakes with a fork. Calculate cooking time as 10 minutes per inch of thickness of fish at its thickest point. Transfer to large platter. Garnish with lime slices; serve with salsa.

balsamic baked fish with onions and mushrooms

This is also
excellent with
halibut or sea
bass. Cooking
the fish and
vegetables
together in one
pan saves time
and clean-up!

Yield: 4 servings.

2 large onions, cut in quarters	4 Tbsp. balsamic vinegar
2 cups mushrooms	2 Tbsp. honey
2 Tbsp. olive oil	salt, freshly ground black pepper
4 salmon fillets (about 2 lbs.)	and dried basil to taste

SLICER: Slice onions and mushrooms, using medium pressure. Place on sprayed, foil-lined baking sheet and drizzle with olive oil.

Place salmon on baking sheet. Drizzle salmon, onions and mushrooms with balsamic vinegar and honey. Season with salt, pepper and basil. Marinate for 15 to 20 minutes.

Bake uncovered in preheated 425°F oven for 15 minutes. Salmon will be nicely browned on the outside, but still juicy inside. Onions and mushrooms should be tender and golden. Serve immediately.

orange teriyaki grilled salmon

Halibut or sea bass may be substituted for salmon. Also excellent with chicken, tofu or vegetables. Grill over heat, not flame, to prevent flare-ups. You can also use an indoor grill, following manufacturer's directions for cooking times.

Yield: 4 servings.

1 slice fresh ginger, peeled (1 Tbsp.)	2 tsp. sugar
1 clove garlic	1 tsp. toasted sesame oil
2 Tbsp. soy sauce	$1/4$ tsp. dried basil
2 Tbsp. orange juice	4 salmon steaks or fillets
2 Tbsp. orange marmalade	1 tsp. cornstarch dissolved in 3 Tbsp. orange juice

STEEL BLADE: Drop ginger and garlic through feed tube while machine is running; process until minced. Add soy sauce, 2 Tbsp. orange juice, marmalade, sugar, sesame oil and basil. Process until combined, 8 to 10 seconds.

Arrange salmon in single layer in glass baking dish. Pour marinade over salmon and marinate at room temperature for 30 minutes (or refrigerate up to 2 hours).

Preheat barbecue or grill. Remove fish from marinade, reserving any leftover marinade. Grill for 3 to 4 minutes per side, basting occasionally. Do not overcook or fish will be dry.

Meanwhile, bring leftover marinade to a boil. Stir cornstarch mixture into boiling marinade and simmer for 2 to 3 minutes, until thickened, stirring often. Drizzle sauce over fish and serve immediately. Delicious over rice.

chef's tip:
• If you don't have a grill, place marinated salmon on a sprayed foil-lined baking sheet. Bake uncovered in preheated 425°F oven for 15 minutes, until fish flakes with a fork.

wood chips tips! Soak 3 or 4 handfuls of wood chips (mesquite, applewood, hickory) in water while food is marinating. Toss the soaked chips on top of the hot coals just before placing food on the barbecue.

baked halibut and potato casserole

Yield: 4 servings.
Do not freeze.

4 large potatoes, peeled
salt, freshly ground black pepper
    and paprika to taste
4 halibut steaks (about
    $3/4$ inch thick)

2 medium onions, halved
1 Tbsp. butter or oil
$1 1/2$ cups milk or tomato
    juice (approximately)

Preheat oven to 350°F.

SLICER: Cut potatoes to fit feed tube. Slice potatoes, using firm pressure. Arrange half of potatoes in sprayed 9 x 13-inch glass baking dish. Sprinkle with salt, pepper and paprika. Season fish and arrange over potatoes.

Cut onions to fit feed tube. Slice, using light pressure. Top fish with onions and remaining potatoes. Season again and dot with butter or drizzle with oil. Cover with milk or tomato juice. Bake, uncovered, for about 1 hour, until tender.

salsa just for the halibut!

So quick, so easy, so good! To make this pizza-style, top with grated Mozzarella cheese. It's equally good with red snapper or sea bass

Yield: 6 servings.
Delicious hot or at room temperature.

$1/4$ cup fresh parsley
Simply Salsa (p. 44)
4 halibut steaks or
    fillets (about 2 lbs.)

salt and lemon pepper to taste
$1/4$ cup grated Parmesan
    cheese (optional)

STEEL BLADE: Process parsley until minced, about 10 seconds. Empty bowl and set aside. Prepare salsa as directed. (Salsa can be prepared up to a day in advance and refrigerated.)

Spoon some salsa into bottom of sprayed 9 x 13-inch glass baking dish. Arrange halibut in single layer on top of salsa. Sprinkle fish lightly with salt and lemon pepper. Top with remaining salsa and sprinkle with cheese, if desired.

Bake in preheated 400°F oven for 10 to 12 minutes, just until fish flakes. (Cooking time depends on thickness of fish; allow 10 minutes per inch, measured at the thickest point.) Sprinkle with parsley.

stuffed fish fillets au gratin

An easy do-ahead company dish.

Yield: 4 servings.

8 sole, tilapia or whitefish fillets (about 2 lbs.)
salt, freshly ground black pepper, paprika and dried thyme to taste
1 large onion, quartered
2 stalks celery, cut in chunks

$1/2$ green or red bell pepper, cut in chunks
1 cup mushrooms
2 Tbsp. butter or margarine
8 slices whole wheat or rye bread
$1/3$ cup grated Parmesan cheese

Sprinkle fish lightly on both sides with salt, pepper, paprika and thyme. Arrange half of fillets in single layer in sprayed 7 x 11-inch glass baking dish.

STEEL BLADE: Process onion and celery with quick on/off pulses, until coarsely chopped. Empty bowl and repeat with bell pepper and mushrooms. Melt butter or margarine in large nonstick skillet; reserve 1 Tbsp. Add vegetables to skillet and sauté on medium heat for about 10 minutes, until fairly dry.

Tear bread into chunks and drop through feed tube while machine is running. Process to make fine crumbs. Add to sautéed vegetables and mix well. Season to taste. Top each fillet in baking dish with stuffing. Place remaining fillets on top. Brush with reserved butter and sprinkle with Parmesan cheese. (May be assembled up to this point and refrigerated.) Bake, uncovered, in preheated 375°F oven for 30 to 35 minutes, until fish flakes with a fork.

variation:
- Instead of topping fish with butter and Parmesan cheese, sprinkle with 1 cup grated Cheddar cheese.

broccoli-stuffed fillets with mushroom sauce

Any firm-fleshed fish fillets will work in this recipe. Try it with sole, tilapia or snapper.

Yield: 6 servings.

10-oz. pkg. frozen chopped broccoli (or 2 cups fresh broccoli)
4 tsp. margarine
1 medium onion, halved

salt, freshly ground black pepper and dried thyme to taste
1 slice bread, quartered
6 fish fillets (about 2 lbs.)
Mushroom Sauce (p. 61)

Cook frozen broccoli according to package directions. Fresh broccoli can be microwaved, covered, on HIGH for 4 to 5 minutes, until tender. Microwave margarine on HIGH for 30 seconds, until melted. Remove 2 tsp. margarine and set aside for crumb topping.

STEEL BLADE: Process onion with quick on/off pulses, until coarsely chopped. Microwave with 2 tsp. margarine on HIGH for 3 minutes, until tender. Process broccoli with 3 or 4 quick on/off pulses, until finely chopped. Add to onions. Season to taste.

For crumb topping: Process bread with reserved margarine until fine crumbs are formed. Set aside.

Season fillets on dark side. Spread each fillet with about 3 Tbsp. of broccoli mixture and roll up. Place seam-side down in a sprayed oven-to-table casserole dish.

Prepare sauce as directed. Pour over fish. Sprinkle with reserved crumb topping. (May be assembled in advance up until this point and refrigerated.) Bake, uncovered, in preheated 375°F oven for 30 to 35 minutes.

variation:

- Substitute spinach for broccoli. Add ½ cup grated cheese to the sauce. Add ¼ tsp. dry mustard if using Cheddar cheese or ⅛ tsp. nutmeg if using Swiss cheese.

fish italian style

Yield: 6 servings.

2 lbs. fish fillets or 6 halibut steaks	1 green or red bell pepper, halved
salt and freshly ground black pepper to taste	1 or 2 cloves garlic
	1 cup tomato sauce
6 oz. chilled Mozzarella cheese (1 ½ cups grated)	¼ cup chili sauce or ketchup
1 cup mushrooms	¼ tsp. each dried oregano and dried basil
	few drops hot sauce (optional)

Wash fish and pat dry. Sprinkle both sides with a little salt and pepper. Place in sprayed 9 x 13-inch glass baking dish.

GRATER: Grate cheese, using medium pressure. Empty bowl and set aside.

SLICER: Slice mushrooms and bell pepper, using medium pressure. Set aside.

STEEL BLADE: Drop garlic through feed tube while machine is running; process until minced. Add tomato sauce, chili sauce or ketchup, seasonings and hot sauce. Process for a few seconds to blend. Pour sauce over fish. Sprinkle with vegetables; top with cheese.

Bake, uncovered, in preheated 375°F oven for 25 to 30 minutes, or until fish flakes with a fork. Halibut takes 35 to 40 minutes, depending on thickness.

sole mornay

A terrific company dish—easy and elegant. Also delicious with halibut —just increase the baking time to 35 or 40 minutes, depending on the thickness of the fish.

Yield: 6 servings.

2 lbs. sole fillets (or any fish fillets)	3 Tbsp. flour
salt, freshly ground black pepper and paprika to taste	4 oz. chilled Swiss cheese, cut in chunks
Mushroom Duxelles (p. 114)	$1/_4$ tsp. dry mustard
3 Tbsp. butter or margarine, cut in chunks	$1 1/_2$ cups hot milk
	$1/_2$ cup bread crumbs
	1 Tbsp. melted butter or margarine

Sprinkle fish lightly with salt, pepper and paprika. Stuff fish with Mushroom Duxelles. Roll up (or fold in half) and fasten with a toothpick. Arrange seam-side down in sprayed 7 x 11-inch glass baking dish.

STEEL BLADE: Process butter or margarine, flour and cheese until cheese is fine, 15 to 20 seconds. Add mustard and a little salt and pepper. Pour hot milk through feed tube while machine is running. Transfer sauce to 4-cup glass measure and microwave on HIGH for 1 to 2 minutes, until thick and bubbling, stirring once or twice. Cool slightly. Pour sauce over fish. Top with crumbs and drizzle with melted butter or margarine. (Can be prepared up to this point and refrigerated up to 24 hours.) Bake, uncovered, in preheated 375°F oven about 30 minutes.

fish patties

Yield: 4 servings.
Freezes well.

1 medium onion, cut in chunks	$1/_2$ cup bread crumbs or matzo meal
$1/_2$ stalk celery, cut in chunks	1 tsp. salt
1 small carrot, cut in chunks	freshly ground black pepper to taste
2 eggs (or 1 egg plus 2 whites)	2 Tbsp. oil for frying
1 lb. fish fillets (sole, haddock or perch), cut in chunks	

STEEL BLADE: Process onion, celery and carrot until minced, about 10 seconds. Add eggs and fish. Process 20 to 25 seconds, until fish is minced. Add crumbs or matzo meal, salt and pepper; process a few seconds longer to mix.

Heat oil in large nonstick skillet. Drop fish mixture from large spoon into hot oil. Flatten slightly with back of spoon. Fry both sides on medium-high heat until golden brown, 3 to 4 minutes per side. Add additional oil if needed. Drain on paper towels.

note:
• To double the recipe, process in 2 batches.

tuna strudel

Perfect for the
buffet table.

Yield: 6 to 8 servings.

Flaky Ginger Ale Pastry (p. 207)
1 medium onion, cut in chunks
1 green and 1 red bell pepper,
   cut in chunks
1 Tbsp. butter or margarine
$1/2$ cup grated Parmesan cheese

$1/2$ cup bread or cracker crumbs
2 7-oz. cans tuna, drained and flaked
1 cup sour cream (regular or low-fat)
1 tsp. dry mustard
dash salt and freshly ground black pepper
1 egg yolk blended with 2 tsp. cold water

Prepare pastry as directed and chill.

STEEL BLADE: Process onion and bell peppers with quick on/off pulses, until coarsely chopped. Sauté in butter or margarine until golden, about 5 minutes.

Process Parmesan cheese with crumbs for 3 or 4 seconds. Remove about ¼ cup of crumb mixture and set aside. Combine tuna, sour cream, mustard, salt, pepper and sautéed vegetables with crumb mixture in processor bowl. Process with several quick on/offs, just until mixed.

Roll out half the dough on a lightly floured surface into an 8 x 10-inch rectangle. Sprinkle with half the reserved crumb mixture. Spoon half the tuna mixture onto pastry along one long edge. Leave a 1-inch border on remaining 3 sides; brush with egg yolk to help seal roll. Roll up, turning in ends. Transfer roll to sprayed baking sheet. Brush with egg yolk and cut several slits on the top. Repeat with remaining dough and filling. (Can be frozen unbaked up to 1 month. Thaw before baking.)

Bake in preheated 375°F oven for 35 to 45 minutes, until golden.

variation:
• Replace tuna with canned or leftover cooked salmon (1½ to 2 cups).

luscious vegetarian lasagna

The name
says it all!

Yield: 10 servings.
Reheats and/or
freezes well.

Vegetarian Spaghetti Sauce (p. 62)	1 cup mushrooms
9 lasagna noodles	3 cups ricotta or creamed cottage cheese
12 oz. chilled Mozzarella cheese (3 cups grated)	1 egg
	3/4 cup grated Parmesan cheese
1 green and/or red bell pepper, halved	

Prepare sauce as directed. Cook lasagna noodles according to package directions. Drain well; lay flat on clean towel. Fresh pasta does not require cooking.

GRATER: Cut Mozzarella cheese to fit feed tube. Grate, using medium pressure. Empty bowl.

SLICER: Slice pepper and mushrooms, using light pressure. Empty bowl.

STEEL BLADE: Process ricotta or cottage cheese with egg until blended, about 10 seconds.

Place about 1½ cups sauce in the bottom of sprayed 9 x 13-inch glass baking dish. Arrange 3 lasagna noodles over sauce. Spread with half the ricotta cheese; sprinkle with half the Parmesan and ⅓ of the Mozzarella cheese. Repeat with sauce, noodles and cheeses. Top with noodles, sauce and Mozzarella cheese. Garnish with peppers and mushrooms. (Can be refrigerated or frozen at this point. Thaw before baking.) Bake in preheated 375°F oven about 45 minutes, until bubbling and golden.

variations:
- Add a 10-oz. package of chopped spinach, drained and squeezed dry, to ricotta cheese mixture. Tofu can replace part or all of the ricotta cheese.

tortilla lasagna florentine

There's no need to
cook pasta for this
quick lasagna. I
like to make it in
two pie plates and
freeze one for a
future meal.

Yield: 8 servings.
Reheats and/or
freezes well.

12 oz. chilled Mozzarella cheese (3 cups grated)	1/2 cup grated Parmesan cheese
2 cloves garlic	1 tsp. salt (or to taste)
1 medium carrot, cut in chunks	freshly ground black pepper to taste
3 cups (1 1/2 lbs.) dry cottage cheese	1/2 tsp. each dried basil and dried oregano
10-oz. pkg. frozen spinach, defrosted and squeezed dry	4 cups vegetarian tomato sauce (store-bought or homemade)
	6 large soft flour tortillas (10-inch round)

GRATER: Grate Mozzarella cheese, using medium pressure. You should have 3 cups. Empty bowl.

STEEL BLADE: Process garlic and carrot until finely minced, about 10 seconds. Add cottage cheese, spinach, Parmesan cheese, salt, pepper, basil and oregano; process until blended. Scrape down sides of bowl as needed.

Spray two 9-inch glass pie plates with nonstick spray. In each pie plate, layer ½ cup of sauce, a tortilla, ¼ of the spinach mixture and ½ cup of grated cheese. Repeat layering, ending with a tortilla. You will have 3 layers of tortillas and 2 layers of spinach mixture in each pie plate. Top with remaining sauce and grated cheese. (Can be prepared in advance up to this point and refrigerated.)

Bake, uncovered, in preheated 350°F oven for 30 minutes, until golden brown. Let stand for 5 minutes for easier slicing. Cut in wedges to serve.

variations:
- Use a combination of grated Mozzarella and Swiss cheeses. Replace part or all of the cottage cheese with ricotta cheese or tofu.

pasta vegetable medley

Yield: 6 servings. Reheats well. If frozen, vegetables may lose some of their texture.

16-oz. pkg. rotini or bow tie pasta	2 Tbsp. fresh chopped basil
3 cups broccoli florets	(or 1 tsp. dried basil)
3 cloves garlic	2 cups tomato sauce
1 medium onion, cut in chunks	¼ cup grated Parmesan cheese,
1 red bell pepper, cut in chunks	plus extra for garnish
1 cup mushrooms	salt and freshly ground black pepper
1 Tbsp. olive oil	to taste

Bring large pot of salted water to a boil. Cook pasta for 8 minutes, until nearly tender. Add broccoli and cook 2 minutes longer, until broccoli is tender-crisp and pasta is al dente. Reserve about ½ cup of cooking liquid. Drain pasta but do not rinse. Return pasta and broccoli to pot.

STEEL BLADE: Drop garlic through feed tube while machine is running; process until minced. Add onion, red pepper and mushrooms; process with quick on/off pulses, until coarsely chopped.

In large nonstick skillet or wok, heat oil. Sauté garlic, onion, red pepper and mushrooms on medium-high heat until tender, 5 to 7 minutes. Stir in pasta, broccoli, basil, tomato sauce and ¼ cup Parmesan cheese. Add reserved cooking liquid; mix well. Season with salt and pepper. Garnish with additional Parmesan cheese.

pasta tips
- Save on clean-up by adding firm vegetables (e.g., broccoli, baby carrots, snow peas, sun-dried tomatoes) to the pasta pot for the last 2 to 3 minutes of cooking, until tender-crisp.
- Don't add oil to the water when cooking pasta and don't rinse it once it's cooked.
- Reserve about $1/2$ cup of the starchy cooking liquid when cooking pasta. It will help thicken the sauce.

penne with roasted tomatoes and garlic au gratin

This could be called "penne from heaven!" Make it when tomatoes and basil are in season. When basil is expensive, chop fresh parsley together with dried basil for a fresh taste.

Yield: 6 servings. Reheats and/or freezes well.

2 dozen Italian plum tomatoes (3 lbs.)
10 to 12 cloves garlic
$1/2$ cup fresh basil, packed (or $1/2$ cup fresh parsley plus 2 tsp. dried basil)

$1/4$ cup extra-virgin olive oil
1-lb. pkg. penne (spirals can be substituted)
8 oz. low-fat Mozzarella cheese, chilled (2 cups grated)

Core tomatoes and cut in half lengthwise. Arrange cut-side-up in a single layer on nonstick baking pan.

STEEL BLADE: Process garlic and basil until minced, 10 to 12 seconds. Add olive oil and process briefly to mix. Spread mixture with a rubber spatula over tomatoes. Roast, uncovered, in preheated 350°F oven for 1½ hours, or until tomatoes are very tender and brown around the edges.

In large pot, cook pasta according to package directions. Reserve about ½ cup of cooking water. Drain pasta well and return to pot.

GRATER: Grate cheese, using medium pressure. Empty bowl.

STEEL BLADE: Coarsely chop tomatoes and pan juices, using several quick on/off pulses. Add to pasta along with reserved cooking water. Mix well. Transfer to sprayed 2-quart casserole and top with grated cheese. (Can be prepared in advance up to this point.)

Bake, uncovered, in preheated 350°F oven for 20 minutes, until cheese is melted and golden.

variations:
- Cut 2 medium onions and 1 red bell pepper in half. Roast with the tomatoes.
- Omit Mozzarella cheese. Mix pasta with roasted chopped tomatoes and ½ cup of cooking water. Place on individual dinner plates. Top with a little crumbled feta or grated Parmesan cheese. Serve immediately.

broccoli cheese squares

Easy and versatile! These make a great vegetarian brunch dish or side dish and can be adapted easily for Passover. For an easy hors d'oeuvre, cut into bite-size squares.

Yield: 4 to 6 servings as a main dish or 8 to 10 servings as a side dish. Freezes well.

8 oz. low-fat Swiss and/or Cheddar cheese (2 cups grated)
1 Tbsp. grated Parmesan cheese
2 cloves garlic
1 medium onion, cut in chunks
1 carrot, cut in chunks
1 Tbsp. olive oil
4 cups cut-up broccoli
2 Tbsp. fresh parsley
3 eggs (or 2 eggs plus 2 egg whites)
$1/4$ cup bread crumbs or matzo meal
$1/4$ tsp. each dried basil and dried oregano
$1/2$ tsp. salt
dash chili powder (optional)

GRATER: Grate Swiss or Cheddar cheese, using medium pressure. Transfer to bowl. Remove 2 Tbsp. grated cheese, combine with Parmesan cheese and reserve as a topping.

STEEL BLADE: Drop garlic through feed tube while machine is running; process until minced. Add onion and carrot; process with several quick on/off pulses, until coarsely chopped. Heat oil in nonstick skillet. Sauté garlic, onion and carrot on medium heat until softened, about 5 minutes.

Meanwhile, rinse broccoli in cold water; drain well. Microwave covered on HIGH for 4 minutes. Cool slightly.

Process broccoli and parsley with several on/off pulses, until coarsely chopped. Add sautéed vegetables and grated cheese (excluding reserved cheese topping), along with all remaining ingredients. Process 8 to 10 seconds longer, until combined. Spread mixture evenly in sprayed 7 x 11-inch glass baking dish. Sprinkle with reserved cheese topping. Bake in a preheated 325°F oven for 30 to 35 minutes, until golden. Cool slightly; cut into squares.

variation:

• Replace cooked broccoli with a 14-oz. can of drained artichoke hearts. Substitute a red bell pepper for the carrot.

onion cheese quiche

My son Steven used to wrap quiche in foil, bring it to school and heat it on the radiator for lunch!

Yield: 6 to 8 servings.
May be frozen.
Reheats well.

Standard Butter Pastry, $1/2$ recipe (p. 206)	2 eggs
3 large onions, quartered	$2/3$ cup milk
2 Tbsp. butter or margarine	1 tsp. salt
1 Tbsp. flour	dash freshly ground black pepper
4 oz. chilled Swiss Cheese (1 cup grated)	and nutmeg

Prepare pastry as directed. Roll out chilled pastry to fit 11-inch quiche pan with removable bottom or 9-inch pie pan. To minimize shrinkage, refrigerate for $1/2$ hour. Line crust with aluminum foil and weigh down with uncooked rice or dried beans.

Bake in preheated 400°F oven for 10 minutes; remove foil and beans or rice, and bake 5 minutes longer. Cool slightly. Reduce oven temperature to 375°F.

STEEL BLADE: Process onions with quick on/off pulses, until coarsely chopped. Sauté onions in melted butter or margarine over medium heat for about 10 minutes. Do not brown. Sprinkle in flour and mix well.

GRATER: Grate cheese, using medium pressure. Remove from bowl and set aside.

STEEL BLADE: Process eggs, milk, salt, pepper and nutmeg for a few seconds. Add onions and **half** of cheese. Process with 2 or 3 quick on/off turns to blend. Place in partially baked pastry shell. (Fill no higher than ¼ inch from top as quiche will puff during baking and may run over.) Sprinkle with remaining cheese. Bake immediately at 375°F for 30 to 35 minutes, until golden. A knife inserted in the center should come out clean.

chef's tip:

- For that just-baked taste, prebake pastry shell, cool and freeze. Prepare filling up to 2 days in advance and refrigerate. About half an hour before serving, pour filling into frozen shell and bake for 30 to 35 minutes.

variations:

- Use 2 cups raw or 1 cup cooked vegetables (e.g., onions, roasted red peppers, spinach, broccoli). Chop with quick on/off pulses. Sauté in butter or margarine until golden. Any gratable cheese may be used.

fish and dairy dishes

no-crust zucchini quiche

Yield: 8 servings of about 140 calories each. Freezes well.

3 medium zucchini, unpeeled
salt and freshly ground black
    pepper to taste
8 oz. chilled low-fat Swiss,
    Mozzarella or Cheddar cheese
    (2 cups grated)

$1/2$ medium onion
3 eggs (or 2 eggs plus 2 egg whites)
$1/2$ tsp. each dried oregano and dried basil
3 Tbsp. grated Parmesan cheese

GRATER: Cut zucchini to fit feed tube. Grate, using firm pressure. Transfer to strainer and sprinkle with salt. Let stand 10 minutes. Press out all liquid. Grate cheese and onion, using medium pressure. Do not empty bowl.

STEEL BLADE: Add zucchini, eggs, oregano and basil to processor bowl. Process with 3 or 4 quick on/off pulses, just until mixed. Place in sprayed 9-inch pie plate or 10-inch ceramic quiche dish. Sprinkle with Parmesan cheese. Bake in preheated 350°F oven for 35 to 40 minutes, until set and golden.

variation:
• Replace zucchini with 2 cups chopped mushrooms. Omit basil and oregano. Add a dash of nutmeg.

luncheon puff

This baked pancake is quick and easy. Serve it with sour cream and berries or fresh fruit.

Yield: 2 servings. Do not freeze.

$1/2$ cup flour
$1/2$ cup milk
2 eggs
dash salt
$1/2$ tsp. ground cinnamon

dash nutmeg
2 Tbsp. butter or margarine
1 Tbsp. lemon juice
2 Tbsp. icing sugar

Preheat oven to 425°F.

STEEL BLADE: Process flour with milk, eggs, salt, cinnamon and nutmeg for 8 to 10 seconds. Melt butter or margarine in shallow 1-quart casserole or two individual casseroles. Pour in batter, but do not stir. Sprinkle lightly with additional nutmeg and cinnamon.

Place immediately into oven and bake for 20 to 25 minutes, until browned on top. Sprinkle with lemon juice and icing sugar. Serve immediately.

fish and dairy dishes

basic crêpe batter

fish and dairy dishes

Crêpes are a terrific way to use up leftovers and make a main course dish or dessert. Let your imagination be your guide!

Yield: 12 to 14 crêpes or blintzes. Can be made in advance and refrigerated for 2 days or frozen for about a month.

³/₄ cup flour (you can use part whole wheat)	3 eggs
¹/₄ tsp. salt	¹/₄ cup canola oil
	1 cup milk or water

STEEL BLADE: Process all ingredients for 10 to 15 seconds, until blended. Refrigerate 30 minutes or overnight. Batter should be like heavy cream. If too thick, add a little milk or water.

Brush 8- or 9-inch nonstick skillet lightly with oil. Heat pan on medium-high heat for 2 minutes. Sprinkle with a few drops water. If it sizzles, pan is hot enough. Quickly pour 3 Tbsp. batter into pan. Tilt in all directions to coat bottom evenly with batter. Immediately pour excess batter back into bowl.

Cook for 1 minute on first side. Flip with a spatula and cook 30 seconds on second side. (If making blintzes, cook only on one side.) Repeat with remaining batter. Place waxed paper between cooked crêpes to prevent sticking and stack them on a plate. Fill as desired.

note:

- In a standard-sized processor, process one batch of batter at a time to avoid leakage from bottom of bowl. Transfer to mixing bowl and repeat as many times as necessary. Recipe can be doubled if you have a large processor.

crêpe shapes

To prevent tearing, crêpes should be at room temperature when filling.

- **Roll-ups:** Either spread filling in a thin layer over entire crêpe, or place 2 to 3 Tbsp. filling on lower ¹/₃ of crêpe; roll up into a cylinder.
- **Envelopes:** Fold bottom edge up over filling, fold sides towards center and roll up (e.g., blintzes). Place seam-side-down.
- **Tortes:** Layers of crêpes, with filling in between, topped with sauce. (Great for people who have trouble rolling blintzes!)
- **Wedges/Triangles:** Fold in half, then in half once again. (Usually used for dessert crêpes.)

florentine crêpes

Although there
are several steps
to this recipe, it is
quite simple.
Delicious!

Yield: 6 servings.
Freezes well.

Basic Crêpe Batter (p. 82)
Béchamel Sauce, double
   recipe (p. 60)
$3/4$ cup grated Parmesan
   cheese, divided
2 slices bread

1 Tbsp. melted butter
2 10-oz. pkgs. frozen or fresh spinach
1 egg
1 cup dry cottage or ricotta cheese
salt and freshly ground black pepper
   to taste

Prepare crêpes as directed and refrigerate or freeze until needed. Prepare double recipe of sauce; stir in half of Parmesan cheese. Let cool.

STEEL BLADE: Tear bread in chunks. Process until fine crumbs are formed. Add melted butter and process a few seconds longer. Set aside.

Cook frozen spinach according to package directions. (Fresh spinach should be washed well and cooked in just the water clinging to the leaves for 4 to 5 minutes.) Drain well; squeeze dry. Process spinach on STEEL BLADE until fine, about 10 seconds. Add egg, cottage or ricotta cheese, salt and pepper and remaining Parmesan cheese. Process until mixed.

Place about 3 Tbsp. filling on lower part of each crêpe and roll up. Place seam-side-down in sprayed 9 x 13-inch glass baking dish. Pour sauce over crêpes; top with crumbs. (May be prepared in advance and refrigerated.) Bake in preheated 350°F oven for 20 to 25 minutes.

fish and dairy dishes

salmon crêpes

Yield: 4 to 6 servings.
May be frozen, but best
prepared fresh.

Béchamel Sauce, double recipe (p. 60), or 10-oz. can condensed mushroom soup plus $1/2$ can milk
1 medium onion, halved
1 cup mushrooms
1 Tbsp. butter or margarine
$1 1/2$ cups cooked or canned salmon, drained
2 oz. chilled Swiss cheese ($1/2$ cup grated)
Basic Crêpe Batter (p. 82)

Prepare sauce as directed, or whisk canned soup with milk, mixing well. Set aside.

STEEL BLADE: Process onion and mushrooms with quick on/off pulses, until coarsely chopped. Sauté in melted butter or margarine in large nonstick skillet over medium heat until golden. Process salmon with quick on/offs, until flaked; do not overprocess. Add to skillet along with half the sauce.

GRATER: Grate cheese, using medium pressure.

Place half the remaining sauce in sprayed 9 x 13-inch glass baking dish. Spread each crêpe with 3 Tbsp. salmon mixture. Roll up and arrange in single layer in baking dish. Top with remaining sauce and sprinkle with grated cheese. (May be prepared in advance and refrigerated.)

Bake in preheated 400°F oven for 15 to 20 minutes, until bubbling hot.

cheese cannelloni (crêpes italiano)

Yield: 4 to 6 servings.
Reheats and/or
freezes well. (I have
used the crêpes
directly from the
freezer, topped them
with sauce and
cheese, then baked
them for 35 to
40 minutes.)

Basic Crêpe Batter (p. 82)
4 oz. chilled Mozzarella cheese (1 cup grated)
$1/2$ cup grated Parmesan cheese
2 cups (1 lb.) dry cottage or ricotta cheese
1 egg
salt and freshly ground black pepper to taste
2 cups tomato sauce
$1/4$ tsp. each garlic powder, dried basil and dried oregano

Prepare crêpes as directed.

GRATER: Grate Mozzarella cheese, using medium pressure. Set aside.

STEEL BLADE: Process Parmesan, cottage or ricotta cheese, egg, salt and pepper until mixed, about 15 seconds. Place 2 to 3 Tbsp. cheese mixture on each crêpe. Roll up and place in sprayed 9 x 13-inch glass baking dish.

Combine tomato sauce with garlic, basil and oregano; pour over crêpes. Top with grated cheese. Bake in preheated 350°F oven for 25 to 30 minutes, until bubbly and golden.

meat and poultry

- Chop, purée or slice meats and poultry in moments in your processor (e.g., lean boneless beef, veal, chicken or turkey breasts). An added benefit is that you can also control the fat and cholesterol content. Refer to the Smart Chart (pp. 18, 27) for basic techniques.
- Grind your own meat or poultry (see p. 27).
- Combine ground meat or poultry with remaining ingredients in a large mixing bowl. Too large a quantity won't mix properly in the processor. Meat at the bottom of the bowl will become overprocessed and meat at the top won't be mixed at all.
- If you don't have a scale, remember that 2 cups meat cubes or 3 single, boneless, skinless chicken breasts weigh about 1 lb.
- Bone your own: Pull the skin off the chicken breast; remove the breastbone and smaller bones with your fingers and a sharp knife. Pull out the white tendons from the breast meat. No need to be perfect—you will improve with practice!
- Slice your own uncooked boneless meat or poultry (see p. 27). You will have perfect, paper-thin slices that are perfect for stir-fries!
- Slice across the grain for maximum tenderness. To check which way the grain (muscle fiber) runs, slice off a thin piece from raw or cooked meat. Muscle fibers in chicken and turkey breasts run lengthwise, so cut across the width.

- Use ground meat within 24 to 48 hours of purchase. Stewing meat, steaks, chicken and chops should be used within 2 days, and roasts within 3 days. Store in the coldest part of your refrigerator at 40°F or lower.
- You can freeze raw ground meat for 2 to 3 months. Roasts and steaks can be frozen for 8 to 12 months. Whole chicken and turkey can be frozen for 8 to 10 months, or 5 to 6 months if cut up. Freeze cooked meat and poultry dishes no longer than 2 months for maximum quality.
- Never stuff poultry or roasts in advance. Prepare stuffing and refrigerate; stuff just before cooking. Allow ½ cup stuffing for each pound of poultry. Stuff loosely as stuffing expands during cooking. Stuffing must be cooked to 165°F; check the temperature with an instant read thermometer.
- Stuffing may be baked separately in a covered casserole to prevent it from absorbing the fatty drippings. Bake at 350°F for about 45 minutes.
- Remove stuffing from poultry or roast before refrigerating or freezing leftovers.
- For maximum flavor, season poultry with desired marinade or spices, cover and marinate in the refrigerator for at least 1 hour or up to 48 hours.
- Brush up on food safety! Beware of cross-contamination from raw meat, poultry or the basting brush used during cooking. Boil marinade for 1 to 2 minutes; then you can use it as a sauce on cooked food. (Be sure to use a clean basting brush or spoon.)
- Clean all work surfaces, cutting boards, blades and processor bowl thoroughly; wash your hands with soap and hot water to help prevent cross-contamination.
- Do not leave raw or cooked meats and poultry at room temperature for more than 1 to 2 hours.
- Use your processor to slice, chop or shred foods quickly into uniform pieces; then stir-fry. Dinner will be ready in minutes! Use the recipe for Teriyaki Turkey or Chicken Stir-Fry (p. 96) as a guideline on how to slice meat and vegetables for stir-fries using expanded feed tube techniques.
- Leftover cooked meat or poultry is a blessing in disguise! Use it in fajitas, sandwiches, salads, stir-fries, pasta, stuffed bell peppers, crêpes, soufflés or omelets.

herbed rack of lamb

This elegant, quick recipe is excellent for company. It multiplies easily—each rack serves two people.

Yield: 4 servings.

2 trimmed racks of lamb, about
    2 lbs. each
salt and freshly ground black
    pepper to taste
4 cloves garlic
2 Tbsp. fresh rosemary
    (or $1/2$ tsp. dried rosemary)
2 Tbsp. fresh thyme
    (or $1/2$ tsp. dried thyme)

2 Tbsp. olive oil
2 Tbsp. lemon juice
2 Tbsp. honey
2 Tbsp. Dijon mustard
$1/2$ cup fresh parsley
2 slices bread, torn into pieces
$1/4$ cup pecans

Rub lamb with salt and pepper.

STEEL BLADE: Drop garlic through feed tube while machine is running; process until minced. Add rosemary, thyme, oil, lemon juice, honey and mustard; process until blended, about 10 seconds. Rub mixture over lamb. Marinate at room temperature for 30 minutes or overnight in refrigerator.

Place lamb, meat-side down, on rack in roasting pan. Roast in preheated 450°F oven for 10 minutes, until browned.

STEEL BLADE: Process parsley, bread and pecans until finely minced, 15 to 20 seconds. Turn lamb meat-side up; pat crumb mixture evenly over meat. Return lamb to oven and roast about 10 minutes longer, or until meat thermometer registers 140°F for rare. Let stand for 10 minutes. Carve into chops and serve immediately.

meat and poultry

marinated brisket

Marinating, then long, slow cooking are the secrets to this mouth-watering brisket.

Yield: 8 to 10 servings. Freezes well. Can be prepared in advance and refrigerated overnight. Discard congealed fat from gravy, slice and serve.

3 or 4 medium onions,
   cut in chunks
4- to 5-lb. brisket
2 tsp. salt
freshly ground black pepper
   to taste

1 Tbsp. paprika
1 tsp. dry mustard
4 cloves garlic
$1/2$ cup soy sauce
2 to 3 Tbsp. honey or maple syrup

SLICER: Slice onions, using medium pressure. Place in large, sprayed roasting pan. Rub brisket on all sides with salt, pepper, paprika and mustard; place in pan.

STEEL BLADE: Drop garlic through feed tube while machine is running; process until minced. Add soy sauce and honey or maple syrup; process 2 or 3 seconds longer. Pour mixture over brisket and rub into meat on all sides. Cover pan with aluminum foil. Marinate in refrigerator for at least 1 hour or up to 24 hours.

Bake, covered, in preheated 325°F oven. Allow 45 minutes per pound, or until meat is fork tender. Uncover for the last hour and baste occasionally. Let stand for 20 to 30 minutes before slicing. Reheat for a few minutes in pan gravy.

super roast brisket

A tried and true favorite and an excellent holiday dish.

Yield: 10 to 12 servings. Freezes well.

5- to 6-lb. brisket
2 or 3 cloves garlic
1 small onion, halved
2 Tbsp. vinegar or lemon juice
$1/4$ cup red wine
$1/4$ cup oil

$1/4$ cup honey
$1/4$ cup cola
3 Tbsp. ketchup
1 Tbsp. salt
$1/4$ tsp. freshly ground black pepper
1 tsp. paprika

Place brisket in large, sprayed roasting pan.

STEEL BLADE: Process garlic and onion until minced. Add remaining ingredients and process a few seconds longer to blend. Pour over brisket, making sure to cover all surfaces. Cover pan with aluminum foil. Marinate in refrigerator for 1 to 2 hours, or up to 24 hours. Baste occasionally.

Bake, covered, in preheated 300°F oven for 5 hours, until very tender (about 1 hour per pound). When cool, refrigerate. Slices better the next day. Remove hardened fat and discard.

italian roasted veal

meat and poultry

The seasonings for this recipe may be used on any cut of veal (shoulder, breast, steaks, chops). Thinly sliced cold roast is delicious in sandwiches.

Yield: 6 to 8 servings. Allow $1/2$ lb. per person for boneless roasts and $3/4$ to 1 lb. per person if there is a large percentage of bone. Freezes well.

4- to 5-lb. veal roast (or 6 veal steaks or chops)
2 tsp. seasoning salt
freshly ground black pepper to taste
2 tsp. Italian seasoning (or 1 tsp. each dried oregano and dried basil)
1 tsp. dry mustard
4 cloves garlic, cut in slivers
2 large onions
4 large carrots
$1/2$ cup tomato sauce or chicken broth
$1/2$ cup dry red wine
6 to 8 potatoes (optional)

Rub meat with salt, pepper, Italian seasoning and mustard. Cut several slits in meat and insert garlic. Place in large sprayed roasting pan.

SLICER: Cut onions and carrots to fit feed tube. Slice, using firm pressure. Add vegetables, tomato sauce or broth and wine to roasting pan. Cover and bake in preheated 300°F oven about 3 hours for a roast or 1½ hours for steaks or chops (see note). Uncover and roast 45 minutes longer, basting occasionally. If desired, sliced or quartered potatoes may be added when you uncover the meat.

Let roast stand for 20 minutes before slicing, or slice when cold and reheat in the pan gravy.

note:
- The low cooking temperature is important. Allow 50 to 60 minutes cooking time per pound of meat and cook until fork tender.

passover variation:
- Omit mustard. Have butcher make a pocket in roast. Stuff with your favorite Passover stuffing. Allow an extra ½ hour cooking time.

rozie's osso bucco with gremolata

Thanks to my
friend Roz Brown
of Montreal for this
awesome Italian
dish. It tastes even
better the next
day. Delicious
over rice. Buono
appetito!

Yield: 4 to 6 servings.
Reheats and/or freezes
well. Before reheating,
skim off fat.

4 to 6 veal shanks (about 3 lbs.)
$1/3$ cup flour
salt and freshly ground black
 pepper to taste
$1/4$ cup olive oil
3 or 4 cloves garlic
3 carrots, cut in chunks
2 medium onions, cut in chunks
2 cups mushrooms

2 stalks celery
$3/4$ to 1 cup dry white wine
$1 1/2$ cups chicken broth
28-oz. can crushed Italian tomatoes
$1/4$ cup fresh basil, minced
 (or 1 tsp. dried basil)
1 tsp. dried rosemary
$1/2$ tsp. dried thyme (optional)
Gremolata

Coat veal on all sides with flour, shaking off excess. Sprinkle with salt and pepper. Heat 3 Tbsp. of the oil in a large skillet. Add veal and brown slowly on all sides, about 10 minutes. Transfer to a platter. Discard fat from skillet.

STEEL BLADE: Drop garlic through feed tube while machine is running; process until minced. Add carrots and onions and process with quick on/off pulses, until coarsely chopped.

SLICER: Slice mushrooms and celery, using medium pressure. Heat remaining 1 Tbsp. oil in skillet. Add vegetables and sauté on medium heat for 6 to 8 minutes, stirring occasionally. Add wine, reduce heat and cook 1 minute longer. Add broth, tomatoes and herbs. Season with salt and pepper. Add veal.

Cover and simmer for 2 hours, until tender. At serving time, sprinkle Gremolata over veal.

gremolata

2 Tbsp. lemon rind
$1/4$ cup fresh parsley

2 to 3 cloves garlic

STEEL BLADE: Process until finely minced, about 10 seconds. Delicious with veal, chicken or fish.

baked veal chops

Yield: 4 to 6 servings.
May be frozen.

30 crackers (or 1 cup bread
  crumbs)
1 tsp. salt
$1/4$ tsp. each freshly ground
  black pepper, paprika and
  garlic powder
1 tsp. Italian seasoning
1 egg plus 2 Tbsp. water

4 to 6 large veal chops
2 Tbsp. oil for frying
2 cloves garlic
2 cups tomato sauce
1 green and/or red bell pepper,
  cut in chunks
1 medium onion, cut in chunks

STEEL BLADE: Process crackers with salt, pepper, paprika, garlic powder and Italian seasoning until fine crumbs are formed, about 30 seconds. Transfer to a flat plate or plastic bag. Process egg with water for 2 or 3 seconds. Transfer to a pie plate.

Dip chops in egg mixture, then in crumbs. Heat oil in large nonstick skillet over medium-high heat. Brown chops quickly on both sides, adding more oil if needed. Drain well on paper towels. Arrange in a single layer in large casserole.

STEEL BLADE: Drop garlic through feed tube while machine is running; process until minced. Add tomato sauce and dash of Italian seasoning. Process for a few seconds to blend. Pour over chops.

SLICER: Slice peppers and onion, using medium pressure. Add to casserole. Cover and bake in preheated 350°F oven for ½ hour. Uncover and bake ½ hour longer, or until tender.

passover variation:

• Replace cracker crumbs with matzo crackers or matzo meal. Replace Italian seasoning with mixture of fresh or dried basil, oregano and thyme.

cantonese short ribs

Yield: 6 servings.
Reheats well. If freez-
ing, add pineapple and
vegetables when
reheating.

14-oz. can pineapple chunks
Cantonese Marinade (p. 66)
4 lbs. short ribs (flanken or
  Miami ribs), cut in serving
  size pieces

1 green or red bell pepper, cut in chunks
2 medium onions, cut in chunks
2 cups mushrooms
2 cups bean sprouts
1 cup snow peas or sugar snap peas

Drain pineapple. Reserve ¾ cup of the juice and use to prepare marinade as directed. Refrigerate pineapple until needed.

Place short ribs in sprayed 9 x 13-inch ovenproof dish. Pour marinade over ribs. Cover and marinate for 2 to 3 hours or up to 24 hours in the refrigerator, turning meat over several times.

Bake, covered, in preheated 300°F oven about 3 hours, or until tender, basting occasionally.

SLICER: Slice bell pepper, onions and mushrooms, using medium pressure. Add sliced vegetables, bean sprouts, peas and reserved pineapple to meat. Cook 10 minutes longer, until heated through. Serve over rice.

honey garlic ribs

Yield: 4 servings as a main course, 6 to 8 servings as an appetizer. Reheats and/or freezes well.

3 lbs. spareribs
salt and freshly ground black pepper to taste
1 slice fresh ginger, peeled (1 Tbsp.) (or 1 tsp. ground ginger)

2 or 3 cloves garlic
1 cup brown sugar or honey
¼ cup soy sauce
2 tsp. white or rice vinegar
½ cup water

Place ribs in a single layer on broiling rack. Sprinkle with salt and pepper. Broil on both sides until brown. Drain on paper towels. Cut into individual ribs and place in sprayed 2-quart casserole.

STEEL BLADE: Drop ginger and garlic through feed tube while machine is running; process until minced. Add remaining ingredients and process a few seconds, until mixed. Pour over ribs. Bake, uncovered, in preheated 300°F oven for 1½ hours, basting every 15 minutes.

variation:

• Cut spareribs into individual ribs. Place in saucepan, cover with water and simmer, covered, for ½ hour. Drain well. Place in sprayed casserole; pour Honey Garlic Sparerib Sauce (p. 98) over ribs. (No need to cook the sauce first!) Bake, uncovered, at 350°F about 1 hour, basting occasionally.

spicy short ribs/miami ribs

Yield: 4 to 6 servings.
Reheats and/or
freezes well.

8 strips short ribs (flanken or
  Miami ribs)
3 cloves garlic
14-oz. can peaches, drained (or
  1 cup baby food peaches)
$1/_2$ cup ketchup or chili sauce

3 Tbsp. soy sauce
1 Tbsp. Worcestershire or steak sauce
$1/_4$ cup brown sugar
$1/_4$ cup lemon juice or vinegar
$1/_2$ tsp. dry mustard

Arrange ribs in a single layer in sprayed 9 x 13-inch baking dish.

STEEL BLADE: Drop garlic through feed tube while machine is running; process until minced. Add remaining ingredients and process until smooth. Pour sauce over meat, cover and marinate 1 to 2 hours or up to 24 hours in refrigerator, basting occasionally.

Bake in preheated 325°F oven for 2½ hours. Uncover and bake ½ hour longer, or until very tender. Baste occasionally. Serve with rice or noodles.

variation:

- To make an oven stew, replace short ribs with 2½ lbs. lean stewing beef or veal. Add sauce and bake as above. Slice 3 large carrots, 2 onions, 4 large potatoes and 3 stalks celery on the SLICER, using medium pressure. Add vegetables to stew the last hour of cooking. Omit potatoes if freezing.

meat and poultry

super spaghetti sauce

For a vegetarian version, omit salami and replace ground meat with vegetarian meat substitute.

Yield: 8 servings. Reheats and/or freezes well.

3 cloves garlic

2 medium onions, quartered

1 to 2 Tbsp. oil

1 green or red bell pepper, cut in chunks

1 cup mushrooms

$1/4$ lb. salami or pepperoni, cut in chunks (optional)

2 lbs. lean ground beef or veal (or Grind Your Own, p. 27)

28-oz. can tomatoes

2 $5^1/2$-oz. cans tomato paste

$1/4$ cup red wine

1 to 2 tsp. salt (to taste)

$1/2$ tsp. each freshly ground black pepper, dried basil, dried oregano and sugar

1 bay leaf

red pepper flakes or chili powder to taste

STEEL BLADE: Drop garlic through feed tube while machine is running; process until minced. Process onions with 3 or 4 quick on/off pulses, until coarsely chopped. Brown garlic and onions slowly in hot oil in a Dutch oven for 5 minutes. Process green or red pepper and mushrooms with 3 or 4 quick on/offs, until coarsely chopped. Add to pot and cook 2 minutes longer. Remove vegetables from pot.

If using salami or pepperoni, process with several quick on/offs, until coarsely chopped. Add to pan along with ground meat. Brown slowly over medium heat for 10 minutes, stirring often.

Add remaining ingredients to pot, stirring well to break up tomatoes. Cover and simmer for 1½ to 2 hours, stirring occasionally. Taste to adjust seasonings.

meat and poultry

stir-fried beef and broccoli

meat and poultry

I've simplified the preparation for this delicious family favorite. You can add snow peas, bean sprouts, bok choy or any vegetables you like. It's also scrumptious with chicken breasts.

Yield: 6 servings.
If frozen, vegetables will become soggy.

1$^1/_2$ lbs. lean boneless steak
4 cloves garlic
$^1/_4$ cup soy sauce
1 Tbsp. lemon juice
1 Tbsp. honey or maple syrup
1 Tbsp. ketchup
1 pint mushrooms

2 large onions, quartered
1 bunch fresh broccoli (about 1 lb.)
oil for frying (about 3 Tbsp.)
2 Tbsp. cornstarch dissolved in $^1/_4$ cup
   cold water or broth
1 tsp. toasted sesame oil
4 cups cooked rice

Cut meat in pieces to fit feed tube snugly. Trim fat. Freeze until semi-frozen, about 1 hour. It should be firm to the touch but easily pierced with the point of a sharp knife. If necessary, let meat stand for a few minutes until you can do the knife test.

SLICER: Slice meat, using firm pressure. Place in large bowl.

STEEL BLADE: Drop garlic through feed tube; process until minced. Remove half of garlic and reserve. Add soy sauce, lemon juice, honey or maple syrup and ketchup to processor. Process a few seconds longer. Pour marinade over meat, cover and marinate for 1 hour or up to 24 hours in the refrigerator, stirring occasionally. Wash and dry processor bowl.

SLICER: Slice mushrooms and onions, using medium pressure. Transfer to mixing bowl. Cut florets from broccoli and add to vegetables. Slice broccoli stems, using medium pressure. Add to vegetables.

Heat 1 Tbsp. oil in wok or large nonstick skillet. Stir-fry vegetables for 2 minutes on high heat. Add reserved garlic and stir-fry 30 seconds longer. Transfer to a bowl.

Remove half of meat from marinade with a slotted spoon; stir-fry in 1 Tbsp. hot oil about 2 minutes. If necessary, sprinkle with a little cornstarch to prevent splattering. Remove from wok and repeat with remaining meat.

Return meat and vegetables to wok and mix well. Add marinade and bring to a boil. Make a well in the center and stir in cornstarch mixture and sesame oil. Cook 1 to 2 minutes longer, until thickened, stirring constantly. Serve over rice.

teriyaki turkey or chicken stir-fry

This colorful, versatile stir-fry is full of flavor! For a vegetarian version, substitute extra-firm tofu, cut in strips, for the meat.

Yield: 6 servings. Do not freeze or vegetables will lose their crispness. Leftovers can be reheated in the microwave.

Teriyaki Marinade (p. 65)
1 1/2 lbs. turkey or chicken breasts
4 green onions
2 stalks celery
1 red and 1 yellow bell pepper
4 stalks bok choy
1 cup sugar snap peas, trimmed
2 cups bean sprouts
1 to 2 Tbsp. oil
1 Tbsp. cornstarch dissolved in 2 Tbsp. cold water
4 cups cooked rice

Prepare marinade and set aside. Cut turkey or chicken breasts in half to fit feed tube snugly. Wrap and freeze for about 30 minutes, or until semi-frozen. They are ready to slice when easily pierced with the tip of a sharp knife.

SLICER: Place turkey or chicken in feed tube cut-side down. Slice, using firm pressure. Mix marinade and meat in nonreactive dish, cover and marinate for 1 hour or up to 24 hours in the refrigerator, stirring occasionally.

Cut green onions, celery and peppers to fit feed tube. Slice, using medium pressure. (Use small feed tube if your machine has one.) Trim bok choy and cut to fit feed tube. Slice, using medium pressure. (Use expanded feed tube if your machine has one.) Combine with peas and bean sprouts in large bowl.

Heat oil in wok or large nonstick skillet. Drain turkey or chicken, reserving marinade. Stir-fry on high heat for 2 minutes, or until chicken is white. Add vegetables and stir-fry 2 minutes longer. Add reserved marinade and bring to a boil. Stir in cornstarch mixture and cook 1 to 2 minutes longer, until sauce is bubbling and thickened. Serve over rice.

meat and poultry

mushroom almond chicken stir-fry

Yield: 4 servings.
If frozen, vegetables
will not be crispy.

4 single boneless, skinless
    chicken breasts
2 cups mushrooms
1 medium onion, halved
1 to 2 Tbsp. oil
1 cup frozen peas (no need to thaw)
2 cloves garlic, crushed

$1/4$ cup chicken broth
1 to 2 Tbsp. soy sauce
1 Tbsp. cornstarch dissolved in
    2 Tbsp. cold water
freshly ground black pepper to taste
3 cups cooked rice
$1/2$ cup slivered almonds, toasted

Cut chicken breasts to fit feed tube snugly. Freeze for about 30 minutes, or until semi-frozen. They will be ready to slice when easily pierced with the tip of a sharp knife.

SLICER: Slice chicken, using firm pressure. Empty bowl. Slice mushrooms and onion, using light pressure.

Heat oil in wok or large nonstick skillet. Add chicken and stir-fry over high heat for 2 minutes, until chicken is white. Add mushrooms, onion and peas; stir-fry 1 to 2 minutes longer.

Add garlic, broth and soy sauce and bring to a boil. Stir in cornstarch mixture; cook 1 to 2 minutes longer, until sauce is bubbling and thickened, stirring constantly. Add pepper. Serve over rice; top with almonds.

chicken guy kew

Yield: 8 to 10 servings
as an hors d'oeuvre,
6 servings as a main
course. Allow for
second helpings!
Freezes well.

Chinese Sweet and Sour
    Sauce (p. 65)
6 single boneless, skinless
    chicken breasts
1 cup flour
$1/2$ tsp. baking powder

1 tsp. salt
1 Tbsp. paprika
$1/2$ cup water or beer
2 Tbsp. oil
2 eggs
additional oil for frying (about $1/4$ cup)

Prepare sauce as directed. Cut chicken into 1-inch pieces with a sharp knife.

STEEL BLADE: Process flour, baking powder, salt, paprika, water or beer, 2 Tbsp. oil and eggs until smooth, 10 to 15 seconds. Dip chicken pieces in batter. Fry in hot oil until brown on all sides, 2 to 3 minutes. Drain well on paper towels. Serve with sauce.

To reheat: Bake, uncovered, on foil-lined baking sheet in preheated 450°F oven until hot and crispy, 6 to 8 minutes.

moo goo guy kew

Yield: 6 servings.
If frozen, vegetables
will not be crispy.

Chicken Guy Kew (p. 97)
1 large onion, cut in chunks
1 green or red bell pepper,
   cut in chunks
1 stalk celery, cut in chunks
1 cup mushrooms
2 cups broccoli florets

8-oz. can sliced water
   chestnuts, drained
2 or 3 cloves garlic, crushed
1 to 2 Tbsp. oil
1 to 2 Tbsp. soy sauce (or to taste)
1 Tbsp. cornstarch dissolved in
   $1/4$ cup chicken broth
4 cups cooked rice

Prepare chicken as directed; drain well. Keep warm. (May be prepared in advance and reheated.)

SLICER: Slice onion, green or red pepper, celery and mushrooms, using medium pressure. Pat dry with paper towels. Combine with broccoli, water chestnuts and garlic in large bowl.

Heat oil in wok or large nonstick skillet. Stir-fry vegetables for 2 minutes on medium-high heat. Add soy sauce and cornstarch mixture and cook 1 to 2 minutes longer, stirring constantly. Add chicken and mix well. Serve over rice.

variation:

• Replace water chestnuts with 1 cup snow peas. Omit soy sauce. Add Chinese Sweet and Sour Sauce (p. 65) and 1 cup drained pineapple chunks to cooked chicken and vegetable mixture. Sprinkle with toasted sesame seeds.

chinese chicken dinner-in-a-dish

My student
Rivanna Stuhler
said, "This dish will
tempt even a veg-
etarian like me!"

Yield: 4 to 6 servings.
Reheats well. Chicken
freezes well but rice
may get hard if frozen.

2 medium onions, cut in chunks
1 cup brown rice
1 red and/or green bell
   pepper, halved
1 cup mushrooms
3 lbs. chicken pieces
3 Tbsp. soy sauce

1 Tbsp. rice vinegar
1 Tbsp. honey
1 tsp. toasted sesame oil
2 cups water
freshly ground black pepper and
   paprika to taste

SLICER: Slice onions, using medium pressure. Place in sprayed 9 x 13-inch oven-proof casserole. Top with rice. Slice peppers and mushrooms, using light pressure. Add to casserole.

Remove skin and excess fat from chicken. Arrange chicken pieces in a single layer over rice and vegetables. Combine soy sauce, vinegar, honey and sesame oil. Drizzle over chicken pieces and marinate for 30 minutes.

Add water to casserole. Sprinkle chicken with pepper and paprika. Cover dish with foil. Bake in preheated 350°F oven for 1¾ hours, until chicken is tender. If necessary, add a little more water. Uncover and bake 15 minutes longer.

chicken in pineapple-orange sauce

Yield: 8 servings. Freezes well, but do not garnish until serving time.

2 chickens, each cut in 8 pieces
salt and freshly ground black pepper to taste
1 Tbsp. paprika
2 cloves garlic
1 cup tomato sauce
6-oz. can frozen concentrated orange juice (unthawed)

$1/4$ cup brown sugar or maple syrup
$1/2$ tsp. each dry mustard, ground cinnamon and ground ginger
14-oz. can pineapple chunks, drained (reserve juice)
1 medium orange, for garnish
4 cups cooked rice

Sprinkle chicken with salt, pepper and paprika on all sides. Place in a single layer in large sprayed roasting pan.

STEEL BLADE: Drop garlic through feed tube while machine is running; process until minced. Add tomato sauce, orange juice, brown sugar or maple syrup, mustard, cinnamon, ginger and ½ cup pineapple juice. Process for 2 or 3 seconds to blend. Pour over chicken.

Bake, uncovered, about 1½ hours in preheated 350°F oven, basting occasionally. If sauce cooks down too much, add a little more pineapple juice. Add pineapple chunks and cook 5 minutes longer.

SLICER: Cut orange in half lengthwise. Slice, using medium pressure. Serve chicken over rice, spoon sauce over and garnish with orange slices.

maple-glazed garlic chicken breasts

Ginger and garlic combine perfectly with maple syrup for an easy, tasty chicken dish. Great for company!

Yield: 8 servings. Freezes well. Leftovers are delicious cold.

meat and poultry

8 single chicken breasts, with
   bone (or 2 chickens, cut up)
5 or 6 cloves garlic
2 slices fresh ginger,
   peeled (2 Tbsp.)
$1/2$ cup maple syrup

$1/4$ cup soy sauce
3 Tbsp. orange juice
2 tsp. toasted sesame oil
$1/4$ tsp. cayenne pepper
3 or 4 Tbsp. sesame seeds

If desired, remove skin from chicken. Arrange in a single layer in large, sprayed, nonreactive casserole or roasting pan.

STEEL BLADE: Drop garlic and ginger through feed tube while machine is running; process until minced. Add maple syrup, soy sauce, orange juice, sesame oil and cayenne. Process until blended, about 10 seconds. Pour mixture over chicken, cover and marinate for 1 hour or up to 24 hours in refrigerator. Turn chicken pieces over once or twice for even marinating.

Bake, covered, in preheated 350°F oven for 45 minutes. Uncover, baste chicken with sauce and sprinkle with sesame seeds. Bake, uncovered, 20 minutes longer. Chicken should be glazed and nicely browned. Baste occasionally.

sticky chicky

Tried and true! Be sure to check out Sticky Tofu (p. 117) for the vegetarians at your table.

Yield: 6 servings. Freezes well.

4 lbs. chicken pieces
salt and freshly ground black
   pepper to taste
1 tsp. paprika
$1/2$ tsp. garlic powder
1 tsp. dry mustard
2 cloves garlic

$1/2$ cup soy sauce
$1/2$ cup honey or corn syrup
2 Tbsp. vinegar or lemon juice
$1/2$ tsp. ground ginger
1 Tbsp. cornstarch dissolved in
   2 Tbsp. cold water
2 to 3 Tbsp. sesame seeds, for garnish

Rub chicken pieces with salt, pepper, paprika, garlic powder and mustard. Place skin-side down in large sprayed casserole or roasting pan. Do not add any liquids. Roast, uncovered, in preheated 400°F oven for 20 minutes, then turn skin-side up and roast 15 minutes longer.

STEEL BLADE: Drop garlic through feed tube while machine is running; process until minced. Add soy sauce, honey or syrup, vinegar or lemon juice and ginger. Process 2 or 3 seconds, until blended. Pour sauce over chicken pieces. Reduce heat to 350°F. Roast ½ hour longer, basting occasionally.

Stir cornstarch mixture into bubbling sauce. Return chicken to oven and cook 2 or 3 minutes longer. Sprinkle with sesame seeds.

roasted turkey breast balsamico

This is a wonderful alternative to roasting a whole turkey, no bones about it! Marinating keeps the turkey moist and flavorful. You can also use an unrolled boneless turkey breast.

Yield: 8 to 10 servings. Reheats and/or freezes well.

Balsamic Vinaigrette (p. 132)
3 medium onions, cut in chunks
3 cloves garlic
1 boneless rolled turkey breast, about 4 lbs. (see Chef's Tip)

salt, freshly ground black pepper and paprika to taste
$1/_2$ tsp. each dried basil and dried thyme

Prepare Balsamic Vinaigrette as directed; measure ½ cup. Refrigerate remaining mixture to use another time.

STEEL BLADE: Process onions with several quick on/off pulses, until coarsely chopped. Place in the bottom of a sprayed casserole. Drop garlic through feed tube while machine is running; process until minced.

Place turkey in casserole; rub with garlic, salt, pepper, paprika, basil and thyme. Pour ½ cup vinaigrette over top, turning turkey to coat on all sides. Cover and marinate in refrigerator for at least 1 hour or up to 24 hours, turning occasionally.

Cook, covered, in preheated 350°F oven. Calculate 30 minutes per lb. as the cooking time. Uncover the last ½ hour of cooking and baste occasionally. When done, a meat thermometer should register an internal temperature of 170°F to 175°F and juices will run clear when turkey is pierced. Let stand, covered, for 20 minutes for easier slicing. Slice turkey thinly. Serve with pan juices.

chef's tip:

- Rolled turkey breast is not always available. If you use an unrolled turkey breast, cooking time will be 20 to 25 minutes per lb. If you can't find one large turkey breast, use two smaller ones. Since two smaller pieces require less cooking time than one large piece, use an instant-read thermometer to prevent overcooking.

variation:

- **Stuffed Turkey Breast:** Ask your butcher to butterfly a boneless, skinless turkey breast. (To do it yourself, cut horizontally through the middle, leaving it hinged on one side, so that it opens flat like a book.) Place between two pieces of plastic wrap and pound lightly to flatten. Rub both sides with garlic and seasonings. Spread with your favorite stuffing mixture. Starting at the narrow end, roll up tightly. Tie with string in several places, about 3 inches apart. Place in casserole, pour vinaigrette over and roast as directed. Calculate 30 minutes per lb. as the cooking time.

marinated roast turkey with cranberry relish

Yield: 12 to 14 servings. Leftovers may be refrigerated or frozen. Remove stuffing and wrap separately.

Marinated Turkey

12- to 14-lb. turkey
1 seedless orange
2 cloves garlic
2 Tbsp. olive oil
2 Tbsp. each lemon, orange and lime juice
2 Tbsp. honey or maple syrup (or to taste)
1 tsp. salt
$1/4$ tsp. each freshly ground black pepper, dried basil and dried thyme
$1/2$ tsp. dry mustard (optional)
1 tsp. paprika

Turkey Stuffing

6 cups soft bread crumbs (12 slices bread)
$1/2$ cup fresh parsley
2 medium onions, cut in chunks
2 stalks celery, cut in chunks
2 Tbsp. oil
1 apple, peeled and cut in chunks
2 eggs (or 1 egg plus 2 egg whites)
1 tsp. salt
1 tsp. paprika
$1/2$ tsp. each freshly ground black pepper, dried basil and dried thyme
$1/4$ tsp. each dried savory and dried sage (optional)
$1/2$ cup chicken broth or water (approximately)

For marinated turkey: Remove excess fat and giblets from turkey cavity. Place turkey in large sprayed roasting pan.

SLICER: If necessary, cut orange to fit feed tube; slice, using medium pressure. Place orange slices under turkey skin to keep turkey moist during cooking.

STEEL BLADE: Drop garlic through feed tube while machine is running; process until minced. Add oil, juices, honey or maple syrup and seasonings; process for 5 seconds to blend. Rub mixture over turkey. Cover and refrigerate overnight or up to 2 days. Remove from refrigerator about an hour before cooking.

For turkey stuffing: Drop chunks of bread through feed tube while the machine is running. Process on the STEEL BLADE until fine crumbs are formed; measure 6 cups. Place crumbs in large mixing bowl. Process parsley until minced, 8 to 10 seconds. Add to crumbs.

Process onions with quick on/off pulses, until coarsely chopped. Empty bowl; repeat with celery. Sauté onions and celery in oil on medium heat until golden, about 5 minutes. Add to crumbs.

Process apple until minced, about 10 seconds. Add eggs and process 2 or 3 seconds longer. Add to crumb mixture along with seasonings and enough broth to moisten; mix well. (May be made up to a day in advance and refrigerated.)

Assembly: Stuff cavity and neck of turkey loosely to allow for expansion during cooking. Close with skewers and string. Fasten legs close to the body with string. (Alternately, bake stuffing separately in large casserole in preheated 325°F oven for 50 to 60 minutes.)

meat and poultry

Place turkey breast-side down on sprayed roasting rack. Roast, uncovered, in pre-heated 325°F oven. Calculate 18 to 20 minutes per pound as your cooking time. (A 12- to 14-lb. stuffed turkey takes 3½ to 4 hours.) Turn breast-side up halfway through cooking. Baste occasionally. If turkey gets too brown, cover loosely with a tent of foil. Let turkey stand for 20 minutes before carving. Serve with Cranberry Relish.

test for doneness Turkey is done when a drumstick moves easily and juices run clear when turkey is pierced. An instant-read thermometer inserted into meaty portion of thigh should read 175°F. Stuffing temperature should be 165°F. Unstuffed turkey needs less cooking time; remove from oven when it reaches 165°F on an instant-read thermometer.

turkey gravy Pour pan juices from turkey into a container and freeze for about 15 minutes, or until fat rises to the top. Skim off fat. Measure 2 Tbsp. fat and place it back in roasting pan. Add 2 Tbsp. flour and cook on low heat, stirring to loosen browned bits from bottom of pan. When golden brown, gradually blend in reserved pan juices from turkey plus enough chicken or turkey broth to make 2 cups liquid. Add 1 tsp. soy or Worcestershire sauce.

Simmer for 5 minutes, scraping any remaining browned bits from bottom of pan. Add salt and freshly ground black pepper to taste. This makes 2 cups thin gravy. For a thicker gravy, use 4 Tbsp. fat and 4 Tbsp. flour.

cranberry relish

Yield: About 3½ cups.
Keeps about 1 month
in the refrigerator or
may be frozen.

1 large seedless orange, cut in chunks	½ cup apricot jam
3 cups cranberries	1 cup sugar
	1 tsp. lemon juice

STEEL BLADE: Process orange until fine, about 15 seconds. Add cranberries and process until finely ground, 25 to 30 seconds. Scrape down sides of bowl as necessary. Add remaining ingredients and process until combined, about 10 seconds. Refrigerate for several hours to blend flavors.

turkey cutlets with peppers and mushrooms

This makes a quick, healthy and delicious dinner! It is equally good using chicken breasts and is perfect over rice or pasta. Garnish with toasted slivered almonds for company.

Yield: 4 servings. Vegetables will become soggy if frozen.

1 1/2 lbs. thin turkey cutlets
salt and freshly ground black pepper to taste
1/4 cup flour (approximately)
2 Tbsp. olive oil
1/4 cup fresh parsley
2 cloves garlic
4 green onions (or 1 medium onion)

1 red and 1 yellow bell pepper, halved
2 cups mushrooms
1/2 cup chicken broth
1/4 cup dry white wine
2 Tbsp. fresh lemon juice
2 tsp. Dijon or honey mustard
1/2 tsp. each dried basil and dried thyme (or 1 Tbsp. fresh basil and fresh thyme)

Sprinkle cutlets with salt and pepper. Coat with flour, shaking off excess. Heat 1 Tbsp. oil in large nonstick skillet. Brown turkey about 1 to 2 minutes on each side. Transfer cutlets to a plate and cover with foil to keep warm.

STEEL BLADE: Process parsley until minced, about 10 seconds. Remove from bowl and reserve. Drop garlic through feed tube and process until minced.

SLICER: Slice green onions, bell peppers and mushrooms, using medium pressure. Heat remaining oil in skillet. Sauté garlic, onions, peppers and mushrooms for 3 to 4 minutes, until golden. Add broth, wine, lemon juice, mustard, basil and thyme. Return turkey to skillet. Simmer, uncovered, for 2 or 3 minutes, stirring occasionally, until sauce is slightly thickened. Adjust seasonings to taste. Sprinkle with reserved parsley.

vegetables and side dishes

- Side dishes that do not contain any dairy products can be served with either meat or dairy meals, so they are in this chapter. For side dishes containing dairy products, see the Fish and Dairy chapter.
- Refer to the Smart Chart (p. 18) for basic processing techniques.
- Choose vegetables that are firm and not too ripe. Remove the core, large pits and seeds before processing.
- The expanded feed tube is excellent for slicing or grating whole round fruits and vegetables (e.g., lemons, tomatoes, onions).
- The small feed tube (mini tube) is ideal for single or small items. If vegetables are wide at one end and narrow at the other (e.g., carrots), pack them in pairs, alternating one wide end up and one narrow end up.
- Before slicing or grating/shredding vegetables, cut the bottom ends flat; place them in the feed tube flat-side down. Pack the feed tube snugly, but not so tightly that the pusher can't move.
- Cut vegetables in lengths to fit the feed tube. Some newer models of food processors have a marking on the feed tube to indicate the maximum height for filling. Don't overfill the feed tube or the machine won't start when you press down on the pusher!
- If the vegetables don't fit, try inserting them from the bottom of the feed tube where the opening is slightly larger.
- The mini feed tube (if your machine has one) is ideal for slicing or shredding long vegetables or small items (e.g., 1 or 2 carrots, zucchini, green onions, celery).

- For short shreds, pack the vegetables (e.g., carrots, zucchini) in the feed tube upright. For long, narrow shreds, pack the feed tube horizontally.

- The pusher assembly for the expanded feed tube has a small pusher that fits inside the small feed tube. The small pusher must be in place when using the expanded feed tube; otherwise, food will bounce up and down in the small feed tube instead of being sliced or grated. (I speak from experience!)

- In general, use medium pressure for most vegetables (e.g., potatoes, celery, zucchini). Use firm pressure for hard vegetables (e.g., carrots, sweet potatoes). Use light pressure for tomatoes or cabbage.

- For an easy way to "chop" vegetables, cut them in 1-inch chunks, place them in the feed tube and process on the **Slicer**, using light pressure.

- For more control when slicing or grating vegetables, use the PULSE button. Press down on the pusher with one hand and press PULSE with the other; release PULSE as soon as the food is sliced or shredded. The processor will stop instantly!

- For continuous feed, use either the ON or PULSE button. If you use the ON button, one hand will be free to refill the feed tube.

- Cooking time of vegetables varies depending on the type of vegetable and whether they are whole, sliced or chopped. Estimate 3 to 4 minutes for grated vegetables, 5 to 6 minutes for sliced vegetables, and 10 to 15 minutes for whole vegetables. Taste and check.

- To microwave vegetables, soak them in cold water and shake them dry. The water clinging to the vegetables provides enough steam to cook them. Allow 5 to 7 minutes per pound. Stir or turn vegetables over halfway through cooking. If they have a skin (e.g., potatoes, squash), pierce before microwaving.

- **Gratinéed Vegetables**: Top cooked vegetables with Béchamel Sauce (p. 60) or Cheese Sauce (p. 61); sprinkle with buttered seasoned crumbs. Bake 15 to 20 minutes at 350°F, until bubbling and nicely browned.

- Store potatoes and onions separately in a cool, dark place to prevent spoiling. If refrigerated, potatoes will develop a sweet taste.

- **Rescued Mashed Potatoes:** Here's a tried and true remedy to rescue over-processed mashed potatoes based on 3 to 4 potatoes. Add ¼ cup milk, 2 Tbsp. margarine, 1 egg, ½ tsp. baking powder, salt and freshly ground black pepper to mashed potatoes. Process on the **Steel Blade** 30 seconds, until smooth and sticky. Spread in a sprayed 9-inch pie plate, sprinkle with paprika and bake at 375°F about 30 minutes, until brown and crusty.

- To cook pasta, the general rule is 4 quarts of boiling water and 4 tsp. salt for each pound of pasta. Do not cook pasta without salt or it will never taste right.
- Drain pasta as soon as it is cooked. Reheat quickly by placing in boiling water for a minute (or microwave on HIGH, allowing 1 minute per cup) Undercook pasta slightly if you plan to reheat it later.
- Spaghetti and macaroni double when cooked. Noodles swell slightly. One pound of spaghetti yields 5 to 6 servings. One cup uncooked noodles (2½ oz. weight) yields 1¼ cups cooked (2 servings). You can freeze pasta for 4 to 6 months.

roasted asparagus with portobello mushrooms

Deliciously easy!
You can use
shiitake or button
mushrooms with
equally good
results.

Yield: 4 servings.

1 bunch asparagus
4 medium portobello mushrooms
   ($^1/_2$ to $^3/_4$ lb.)

$^1/_4$ cup Balsamic Vinaigrette (p. 132)
salt and freshly ground black pepper
   to taste

Preheat oven to 425°F. Soak asparagus in cold water; drain well. Bend asparagus and snap off ends at the point where it breaks off naturally. (The ends can be peeled and used in soups.) Remove stems from mushrooms. Rinse mushrooms briefly and pat dry. If necessary, trim caps to fit feed tube. Insert SLICER. Slice, using medium pressure.

Place asparagus and mushrooms in a single layer on a sprayed baking sheet. Drizzle with vinaigrette, and season with salt and pepper. Roast at 425°F for 10 to 12 minutes, or until tender and browned. Serve immediately.

french-cut green beans

Yield: 4 servings.

1 lb. fresh green beans
2 Tbsp. butter or margarine

salt and freshly ground black pepper
   to taste
1 Tbsp. fresh lemon or lime juice

SLICER: Wash and trim beans to fit width of feed tube. Stack horizontally in feed tube to within 1 inch of top. Slice, using medium pressure. Repeat with remaining beans in as many batches as necessary.

Place in saucepan with boiling salted water to cover. Cover and cook on medium heat for 6 to 8 minutes, until tender but still slightly crunchy. Drain well. Combine with remaining ingredients. Serve immediately.

variation:

- Cook and drain sliced green beans as directed. Sauté 1 chopped onion in 2 Tbsp. butter until golden. Add green beans and ¼ cup slivered almonds; cook 2 to 3 minutes longer. Season to taste.

carrot ring

Yield: 8 servings.
Reheats and/or
freezes well.

5 or 6 medium carrots, cut in
   chunks (about 1$\frac{1}{2}$ cups)
2 eggs
$\frac{1}{2}$ cup canola oil
$\frac{1}{2}$ cup brown sugar, packed
$\frac{1}{4}$ cup orange juice or water

1$\frac{1}{2}$ cups flour
2 tsp. baking powder
1 tsp. baking soda
1 tsp. ground cinnamon
dash salt
1 cup green peas or broccoli (optional)

STEEL BLADE: Process carrots until finely minced, 12 to 15 seconds. Add eggs, oil and brown sugar. Process until well mixed, about 45 seconds. Add remaining ingredients and process with 4 or 5 quick on/offs, just until flour disappears.

Pour into sprayed 6-cup ring mold or small fluted tube pan. Bake in preheated 350°F oven for about 40 minutes, or until done. Invert onto serving plate. If desired, cook green peas or broccoli and fill center of ring. Serve warm.

variation:

• Replace oil with margarine and reduce baking powder to 1 tsp. Fill sprayed muffin tins ¾ full. Bake at 350°F about 30 minutes. Serve hot. Makes 12 muffins.

eggplant italiano

If you don't tell them it's eggplant, I won't! It tastes like pizza without the crust. Serve as a side dish or main dish.

Yield: 4 to 6 servings.

2 cloves garlic
1 large onion, cut in chunks
1 stalk celery
1 green or red bell pepper
1 to 2 cups mushrooms
1 Tbsp. oil
1 medium eggplant, peeled

salt and freshly ground black pepper
   to taste
$\frac{1}{2}$ tsp. each dried basil and dried oregano
19-oz. can tomatoes
4 to 8 oz. chilled Mozzarella cheese
   (1 to 2 cups grated)

STEEL BLADE: Drop garlic through feed tube while machine is running; process until minced. Add onion and process with quick on/offs, until coarsely chopped.

SLICER: Cut celery and bell pepper 1 inch shorter than top of feed tube. (If your processor has an expanded feed tube, cut veggies to fit small feed tube.) Slice celery, pepper and mushrooms, using light pressure. Heat oil in large nonstick skillet. Sauté sliced vegetables over medium heat, about 5 minutes, until tender.

Slice eggplant, using firm pressure. (If your processor has a standard feed tube, cut eggplant lengthwise in strips so slices won't be too large.) Add to skillet, stir well and cook 5 minutes longer. Add salt, pepper, basil, oregano and tomatoes. Cover and heat to simmering. Place in sprayed casserole. (May be prepared in advance and refrigerated or frozen.)

GRATER: Grate cheese, using medium pressure. Sprinkle over eggplant mixture. Bake in preheated 375°F oven 25 to 30 minutes, until bubbly and golden.

sweet and sour eggplant

Geitie Kramer of Toronto makes this as an appetizer or side dish. It's delicious either hot or cold. I've even served it as a pasta sauce. Salting eggplant before cooking draws out its bitter juices.

Yield: 8 servings. Reheats and/or freezes well.

2 lbs. eggplant, peeled and cut in 1-inch chunks
1 Tbsp. salt
$1/4$ cup fresh parsley
1 or 2 cloves garlic
1 large onion, cut in chunks

2 Tbsp. olive oil
2 19-oz. cans tomatoes
$1/4$ cup lemon juice
2 Tbsp. balsamic vinegar
3 Tbsp. sugar
$1/4$ tsp. freshly ground black pepper

SLICER: Slice eggplant, using medium pressure. Transfer to a colander and sprinkle with salt. Let drain for 1 hour. Rinse well; squeeze out excess moisture.

STEEL BLADE: Process parsley until minced. Remove from bowl and set aside. Drop garlic through feed tube while machine is running; process until minced. Add onion and process with quick on/off pulses, until coarsely chopped.

Heat oil in large nonstick skillet on medium heat. Sauté onion and garlic until soft and golden, about 5 minutes. Drain tomatoes, adding liquid to skillet.

Process tomatoes for a few seconds, until coarsely chopped. Add tomatoes, eggplant, parsley and remaining ingredients to skillet. Cook on low heat, partially covered, for 20 to 25 minutes, until eggplant is tender. Stir occasionally. Serve hot or cold.

no-fry eggplant parmesan

This recipe may be halved for a small family, but I like to prepare the full recipe and freeze the leftovers.

Yield: 6 to 8 servings as a main dish, 12 servings as a side dish. If frozen, eggplant may become soggy.

2 eggplants (about 1$^1/_2$ lbs. each)
$^1/_2$ cup grated Parmesan cheese
1 cup bread or cracker crumbs
dash salt and freshly ground
    black pepper
$^1/_4$ tsp. garlic powder and
    dried basil

8 oz. chilled Mozzarella cheese
    (2 cups grated)
2 eggs mixed with 2 Tbsp. cold water
1$^1/_2$ cups tomato sauce (bottled
    or homemade)
$^1/_4$ cup additional Parmesan cheese
    (optional)
1 pkg. dry onion soup mix (optional)

Peel eggplants; slice crosswise into ½-inch slices. Sprinkle with salt and let stand for 20 minutes. Pat dry with paper towels.

STEEL BLADE: Process the ½ cup Parmesan cheese, crumbs, salt, pepper, garlic powder and basil for 3 or 4 seconds to mix. Transfer to a sheet of waxed paper.

GRATER: Grate Mozzarella cheese, using medium pressure. Set aside.

Dip eggplant slices first in egg, then in crumb mixture. Arrange in a single layer on sprayed baking sheets.

Bake in preheated 375°F oven for 15 to 20 minutes. Turn slices over. Top each slice with sauce. Add grated cheese and about 1 tsp. dry onion soup mix, if desired. Bake 10 to 12 minutes longer, until golden.

passover eggplant parmesan:
• Replace crumbs with matzo meal or cake meal.

mom's caponata

My mother changed my recipe and boosted the flavor! Make this in minutes using your processor. Sprinkle with toasted pine nuts and chopped parsley. Serve chilled as an appetizer or hot over rice or pasta.

4 cloves garlic
2 medium onions, cut in chunks
2 stalks celery, cut in chunks
1 Tbsp. olive oil
4 medium bell peppers (2 red,
    1 green, 1 yellow)
1 jalapeño pepper
2 Japanese eggplants, unpeeled
    ($^3/_4$ to 1 lb.)
1 Tbsp. balsamic vinegar

28-oz. can plum tomatoes, drained
    (reserve liquid)
1 Tbsp. sugar
$^1/_4$ tsp. red pepper flakes
$^1/_2$ tsp. each ground cumin and dried basil
salt and freshly ground black pepper
    to taste
$^1/_2$ cup sultana raisins
$^1/_4$ cup capers, rinsed and drained
1 cup pitted black and/or green olives

Yield: 8 servings. This keeps about 10 days in the refrigerator or freezes well.

STEEL BLADE: Drop garlic through feed tube while machine is running; process until minced. Add onions and celery; process with quick on/off pulses, until coarsely chopped.

Heat oil in large pot. Sauté garlic, onion and celery on medium heat for 5 minutes, until soft.

SLICER: Cut bell and jalapeño peppers and eggplants in half; remove core and seeds from peppers. Slice peppers and eggplant, using medium pressure. Add to onion mixture and cook 10 minutes longer, stirring occasionally.

Add balsamic vinegar, drained tomatoes, sugar, pepper flakes, cumin, basil, salt, pepper and raisins. Cover partially and simmer 20 minutes longer, stirring occasionally. Add reserved tomato liquid as needed to prevent the mixture from becoming dry. Mixture should be thick, not watery. Stir in capers and olives at the end of cooking. Adjust seasonings to taste.

ratatouille

Here is my mother's updated recipe—serve it chilled as an appetizer or hot as a sauce over pasta. The flavor is even better the next day!

3 cloves garlic
1 Spanish onion, cut in chunks
1 green and 1 red bell pepper, halved
1 cup mushrooms
3 stalks celery, cut in chunks
1 to 2 Tbsp. olive oil
1 medium eggplant, cut in chunks
2 medium zucchini, cut in chunks

19-oz. can plum tomatoes
1 Tbsp. balsamic vinegar
salt and freshly ground black pepper to taste
1 tsp. sugar
$1/2$ tsp. each dried basil and dried oregano
$1/4$ tsp. red pepper flakes
dash Worcestershire sauce

Yield: 8 servings. Keeps in the refrigerator about a week, or freezes well.

STEEL BLADE: Drop garlic through feed tube while machine is running; process until minced.

SLICER: Slice onion, bell peppers, mushrooms and celery, using medium pressure. Spray a large pot with nonstick spray. Add oil and heat on medium heat. Sauté sliced vegetables 7 to 8 minutes, stirring occasionally.

Slice eggplant and zucchini, using medium pressure. Add to pot and cook 10 minutes more. Add remaining ingredients and simmer, uncovered, 10 minutes longer, stirring occasionally. Adjust seasonings to taste.

chickpea chili

With the help of your processor, you can prepare this tasty, versatile chili in minutes. Serve as a side dish or vegetarian main dish over rice, polenta or pasta.

Yield: 8 servings. Keeps about a week in the refrigerator; freezes well.

3 cloves garlic
1 large onion, cut in chunks
2 Tbsp. olive oil
1 red bell pepper, quartered
2 cups mushrooms
$1/2$ lb. eggplant, cut in long strips
2 medium carrots
$5 1/2$-oz. can tomato paste
1 cup tomato sauce (or
    2 tomatoes, chopped)

3 cups water
salt and freshly ground black pepper
    to taste
$1/2$ tsp. each dried basil, dried oregano
    and chili powder
1 Tbsp. honey or sugar
1 bay leaf
$1/2$ cup bulgur or couscous
19-oz. can chickpeas, drained and
    rinsed

STEEL BLADE: Drop garlic through feed tube while machine is running; process until minced. Add onion and chop coarsely, using quick on/off pulses. Heat oil in 5-quart saucepan. Add garlic and onion; sauté on medium heat until soft, about 5 minutes.

SLICER: Slice bell pepper, mushrooms and eggplant, using medium pressure. Add to saucepan and sauté 6 or 7 minutes longer, until softened, stirring occasionally. Slice carrots. Add to saucepan along with remaining ingredients; mix well. Bring to a boil, reduce heat and simmer, partly covered, for 25 to 30 minutes, until vegetables are tender, stirring occasionally. If mixture gets too thick, add a little water. Adjust seasonings to taste.

sautéed garlic mushrooms

If using wild and cultivated mushrooms, substitute olive oil and balsamic vinegar for margarine and lemon juice.

Yield: 4 servings. Do not freeze.

2 to 3 cloves garlic
2 Tbsp. margarine
1 lb. mushrooms

1 Tbsp. fresh lemon juice
salt and freshly ground black pepper
    to taste

STEEL BLADE: Drop garlic through feed tube while machine is running; process until minced. Heat margarine in a nonstick skillet. Stir in garlic and cook for 1 to 2 minutes on medium heat.

SLICER: Stack mushrooms on their sides. Slice, using light pressure. Add to skillet and sauté on medium heat for 4 to 5 minutes, shaking pan to stir. Sprinkle with lemon juice, salt and pepper. Serve immediately.

mushroom duxelles

Yield: About 1 cup.
Duxelles can be
refrigerated for a
week in a tightly
covered container. To
freeze, spoon mixture
into ice cube trays.
When frozen, transfer
to a resealable plastic
bag. For a "gourmet
touch" add cubes to
stews and soups!

1 medium onion or $1/2$ cup
  shallots, cut in chunks
2 to 3 Tbsp. margarine or butter
1 pint mushrooms (about $1/2$ lb.)

1 Tbsp. lemon juice
$3/4$ tsp. salt
$1/4$ tsp. freshly ground black pepper

STEEL BLADE: Process onion or shallots until finely chopped, about 6 seconds. Melt margarine or butter in a nonstick skillet. Sauté onion on medium heat until transparent, about 5 minutes. Do not brown.

Process mushrooms until finely chopped, about 10 seconds. Wrap mushrooms in a tea towel and wring out excess moisture. Add mushrooms to skillet, sprinkle with lemon juice and cook, stirring, until dry, about 10 minutes. Add salt and pepper.

easy potato latkes

I use Idaho (russet)
potatoes, but some
cooks prefer Yukon
Golds or red-
skinned potatoes.
Serve latkes with
applesauce or
sour cream.

Yield: About 2 dozen,
or 5 dozen miniatures.
Freezes well
(see p. 197).

4 medium potatoes, peeled
  or scrubbed
1 medium onion
2 eggs (or 1 egg plus 2 egg
  whites)

$1/3$ cup flour or matzo meal
1 tsp. baking powder
$3/4$ tsp. salt
freshly ground black pepper to taste
2 Tbsp. oil

STEEL BLADE: Cut potatoes in chunks and onion in half. Place in processor with eggs. Process until puréed, 20 to 30 seconds. Add remaining ingredients except oil; process a few seconds longer to blend into a smooth mixture.

Heat oil in large nonstick skillet over medium-high heat. Drop potato mixture into hot oil by large spoonfuls to form pancakes; brown well on both sides. Drain well on paper towels. Add additional oil to pan as needed. Stir batter before cooking each new batch. Latkes can be placed on a baking sheet and kept warm in a 250°F oven. (To bake latkes instead of frying, place oven racks on lowest and middle position in oven. Preheat oven to 450°F. Drop potato mixture by spoonfuls onto well-oiled baking sheets; flatten slightly. Bake 10 minutes, until bottoms are browned and crispy. Turn latkes over. Transfer pan from upper rack to lower rack and vice versa. Bake 8 to 10 minutes longer.)

breaded zucchini

The zucchini comes out crispy and scrumptious.

Yield: 3 to 4 servings. Do not freeze. May be made ahead and refrigerated until needed. Bake in preheated 425°F oven until hot and crispy.

3 or 4 slender zucchini
   (about 1 lb.)
salt (about 1 tsp.)
1 egg or 2 egg whites,
   lightly beaten
1 cup bread crumbs

$1/2$ tsp. salt
$1/4$ tsp. each freshly ground black
   pepper, garlic powder and
   dried oregano
2 to 3 Tbsp. oil

SLICER: Wash zucchini and pat dry. Trim off ends; cut zucchini to fit feed tube. Use the center mini tube if your processor has one. Slice zucchini, using firm pressure. Sprinkle with salt and let stand 20 minutes to remove excess moisture.

Combine crumbs, salt, pepper, garlic powder and oregano. Pat zucchini dry. Dip slices in beaten egg, then seasoned crumbs.

Heat oil in large nonstick skillet. Brown zucchini slices a few at a time on medium heat, 2 or 3 minutes per side. Watch carefully to prevent burning. Drain on paper towels. Add additional oil to pan as needed.

variations:
- Add 3 to 4 Tbsp. grated Parmesan cheese to bread crumb mixture.
- For crispy fried zucchini, omit egg and substitute flour for bread crumbs. Coat zucchini slices with seasoned flour. Sauté in hot oil.

zucchini puffs

Yield: 10 puffs of about 75 calories each. Freezes well.

3 oz. chilled Mozzarella cheese
   ($3/4$ cup grated)
2 medium zucchini (2 cups grated)
$1/2$ small onion

2 eggs (or 1 egg plus 2 egg whites)
$1/2$ tsp. salt
dash freshly ground black pepper
$1/2$ cup bread crumbs

GRATER: Grate cheese using medium pressure. Empty bowl. Cut zucchini to fit feed tube; grate, using firm pressure. Measure 2 cups, lightly packed.

STEEL BLADE: Process onion until minced, about 6 seconds. Add eggs, salt and pepper and process for 2 seconds. Add bread crumbs, zucchini and cheese to egg mixture. Process with 2 or 3 quick on/offs, just until mixed. Do not overprocess.

Divide mixture evenly among 10 sprayed muffin cups. Bake in preheated 375°F oven for 30 minutes. They will fall slightly upon standing, but taste and texture won't be affected. Serve hot.

vegetables and side dishes

hoisin vegetable stir-fry

It takes more time to read this recipe than to prepare it! Add cauliflower florets, bamboo shoots, bean sprouts and/or baby corn for fiber and color.

Yield: 4 servings. If frozen, vegetables will become soggy.

1 medium onion, halved
1 red and 1 green bell pepper, halved
1 bunch broccoli, trimmed
2 cloves garlic
2 Tbsp. hoisin sauce
2 Tbsp. soy sauce

2 Tbsp. honey
2 Tbsp. orange juice
dash cayenne pepper
1 Tbsp. oil
1 Tbsp. cornstarch dissolved in 2 Tbsp. water
1 tsp. toasted sesame oil

SLICER: Slice onion and peppers, using medium pressure. Transfer to mixing bowl. Cut florets from broccoli and add to onions and peppers. Slice stems, using medium pressure. Add to vegetables.

STEEL BLADE: Drop garlic through feed tube while machine is running; process until minced. Add hoisin, soy sauce, honey, orange juice and cayenne. Process a few seconds longer, until blended.

Heat oil in nonstick wok. Stir-fry vegetables on high heat for 2 minutes. Add sauce mixture and bring to a boil. Stir in cornstarch mixture and sesame oil. Cook 1 to 2 minutes longer, until thickened, stirring constantly.

pea pod, pepper and mushroom stir-fry

Yield: 4 to 6 servings. Do not freeze.

2 medium onions, halved
1 green and 1 red bell pepper, halved
2 cups mushrooms
2 cloves garlic
1 cup snow peas or sugar snap peas

1 Tbsp. oil
2 Tbsp. soy sauce
$1^1/_2$ Tbsp. cornstarch
$^1/_4$ cup cold water, chicken or vegetable broth
salt and freshly ground black pepper to taste

SLICER: Slice onions and peppers, using medium pressure. Repeat with mushrooms, using light pressure. Pat dry with paper towels; set aside in a mixing bowl.

STEEL BLADE: Drop garlic through feed tube while machine is running; process until minced. Add garlic and snow peas or sugar snap peas to mixing bowl.

Heat oil in a wok on medium-high heat. Add vegetables and stir-fry for 2 minutes. Stir in soy sauce. Dissolve cornstarch in water or broth. Stir cornstarch mixture into center of wok and cook until thickened, stirring constantly, about 1 minute. Season to taste.

variation:

• Stir-fry vegetables for 2 minutes. (Omit snow peas if desired.) Add ½ cup water chestnuts, ½ cup bamboo shoots and 2 cups bean sprouts; stir-fry 1 minute longer. Add soy sauce and cornstarch mixture and stir-fry until thickened. Serve over noodles.

sticky tofu

Natalie Frankel of Milwaukee adapted my recipe for Sticky Chicky (p. 100), substituting tofu and adding vegetables and pineapple chunks. This tasty vegetarian dish is the result. Serve it over rice.

Yield: 4 to 6 servings.
Do not freeze.

1 lb. firm tofu, cut in 1-inch squares
2 Tbsp. soy sauce
3 to 4 Tbsp. sesame seeds
1 red and 1 green bell pepper, quartered
4 green onions
8-oz. can water chestnuts, drained and halved
1 cup canned pineapple chunks, drained (reserve 2 Tbsp. juice)
2 cloves garlic
1 Tbsp. fresh ginger (or ½ tsp. ground ginger)
½ cup soy sauce
½ cup honey
2 Tbsp. vinegar or lemon juice
1 Tbsp. cornstarch
1 tomato, cut in chunks

Place tofu in a sprayed casserole; sprinkle with 2 Tbsp. soy sauce and 1 Tbsp. of the sesame seeds. Bake, uncovered, in preheated 350°F oven for 20 minutes.

SLICER: Slice bell peppers and green onions, using medium pressure. Add to tofu along with water chestnuts and drained pineapple chunks.

STEEL BLADE: Drop garlic and ginger through feed tube while machine is running; process until minced. Add the ½ cup soy sauce, honey and vinegar or lemon juice and process until blended. Pour over tofu/vegetable mixture. Bake, uncovered, for 20 minutes longer, stirring occasionally.

Dissolve cornstarch in reserved pineapple juice. Add to casserole along with tomato. Sprinkle with remaining sesame seeds and cook 10 minutes longer.

no-fry fried rice

My assistant,
Elaine Kaplan,
loves this dish, and
so do her guests!
It's great for vege-
tarians and is
oven-ready in
minutes.

Yield: 8 to 10 servings.
May be frozen or pre-
pared in advance.

2 cups rice
1 to 2 Tbsp. oil
1 pkg. dry onion soup mix
3 Tbsp. soy sauce
1 green or red bell pepper, halved
2 cups mushrooms

8-oz. can water chestnuts
8-oz. can bamboo shoots
4 cups liquid (reserved juices from canned vegetables, plus cold water)
salt and freshly ground black pepper to taste

Combine rice, oil, soup mix and soy sauce in a large sprayed casserole. Mix well.

SLICER: Slice pepper and mushrooms, using light pressure. Drain canned vegetables and reserve liquid. Slice water chestnuts, using firm pressure. Combine all ingredients in casserole and mix well. Cover and bake in preheated 350°F oven about 1 hour, or until all liquid is absorbed. Adjust seasonings to taste.

variation:

- Replace onion soup mix with 2 chopped onions. Add ½ cup each of chopped carrots and celery. Coarsely chop vegetables on the STEEL BLADE, using quick on/off pulses. Add 1 cup firm tofu, cut in ½-inch cubes.

chinese fried rice

Rice should be
cold for best
results. Leftover
rice is ideal. It
keeps for 3 or
4 days in the
refrigerator.

Yield: 4 to 6 servings.
Reheats well in the
microwave. If frozen,
rice has a tendency to
become hard.

3 green onions, cut in chunks
1 stalk celery, cut in chunks
1/2 cup cooked chicken (optional)
2 eggs
1 to 2 Tbsp. oil

3 cups cold cooked rice
1/2 cup frozen green peas
2 Tbsp. soy sauce
1 tsp. toasted sesame oil
freshly ground black pepper to taste

STEEL BLADE: Process green onions and celery with quick on/offs, until coarsely chopped. Empty bowl. If using chicken, coarsely chop with quick on/offs. Set chicken aside separately from vegetables. Process eggs for 2 or 3 seconds to mix.

Heat 1 tsp. oil in large nonstick skillet or wok over medium-high heat. Add eggs and scramble them briefly. Remove eggs from pan. Add remaining oil to pan. Stir-fry onions and celery for 1 minute. Add rice and mix thoroughly, until heated through. Add remaining ingredients and stir well. Serve piping hot.

vegetables and side dishes

rice pilaf

To substitute brown rice, increase cooking time to 45 minutes.

Yield: 6 to 8 servings.

If frozen, rice has a tendency to get hard.

2 medium onions, cut in chunks
1 stalk celery, cut in chunks
1 red bell pepper, cut in chunks
1 to 2 Tbsp. olive oil
1$1/2$ cups basmati or long-grain rice, rinsed and drained

3 cups chicken or vegetable broth, boiling
salt and freshly ground black pepper to taste
$1/2$ tsp. each dried dill and dried thyme
$1/4$ cup fresh parsley
$1/2$ cup cooked chicken (optional)

STEEL BLADE: Process onions, celery and pepper with several quick on/off pulses, until coarsely chopped. Heat olive oil in nonstick skillet. Add vegetables and sauté on medium heat for 2 to 3 minutes. Add rice and cook 2 minutes longer, stirring. Add boiling broth, salt, pepper, dill and thyme. Cover and simmer 15 minutes for basmati rice and 20 minutes for long-grain rice.

STEEL BLADE: Process parsley until minced. Add chicken, if using. Process with quick on/offs, until coarsely chopped. Add to rice. Remove from heat and let stand covered for 10 minutes. Fluff with a fork.

leek and rice skillet casserole

Yield: 4 to 6 servings.

Freezes well.

4 leeks
1 green or red bell pepper
2 stalks celery
1 to 2 Tbsp. oil
$1/2$ to $3/4$ cup boiling water

1 cup tomato juice or sauce
1 cup cooked rice
salt and freshly ground black pepper to taste

Clean leeks thoroughly; dry well. (See below.) Cut all vegetables to fit feed tube.

SLICER: Slice leeks, bell pepper and celery, using medium pressure. Sauté in oil on medium heat for about 5 minutes, until golden. Add boiling water just to cover. Simmer, covered, for 5 minutes. Add tomato juice and bring to a boil. Add rice, salt and pepper. Cover and simmer 10 minutes.

preparing leeks — Leeks are difficult to clean. First, remove all but 2 or 3 inches of the green part. Make 4 lengthwise cuts to within 1 inch of the roots, so that the leeks resemble a whisk broom. To remove sand and grit, swish them in cold water. Dry well, then slice or chop.

vegetables and side dishes

stuffing casserole

Yield: 6 to 8 servings.
May be frozen.

5 cups soft bread crumbs (p. 20),
  or 10 slices bread
2 Tbsp. oil or margarine
2 medium onions, halved
1 green bell pepper, cut in chunks
2 stalks celery, cut in chunks
1 cup mushrooms

3 eggs (or 2 eggs plus 2 egg whites)
1 tsp. salt
dash freshly ground black pepper
$1/4$ tsp. garlic powder
1 cup chicken broth
1 tsp. baking powder

STEEL BLADE: Make crumbs from stale bread or rolls. Tear into chunks and drop through feed tube while machine is running. Process until fine crumbs are formed. Measure 5 cups crumbs, loosely packed.

Heat oil or margarine in large nonstick skillet. Meanwhile, process onions with quick on/offs, until coarsely chopped. Add to skillet. Repeat with bell pepper, then celery, then mushrooms, adding each in turn to skillet. Brown vegetables quickly on medium-high heat. Remove from heat and cool slightly.

Process eggs for 2 or 3 seconds. Add with bread crumbs and remaining ingredients to skillet and mix well. Place in sprayed 7 x 11-inch glass baking dish. Bake, uncovered, in preheated 350°F oven for 40 to 45 minutes, until golden brown.

variation:

• To use as a stuffing for veal brisket or turkey, omit baking powder and increase mushrooms to 2 cups. Add ½ tsp. each of dried sage and dried thyme.

super salads and dressings

- Refer to the Smart Chart (p. 18) for basic processing techniques.
- Before processing, wash and dry vegetables well. Peel and core; remove seeds and any pits to prevent damage to the processor blades.
- See Vegetables and Side Dishes chapter (pp. 105–107) for vegetable processing techniques.
- Vegetables with a high water content (e.g., cucumbers, bell peppers) should be patted dry with paper towels after processing to absorb excess moisture.
- Use a salad spinner to dry salad greens, then wrap in a towel to absorb remaining moisture. Greens can be stored in a resealable plastic bag for a day or two in your refrigerator.
- Salad bore or salad bar? There is an amazing selection of fresh produce available today, including local and organic. Many are washed, trimmed and ready to serve.
- Take your pick of salad greens! Reach for arugula, Bibb/butterhead, Boston, curly leaf lettuce, endive, escarole, iceberg, Romaine, mesclun/ mixed salad greens, oak leaf, radicchio, spinach/baby spinach or watercress.
- To give color, texture and flavor to salads, add avocado, broccoli slaw, carrots/baby carrots, red or green cabbage, celery, cucumbers, fennel, bell peppers, onions (Spanish, Vidalia, red), green onions/scallions or chives, and alfalfa, bean or broccoli sprouts.
- Tomatoes are available in many shapes, sizes and colors, from grape tomatoes to beefsteaks. For maximum flavor, store them at room temperature.

- Roasted and grilled vegetables add terrific flavor to salads. Choose from bell peppers, garlic, beets, eggplant, mushrooms or zucchini.
- Lightly steamed broccoli or cauliflower florets, asparagus, green or yellow beans add crunch and flavor to salads.
- Use baked, microwaved or boiled potatoes for potato salad. When cool, remove peel. (New potatoes do not need to be peeled.) Slice or cut into cubes by hand; potatoes may crumble if sliced on the processor.
- Jarred or canned marinated artichoke hearts, olives, sun-dried tomatoes, roasted bell peppers, canned beets, kidney beans, black beans, chickpeas, lentils or corn niblets add variety with no fuss or muss.
- Use pasta, rice, bulgur, couscous, quinoa, barley, kasha or other cooked grains for a hearty salad base.
- Add color, zing and nutrients to salads with fresh fruit. Dried fruits make a quick, delicious addition (e.g., apricots, cranberries, raisins). Pomegranate seeds are beautiful as a garnish!
- Finish off your salads with toasted sunflower seeds, sesame seeds, almonds, walnuts, flax seed, wheat germ, croutons or chow mein noodles.
- Try adding Cheddar, Swiss, Mozzarella, Muenster or Parmesan, crumbled feta, goat or cottage cheese to salads for flavor and extra protein.
- Add cooked chicken, turkey, cold cuts, hard-cooked egg wedges, cooked or canned fish (e.g., salmon, tuna) for hearty main-dish salads. Allow 1 to 2 cups salad per person as a main dish.
- Use the **Steel Blade** to make salad dressings. Transform dips into dressings by thinning them down with a little milk or buttermilk.
- Replace part of the oil in salad dressings with fruit juice, chicken or vegetable broth. Experiment with different vinegars (balsamic, cider, rice or wine vinegar) and fruit juices (lemon, lime, grapefruit, mango or orange juice). For variety, use extra-virgin olive oil, toasted sesame oil or walnut oil.
- Add salad dressing just before serving; otherwise salad will become limp and watery.
- **Instant Gazpacho!** Transform limp, leftover salad into delicious soup. Process on the **Steel Blade** until finely chopped. Combine with tomato or vegetable juice and a squeeze of fresh lemon juice. Season to taste. Serve chilled. Garnish with chopped tomatoes, bell peppers and green onions.

marinated bean salad

To substitute fresh or frozen beans for the canned ones in this recipe, undercook them slightly, and drain well.

Yield: 12 servings. Keeps about 10 days in the refrigerator.

14-oz. can cut green beans
14-oz. can cut yellow beans
10-oz. can baby lima beans
1 cup canned kidney beans
  or chickpeas
1 large Spanish or Vidalia onion,
  cut in chunks
1 green and 1 red bell pepper,
  halved

2 cups raw cauliflower florets (optional)
$1/3$ cup olive or canola oil
$1/4$ cup vinegar (white, wine or balsamic)
salt and freshly ground black pepper to
  taste
1 tsp. dry mustard
1 tsp. Italian seasoning
2 to 3 Tbsp. sugar (or to taste)

SLICER: Place beans in a colander, rinse and drain well. Slice onion and bell peppers, using medium pressure.

Combine all ingredients in a large bowl and mix well. Cover and refrigerate for at least 24 hours before serving.

super coleslaw

I've made this family favorite for years—it's a winner! The hot marinade keeps the coleslaw mixture crisp. For a colorful slaw, use a mixture of red and green cabbage.

Yield: 12 to 16 servings.

1 head cabbage (about 3 lbs.)
1 green bell pepper, cut in chunks
3 carrots (or 12 mini carrots)
2 cloves garlic
3 green onions, cut in chunks

1 cup white vinegar
$1/2$ cup sugar (see below)
$3/4$ cup oil
1 tsp. salt
$1/4$ tsp. freshly ground black pepper

SLICER: Discard soft, outer leaves. Cut cabbage into wedges to fit feed tube. Discard core. Slice, using very light pressure. If too thick, chop in batches on the STEEL BLADE, using quick on/off pulses. Slice green pepper, using medium pressure. Empty into a large bowl.

GRATER: Use the mini feed tube if your machine has one. Grate carrots, using firm pressure. Add to cabbage.

STEEL BLADE: Drop garlic and green onions through feed tube while machine is running; process until minced. Add to cabbage.

Combine remaining ingredients in a saucepan or microwavable bowl. Heat until almost boiling (2 to 3 minutes on HIGH in the microwave), stirring occasionally. Pour hot marinade over coleslaw mixture and mix well. Refrigerate. Keeps about 1 month in the refrigerator.

moroccan pepper salad (salade cuite)

My daughter-in-law Ariane prepares this dish for me whenever I visit Montreal. She roasts and peels the peppers first, but my son Doug, who is a chef, omits this step. Either way, it's delicious.

Yield: 4 to 6 servings.
Serve hot or cold.
Freezes well.

6 Roasted Red Peppers (p. 43)
8 Italian plum tomatoes
2 cloves garlic
1 medium onion, cut in chunks
1 Tbsp. olive oil

1 cup tomato sauce
1 to 2 Tbsp. sugar (or to taste)
salt and freshly ground black pepper
   to taste
few drops hot sauce (optional)

Prepare roasted peppers as directed. Peel and remove seeds, then cut into strips. Set aside.

Bring water to a boil in a large saucepan. Cut an "x" in the bottom of each tomato. Drop into boiling water for 30 seconds; plunge into cold water immediately. Peel tomatoes, cut in half and squeeze gently to remove seeds. Set aside.

STEEL BLADE: Drop garlic through feed tube while machine is running; process until minced. Add onion and process with quick on/off pulses, until coarsely chopped. Heat oil in a large skillet. Add garlic and onion. Sauté on medium heat until tender, 5 to 7 minutes.

Process tomatoes with quick on/off pulses, until coarsely chopped. Add to skillet and cook 3 or 4 minutes longer. Add roasted peppers along with remaining ingredients. Simmer for 20 minutes, stirring occasionally. Adjust seasonings to taste.

variation:

• Instead of roasting the peppers, cut fresh red peppers in half; remove seeds and core. Slice on SLICER, using medium pressure. Sauté with garlic and onion until tender. Roasted red peppers from a jar can also be substituted.

super salads and dressings

faux-tato salad

Cauliflower replaces potatoes in this low-carb version of potato salad!

Yield: 6 servings.
Do not freeze. Recipe may be doubled.

1 medium cauliflower, cut up
3 hard-cooked eggs (or 5 hard-cooked egg whites)
2 Tbsp. fresh dill
2 stalks celery, cut in chunks

2 green onions, cut in chunks
$1/2$ cup light or regular mayonnaise (approximately)
$1/2$ tsp. dry mustard
salt and freshly ground black pepper to taste

Cook cauliflower in boiling water to cover until very tender, 15 to 20 minutes. Drain well. (Or microwave, covered, on HIGH for 7 to 8 minutes.) You should have about 4 cups. Let cool. Eggs should be cooked in advance and cooled.

STEEL BLADE: Process dill until minced. Add celery and green onions; process with quick on/off pulses, until coarsely chopped. Add eggs and process with quick on/offs, until coarsely chopped. Transfer to a large bowl, add remaining ingredients and mix gently. Cover and refrigerate.

caesar salad

A tried and true favorite!

Yield: 8 servings.

2 to 3 heads Romaine lettuce (depending on size)
1 can flat anchovies (optional)
$1/2$ cup canola or olive oil (approximately)
1 or 2 cloves garlic
$1/4$ cup wine vinegar

1 Tbsp. lemon juice
$1/2$ tsp. salt
freshly ground black pepper to taste
$1/2$ tsp. sugar
1 tsp. Worcestershire sauce
$1/4$ to $1/3$ cup Parmesan cheese
Croutons (p. 126)

Wash lettuce; dry thoroughly. Tear into bite-sized pieces. (May be wrapped in paper towels and stored in a plastic bag in refrigerator until serving time.)

Drain oil from anchovies into measuring cup; add oil to measure ¾ cup. (If you don't use anchovies, increase canola or olive oil to ¾ cup.)

STEEL BLADE: Drop garlic through feed tube while machine is running; process until minced. Add oil, vinegar, lemon juice, salt, pepper, sugar, Worcestershire sauce and Parmesan cheese. Process 8 to 10 seconds to blend. (May be prepared in advance and refrigerated.)

Combine approximately 1 cup dressing with lettuce, anchovies and croutons in a large salad bowl; mix well. Add additional dressing if needed. Serve immediately.

variations:

- Omit anchovies. Increase oil to 1 cup and increase Parmesan cheese to ½ cup. Process until blended. Makes about 1¾ cups dressing. Keeps about 7 to 10 days in the refrigerator. If desired, add 3 Tbsp. mayonnaise to make a creamier dressing. (This will give the same texture as using a coddled egg, which was called for in my original recipe.)

croutons

2 cups cubed stale French bread, crusts trimmed (freeze crusts for bread crumbs)	2 Tbsp. canola or olive oil 1 clove garlic, minced (optional)

Spread bread cubes on baking sheet and bake in preheated 325°F oven for 10 to 15 minutes, until dry. Cool slightly. Toss with oil and garlic. Return to oven for a few minutes, until lightly toasted and completely dry and crisp.

cucumber salad

Yield: 8 to 10 servings.

¹/₄ cup fresh dill, loosely packed	1 medium onion, cut in chunks
4 English cucumbers, unpeeled	1 small red bell pepper, cut in chunks
2 tsp. salt	Best Vinaigrette Dressing (p. 132)

STEEL BLADE: Process dill until minced, 6 to 8 seconds. Remove from bowl and reserve.

SLICER: Cut cucumbers to fit feed tube. Slice, using medium pressure. Transfer to a colander, sprinkle with salt and mix well. Weigh down cucumbers with a heavy plate and let drain for ½ hour. Press to remove excess liquid; rinse well. Pat dry with paper towels.

Slice onion and bell pepper, using light pressure. Prepare dressing as directed, adding reserved dill. In a large bowl, combine about ¾ cup dressing with all ingredients and mix well. Marinate for at least 1 hour before serving. Serve chilled.

asian spinach salad

Yield: 6 to 8 servings.

10-oz. pkg. fresh spinach
 (or baby spinach can
 be substituted)
Asian Salad Dressing (p. 134)
1 red and 1 yellow bell pepper,
 quartered
4 green onions
$1/2$ cup radishes
2 carrots

2 cups bean sprouts or broccoli
 sprouts
salt and freshly ground black pepper
 to taste
2 Tbsp. toasted sesame seeds,
 for garnish
$1/2$ cup toasted slivered almonds,
 for garnish

Trim tough stems from spinach leaves. Wash and dry thoroughly. Tear into bite-sized pieces if using large spinach leaves. Place in large bowl. Prepare salad dressing as directed and set aside.

SLICER: Slice bell peppers, green onions and radishes, using medium pressure. Add to spinach.

GRATER: Grate carrots, using medium pressure. Add to spinach along with sprouts. (Vegetables and dressing can be prepared in advance and refrigerated separately for several hours.)

At serving time, combine vegetables with dressing and mix gently. Season with salt and pepper. Sprinkle with sesame seeds and almonds. Serve immediately.

variations:
- Add sliced water chestnuts, bamboo shoots, baby corn, snow peas and/or mandarin oranges. For a main dish salad, top with slices of cooked chicken breast.

raspberry spinach salad

This crunchy salad comes from Lisa Kaufman of Toronto. She uses raspberries but sliced strawberries are a delicious alternative.

$1/2$ cup slivered almonds
$1/4$ cup sugar
2 tsp. water
$1/4$ of a small onion
 (about 1 Tbsp.)
$1/4$ cup sugar
2 tsp. poppy seeds

$1/4$ tsp. paprika
$1/2$ cup canola oil
$1/4$ cup raspberry vinegar
$1/4$ tsp. Worcestershire sauce
1 lb. fresh spinach, baby spinach
 or mixed salad greens (mesclun)
2 cups fresh raspberries

Yield: 6 servings.

In a heavy skillet, combine almonds with ¼ cup sugar and water. Stir over medium heat until sugar melts and coats the almonds. Set aside to cool; break into small pieces.

STEEL BLADE: Process onion until minced. Add remaining ¼ cup sugar, poppy seeds, paprika, oil, vinegar and Worcestershire sauce; process for 10 to 12 seconds. (Can be made ahead and refrigerated.)

Wash and dry greens. If using large spinach leaves, remove stems. At serving time, gently toss dressing with greens. Transfer to a serving platter or bowl. Sprinkle with raspberries and almonds.

greek salad

In Detroit, cut-up cooked beets are added to Greek Salad!

Yield: 8 servings.

2 heads Romaine lettuce	1 large clove garlic
1 red onion or $^1/_4$ Spanish onion	$^1/_2$ cup olive oil
1 red and 1 green bell pepper, halved	juice of 1 lemon (3 Tbsp.)
2 cups cherry tomatoes or 2 large ripe tomatoes, cut in wedges	$^1/_2$ tsp. dry mustard
	$^1/_2$ tsp. dried oregano
	salt and freshly ground black pepper to taste
2 dozen black olives	1 can flat anchovies, drained
$^1/_2$ lb. feta cheese	

Wash lettuce; dry well. Tear into bite-sized pieces and place in large salad bowl.

SLICER: Slice onion and peppers, using medium pressure. Pat dry with paper towels. Add to salad bowl along with tomatoes and olives, reserving a few olives for garnishing.

STEEL BLADE: Process feta cheese with quick on/offs, until crumbled. Add to salad. Wipe out processor bowl and blade with paper towels.

Drop garlic through feed tube while machine is running; process until minced. Add oil, lemon juice, mustard and oregano. Process for a few seconds to blend. (Can be prepared in advance up to this point and refrigerated until serving time.)

Pour dressing over salad. Season lightly with salt and pepper and toss well. Arrange anchovies like the spokes of a wheel on top of salad. Place reserved olives between anchovies.

pesto pasta salad

I love to combine pesto with pasta. It's the best!

Yield: 8 servings. Keeps 2 or 3 days in the refrigerator.

12-oz. pkg. fusilli or penne (about 4 cups)
$3/4$ cup sun-dried tomatoes
$1/4$ cup fresh parsley
6 green onions

1 red and 1 yellow bell pepper, quartered
$1/4$ to $1/3$ cup Pesto (p. 63)
$1/2$ cup mayonnaise (approximately)
salt and freshly ground black pepper to taste
$1/4$ cup grated Parmesan cheese

Cook pasta in boiling salted water according to package directions; drain well. Place in large bowl. Cover sun-dried tomatoes with boiling water; soak for 10 minutes. (If using sun-dried tomatoes packed in oil, drain well.)

STEEL BLADE: Process parsley until minced, about 10 seconds. Add drained sun-dried tomatoes and process with quick on/off pulses, until coarsely chopped. (No need to empty the work bowl.)

SLICER: Slice green onions and peppers, using light pressure. Combine all ingredients with pasta and mix well. Adjust seasonings to taste. Chill before serving.

bev's colorful couscous salad

This nutritious, delicious salad from my friend Bev Binder of Winnipeg is an excellent vegetarian dish for a buffet and can be made in advance.

Yield: 12 servings. Leftovers keep for 4 or 5 days in the refrigerator.

$1 1/2$ cups vegetable broth
1 cup couscous
19-oz. can chickpeas, drained and rinsed
$1/2$ cup fresh parsley
$3/4$ to 1 cup dried apricots
$1/2$ cup pitted prunes
$1/2$ cup dried cranberries
$1/2$ cup raisins
1 small red onion, cut in chunks
1 red bell pepper, cut in chunks

1 medium zucchini, cut in chunks
2 cloves garlic
$1/3$ cup olive or canola oil
3 Tbsp. lemon juice
3 Tbsp. orange juice
1 tsp. ground cumin
1 tsp. curry powder
salt and freshly ground black pepper to taste
$1/2$ cup toasted slivered almonds, for garnish

Combine broth with couscous in a large bowl. Cover and let stand 5 to 10 minutes, then stir with a fork. Add chickpeas.

STEEL BLADE: Process parsley until minced, about 10 seconds. Add apricots, prunes, cranberries and raisins and process with quick on/off pulses, until coarsely chopped. Add to couscous. Process onion, bell pepper and zucchini with quick on/off pulses, until coarsely chopped. Add to couscous mixture.

Drop garlic through feed tube while machine is running; process until minced. Add remaining ingredients and process until blended. Pour dressing over

So versatile, so easy!

couscous mixture and mix well. Adjust seasonings to taste. Garnish with toasted almonds at serving time.

Yield: 6 servings. Keeps in the refrigerator up to 3 days.

variations:
• Add other dried fruits such as dates, figs, dried cherries, etc. Toasted sesame or sunflower seeds also make a nice garnish. For a flavor boost, add 1 Tbsp. freshly grated ginger.

quick couscous salad

1 1/2 cups couscous	4 green onions, cut in 2-inch pieces
3 cups water, chicken or	2 carrots
vegetable broth	2 Tbsp. extra-virgin olive oil
2 cloves garlic	3 Tbsp. lemon juice
1/4 cup fresh parsley	salt and freshly ground black
1 red and 1 yellow bell pepper,	pepper to taste
cut in chunks	1/2 tsp. each chili powder, dry
	mustard and ground cumin

In a large mixing bowl, combine couscous with water or broth. Let stand for 10 minutes to absorb liquid. Fluff with a fork.

STEEL BLADE: Drop garlic and parsley through feed tube while machine is running; process until minced. Add bell peppers and green onions; process with quick on/off pulses, until coarsely chopped. Add to couscous.

GRATER: Grate carrots, using medium pressure. Add to couscous along with remaining ingredients. Adjust seasonings to taste. Cover and refrigerate.

variations:
• To turn this into a main dish, add 2 cups of cooked chicken, cut in chunks.
• For vegetarians, add a can of drained chickpeas or kidney beans. Replace chili powder, mustard and cumin with ¼ cup each of chopped sun-dried tomatoes, minced fresh basil and parsley, if desired.

tabbouleh salad

This nutritious Middle Eastern salad is packed with vitamins, minerals and flavor. For best results, dry parsley and mint thoroughly before chopping them in the processor. Save the parsley stems and use them when making chicken or vegetable broth.

Yield: 4 to 6 servings. Leftovers will keep for a day or two in the refrigerator.

1/2 cup bulgur (cracked wheat)
2 cups boiling water
1 large bunch flat-leaf parsley
   (about 1 cup chopped)
1 small bunch mint
   (about 1/4 cup chopped)

4 firm, ripe tomatoes, cored and quartered
4 green onions, cut in chunks
1/4 cup olive oil (preferably extra-virgin)
1/4 cup fresh lemon juice
salt and freshly ground black pepper
   to taste

In a medium bowl, soak bulgur in boiling water for 15 minutes. Drain in a fine strainer. Soak parsley and mint in cold salted water for 10 minutes. Drain and dry well. Trim stems from parsley and mint.

STEEL BLADE: Process tomatoes with on/off pulses, until coarsely chopped. Place in a large bowl. Add drained bulgur to tomatoes. Wipe processor bowl dry with paper towels. Process parsley with mint until finely minced. Add green onions and process with on/off pulses, until chopped. Add to bulgur mixture along with remaining ingredients and mix gently. Refrigerate at least 1 hour before serving. Serve chilled.

variations:
• For a grain-based tabbouleh, increase bulgur to 1 cup. If you prefer a greener tabbouleh, use only ¼ to ⅓ cup bulgur. Couscous can be substituted for the bulgur. If desired, add ½ cup sliced olives and sprinkle with feta cheese.

chickpea broccoli salad

This tasty salad is an ideal way to use up broccoli stems!

Yield: 4 to 6 servings. Leftovers keep for 2 to 3 days, but you will have to add additional seasonings.

4 green onions, cut in chunks
1/4 cup fresh parsley
2 or 3 carrots
4 thick broccoli stems, peeled
   (reserve florets for
   another time)

19-oz. can chickpeas, drained and rinsed
1/4 cup olive oil
3 Tbsp. honey (or to taste)
3 Tbsp. lemon juice or rice vinegar
1/2 tsp. each dried basil and dried thyme
salt and freshly ground black pepper
   to taste

STEEL BLADE: Chop green onions and parsley with quick on/off pulses.
   GRATER: Grate carrots and broccoli stems, using medium pressure. Transfer to a mixing bowl. Add remaining ingredients and mix well. Refrigerate before serving.

best vinaigrette dressing

Yield: About 1 cup.
Keeps about 10 days.
Shake before using.

1 clove garlic
3 Tbsp. fresh parsley
2 Tbsp. fresh basil (or $^1/_2$ tsp. dried basil)

$^3/_4$ cup olive or canola oil
$^1/_4$ cup red wine vinegar
$^1/_2$ tsp. salt
$^1/_4$ tsp. freshly ground black pepper

STEEL BLADE: Drop garlic, parsley and basil through feed tube while machine is running; process until minced. Add remaining ingredients and process until blended. Refrigerate.

balsamic vinaigrette

This is wonderful on salad greens or roasted vegetables, or as a marinade for chicken or salmon.

2 cloves garlic
2 Tbsp. fresh parsley
$^2/_3$ cup olive oil (preferably extra-virgin)
$^1/_3$ cup balsamic vinegar

2 Tbsp. orange juice
2 to 3 Tbsp. honey (or to taste)
salt and freshly ground black pepper to taste
$^1/_4$ tsp. each dried basil and dried thyme

Yield: 1$^1/_4$ cups.
Refrigerate for up to 2 weeks. Shake before using.

STEEL BLADE: Drop garlic and parsley through feed tube while machine is running; process until minced. Add remaining ingredients and process for 8 to 10 seconds to blend.

sweet and spicy french dressing

Yield: About 2$^3/_4$ cups.
Keeps about 2 months in the refrigerator in a tightly closed jar.

2 cloves garlic
$^1/_2$ cup ketchup
1$^1/_2$ tsp. salt
$^1/_2$ tsp. dry mustard
1$^1/_2$ cups canola oil

$^1/_2$ cup vinegar
$^1/_2$ cup sugar
$^1/_2$ tsp. paprika
$^1/_2$ tsp. Worcestershire sauce

STEEL BLADE: Drop garlic through feed tube while machine is running; process until minced. Scrape down sides of bowl. Add remaining ingredients and process until blended and creamy, 25 to 30 seconds.

marty's garlic cheese dressing

The verdict's in—this creamy, garlicky dressing from Toronto lawyer Marty Kaplan is a winner!

3 or 4 large cloves garlic
4 oz. low-fat Mozzarella
   or brick cheese
2 to 4 Tbsp. grated Parmesan
   cheese
1/2 cup red wine vinegar
1 cup olive or canola oil

1 tsp. lemon juice
1/2 tsp. Worcestershire sauce
1/2 tsp. Italian seasoning
salt to taste
freshly ground black pepper (or mixed
   peppercorns) to taste

Yield: about 2 cups. Keeps about 2 weeks in the refrigerator. If too thick, thin with a little water.

STEEL BLADE: Drop garlic through feed tube while machine is running; process until minced. Cut Mozzarella or brick cheese in 1-inch chunks. Process until finely chopped, 20 to 25 seconds. Add remaining ingredients and process until combined, about 15 seconds longer. Store in a jar in the refrigerator. Wait a few hours before serving to allow flavors to blend. Shake very well before serving.

green goddess salad dressing or dip

Yield: 1 1/2 cups. Keeps about 10 days in the refrigerator.

1 or 2 cloves garlic
4 green onions, cut in chunks
1/4 cup fresh parsley
1 can anchovies, drained
1/2 cup sour cream or yogurt
   (regular or low-fat)

1/2 cup mayonnaise (regular
   or low-fat)
3 Tbsp. white wine vinegar
2 to 3 Tbsp. lemon juice
freshly ground black pepper
   to taste

STEEL BLADE: Drop garlic through feed tube while machine is running; process until minced. Add green onions, parsley and anchovies. Process until minced. Add remaining ingredients and process until blended, scraping down sides of bowl once or twice. Refrigerate.

low-fat ranch dressing

Yield: 1 cup.
Keeps for 5 or 6 days in
the refrigerator. One
tablespoon contains
28 calories.

¹/₄ cup skim milk
¹/₄ cup fat-free yogurt
¹/₂ cup light mayonnaise
1 tsp. Dijon mustard

1 tsp. honey
2 tsp. white vinegar
¹/₂ tsp. dried basil

STEEL BLADE: Process all ingredients until blended, about 10 seconds.

yummy yogurt salad dressing

Yield: 1¹/₄ cups.
Keeps about 10 days
in a tightly covered
container in the
refrigerator. One
tablespoon contains
about 22 calories.

¹/₂ small onion
2 Tbsp. fresh parsley (or
    2 tsp. dried parsley)
1 cup yogurt (fat-free
    or regular)
2 to 3 Tbsp. canola oil

1 Tbsp. white vinegar
¹/₂ tsp. salt
dash freshly ground black pepper
¹/₄ tsp. each dried oregano, dried
    basil and garlic powder
pinch dried tarragon

STEEL BLADE: Process onion with parsley until minced. Add remaining ingredients and process about 10 seconds longer. Chill for 1 hour before serving to blend flavors.

variations:
• Omit dried tarragon and dried basil. Add 2 Tbsp. fresh basil and/or dill. Add 2 Tbsp. chili sauce or ketchup, if desired.

asian salad dressing

Use this on
spinach, mixed
greens or
coleslaw.

Yield: 1 cup.
Keeps about a month
in the refrigerator.

2 cloves garlic
¹/₂ cup rice vinegar
¹/₄ cup canola oil
¹/₄ cup soy sauce

2 Tbsp. toasted sesame oil
3 to 4 Tbsp. honey (or to taste)
2 Tbsp. toasted sesame seeds

STEEL BLADE: Drop garlic through feed tube while machine is running; process until minced. Add remaining ingredients and process until blended, about 10 to 15 seconds. Store in a jar in the refrigerator. Shake well before using.

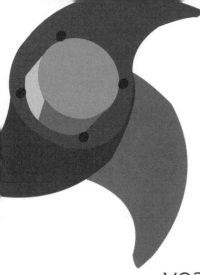

yeast doughs, quick breads and muffins

- Although I have a bread machine and a heavy-duty mixer, I prefer making yeast doughs in my food processor! I can make several batches, shaping them any way I like. If I am busy, I just refrigerate the dough for a few hours (or even days), then take it out and continue.

- Each yeast dough recipe in this book gives step-by-step instructions for mixing, kneading, rising, shaping and baking. You can convert your favorite yeast recipes for the food processor using the following guidelines, so stop loafing around and let's get started!

- Capacity: The recommended maximum amount of flour in a standard processor is 3 cups all-purpose flour. In a large processor, the maximum amount is 6 cups all-purpose flour or 3½ cups whole-grain flour, e.g., oats, rye. (Refer to your manual.) If your recipe calls for more flour than recommended, divide the recipe in half. Process in batches, then combine by hand.

- Use the **Steel Blade** for recipes calling for less than 3½ cups flour. Use the **Metal Dough Blade** and Dough Cycle for recipes using more than 3½ cups flour. The **Plastic Dough Blade** (available with some models) helps prevent dough from overheating.

- Yeast comes in several forms: active dry/traditional, quick-rise/instant, bread machine and fresh cake yeast. Always check the expiry date before using yeast. One package of dry yeast (2¼ tsp.) equals 1 ounce of cake yeast. I buy active dry yeast in bulk and use 1 Tbsp. instead of 2¼ tsp. (It's easier to measure!) My breads are perfect every time.

- I like to proof the yeast first (i.e., test if it is good). Dissolve active dry yeast in warm water (105°F to 115°F) with a pinch of sugar or flour. If the yeast is good, it will become foamy and creamy within 10 minutes. Stir to dissolve. If you're using fresh cake yeast, the water should be 85°F. If it is too hot, it will kill the yeast; if it's too cool, the yeast won't grow. An instant-read thermometer is an excellent investment.

- Process the dry ingredients (e.g., flour, salt, sugar, herbs) until mixed, about 10 seconds. If the recipe calls for solid butter or margarine, cut it in chunks and process with the dry ingredients. Increase processing time to 20 seconds. If using oil, add with liquid ingredients.

- Next, add the yeast mixture to the dry ingredients; process for 10 seconds. Combine the liquid ingredients (oil, water/milk, eggs). Start the processor, then add liquid through the feed tube in a slow, steady stream, a little at a time. If the liquid sloshes or splatters, either stop adding it or drizzle it in more slowly. If the dough is very sticky, it may go under the blade, pushing it up.

- Process until the dough gathers together and forms a mass around the blades. The dough will pull away from the sides of the bowl and should be slightly sticky.

- Have ¼ cup flour handy in case the motor slows down because the dough is too sticky. Dump flour through feed tube while the machine is running; the motor will return to normal speed. If you are worried about adding too much flour, add it a tablespoon or two at a time. If the dough is too dry, just add more water, a tablespoon or two at a time.

- Once all the liquid has been added, let the processor knead the dough 30 to 45 seconds longer. (Add nuts, raisins, etc. a few seconds before you stop processing, or add them when kneading by hand.) Transfer the dough to a lightly floured surface and let it rest briefly while you wash the bowl and blade. Be careful—the blade is very sharp!

- If you are using quick-rise/instant yeast, instead of dissolving the yeast in warm liquid, combine the yeast with the dry ingredients in the processor. Heat the total amount of liquid called for in the recipe to a maximum of 90°F to 100°F. Start the machine and slowly add the liquid through feed tube. Process for 45 seconds, until well-kneaded.

- Bread machine yeast can also be used for processor breads, following the quick-rise method described above. Heat the total amount of liquid to 105°F. According to Fleischmann's (1-800-777-4959), all yeast is interchangeable in recipes. Only the water temperature and method of mixing ingredients are different.

- Technical difficulties? If the motor stops while kneading the dough, let the machine cool down for 5 to 10 minutes. Excessive strain may have caused the motor to overheat. Divide the dough into two batches and process each batch until well-kneaded.
- I like to knead the dough by hand on a lightly floured surface for 1 to 2 minutes, until smooth and elastic. It should be dimpled, like a baby's bottom.
- Place the dough in a large bowl greased with about 1 tsp. of oil. Turn the dough over so that all the surfaces are greased. Make sure the bowl is large enough for the dough to rise at least double in size. Cover the bowl tightly with plastic wrap to prevent the dough from drying out.
- How many times should the dough rise? Let it rise once or twice before shaping, then once after shaping. It can rise either at room temperature or in the refrigerator.
- At room temperature (80°F), the dough will take 1 to 1½ hours to double. Multi-grain breads take slightly longer, 1½ to 2 hours. A second rising takes about half the time, ¾ to 1 hour. Rising time varies, depending on the temperature and humidity. Don't let the dough get too warm during rising or it will develop a yeasty taste.
- If you're letting it rise in the refrigerator, make sure there is enough room between the shelves for the dough to rise. If the dough is made with butter or margarine, let it rise at room temperature for 1 hour before refrigerating.
- If you are busy, refrigerate the dough (or a shaped loaf) at any point to slow down the rising process. Dough made with water will keep 4 to 5 days in the fridge. Dough made with milk will keep 3 to 4 days. Remove from the fridge and let the dough stand at room temperature for about ½ hour before completing the recipe.
- The finger test: To test if the dough has risen enough, poke your finger into the dough. An indentation should remain. If it doesn't, wait 15 to 20 minutes longer and test it again.
- Punch down the dough by plunging your fist into the center. Fold the outside edges into the center to release gases and redistribute the yeast. If you have time, let the dough rise a second time for a finer texture.
- Shaping: Punch down the dough before shaping. Let it rest for about 5 minutes for easier handling. (If you don't, the dough will be very springy when you try to roll it out.)

- Rise and shine! Place the shaped dough in baking pans, cover with a towel and let rise at room temperature until doubled (about 1 hour for room-temperature dough, 2 to 3 hours for refrigerated dough).

- If yeast breads rise too long, the gluten strands will break and the bread will collapse. Once the breads have been shaped, they should not rise to more than double in size before baking.

- Brush the dough with egg glaze (1 egg yolk mixed with 1 to 2 tsp. water) just before baking. Coffee cakes and buns can be brushed with juice from canned fruit 10 minutes before baking is completed.

- Bake yeast breads in the middle or lower third of a preheated oven. There will be a final expansion known as "oven-spring" in the first few minutes of baking.

- When done, yeast dough will be evenly browned and sound hollow when the crust is tapped lightly. If the dough is browning too quickly, cover it loosely with foil.

- Remove breads from pans immediately after baking. Cool on a wire rack away from drafts.

- When a recipe calls for flour, use all-purpose flour (bleached or unbleached) unless otherwise indicated. Do not use self-rising or pastry flour. Bread flour can replace all-purpose flour.

- As a general guideline when substituting other flours, you can replace up to half the flour called for in a recipe with whole wheat, rye or other specialty flours. The amount of flour needed will vary according to the weather. When it is hot and humid, you need to add more flour.

- Fill up on fiber! Add ¼ cup wheat germ or ground flax seeds to your favorite bread doughs and muffins. You can also sprinkle whole flax seeds or sunflower, sesame or poppy seeds on top of loaves after brushing them with egg glaze.

- Freeze with ease! Immediately after shaping, wrap unbaked dough airtight and freeze it for up to 1 month. When needed, remove it from the freezer. Place it on a sprayed baking sheet, cover and defrost at room temperature until doubled, 6 to 7 hours. Bake as directed. Another option is to defrost dough in the refrigerator, then let it rise at room temperature until doubled. Baked breads, rolls, coffee cakes and muffins can be frozen for about 4 months if well wrapped.

- Need more information? Visit cookbook author and bread expert Betsy Openneer's excellent Web site at www.breadworksinc.com.

challah

A delectable braided egg bread that is served on the Sabbath, Jewish holidays and special ceremonial occasions.

Yield: 1 large loaf.
Freezes well.

1 tsp. sugar	1 tsp. salt
$1/2$ cup warm water (105°F to 115°F)	$1/3$ cup oil
1 pkg. yeast (1 Tbsp.)	2 eggs (or 1 egg plus 2 egg whites)
3 cups flour (approximately)	$1/4$ cup lukewarm water
2 to 3 Tbsp. sugar or honey	1 egg yolk beaten with 1 tsp. water
	poppy or sesame seeds

In a measuring cup, dissolve 1 tsp. sugar in ½ cup warm water. Sprinkle yeast over and let stand for 8 to 10 minutes, until foamy. Stir to dissolve.

STEEL BLADE: Place flour, sugar or honey and salt in processor. Pour dissolved yeast mixture over and process 12 to 15 seconds. While machine is running, add oil and eggs through feed tube and process until blended, about 10 seconds. Add water and process until dough gathers and forms a mass around the blades. (Have an additional ¼ cup flour ready in case the machine begins to slow down; add it through feed tube if necessary.) Process 45 seconds longer; dough will be sticky.

Turn out onto lightly floured surface. Knead by hand for 1 to 2 minutes, until smooth and elastic, adding just enough flour to prevent dough from sticking.

Place dough in large greased bowl; turn dough over so all surfaces are lightly greased. Cover bowl with plastic wrap and let rise in warm place until doubled, 1½ to 2 hours. (Dough may also rise in refrigerator; it will keep up to 3 days before shaping and baking.) Punch down. For a lighter texture, let dough rise again until doubled; punch down.

To shape: Divide dough into 3 equal portions. Roll into 3 long strands. Place on sprayed baking sheet. Braid loosely; tuck ends under. Cover with towel and let rise until doubled, about 1 hour. Brush with egg glaze; sprinkle with seeds.

Bake in preheated 400°F oven for 30 minutes, until golden brown. Dough will sound hollow when tapped with your fingers. Cool away from drafts.

variations:

- **Holiday Raisin Challah:** Use 3 Tbsp. honey instead of sugar. Add ¾ cup sultana raisins to dough about 20 seconds after it gathers into a mass around the blades. Process 10 seconds longer. Knead and let rise as directed. To shape, roll dough into a long thick rope. Place on a sprayed baking sheet. Coil up like a snail, starting from the center and working outwards. Tuck end under. When doubled, brush with egg glaze, sprinkle with seeds and bake as directed.
- **Challah Rolls (Bulkas):** Divide dough into 12 equal pieces (or 24 smaller pieces). Roll each piece into a rope and tie in a knot. When doubled, brush with egg glaze and sprinkle with seeds. Bake at 400°F 15 to 18 minutes, until golden.

100% whole wheat bread

Yield: 1 loaf.
May be frozen.

$1/2$ cup milk or water	1 tsp. salt
1 tsp. sugar	2 Tbsp. honey
$1/2$ cup warm water (105°F to 115°F)	2 Tbsp. oil
1 pkg. yeast (1 Tbsp.)	2 eggs (or 1 egg plus 2 whites), lightly beaten
$3^1/4$ cups whole wheat flour (approximately)	

Heat milk or water until steaming, about 45 seconds on HIGH in the microwave. Let cool for 5 minutes, until lukewarm. Meanwhile, dissolve 1 tsp. sugar in $1/2$ cup warm water. Sprinkle yeast over and let stand for 8 to 10 minutes, until foamy. Stir to dissolve.

STEEL BLADE: Reserve $1/4$ cup flour. Process 3 cups flour, salt and honey in processor for 5 seconds. Add dissolved yeast mixture and process 10 seconds longer. In a measuring cup, combine lukewarm milk with oil and eggs. Add through feed tube while machine is running. Batter will be very sticky. Add reserved $1/4$ cup flour as machine begins to slow down. Process until well kneaded, 30 to 40 seconds. (If necessary, add 1 to 2 Tbsp. additional flour.) Batter will **not** form a ball on the blades.

Turn out onto well-floured surface. Flour surface of dough lightly. Knead by hand about 2 minutes, until smooth and elastic, adding flour as necessary to prevent dough from sticking.

Place dough in large greased bowl; turn dough over so all surfaces are lightly greased. Cover bowl and let rise until doubled. Punch down. For a lighter texture, let dough rise once again until doubled; punch down.

To shape: Roll on lightly floured surface into 9 x 12-inch rectangle. Roll up jelly-roll style from shorter side. Seal ends by pressing down with edge of your hand. Place seam-side down in sprayed 9 x 5-inch loaf pan. Cover and let rise until doubled.

Bake in preheated 375°F oven for 35 to 40 minutes. Remove from pan and cool.

variation:

• For whole wheat rolls, divide dough into 12 pieces. Shape each piece into a ball. Baking time will be about 20 minutes.

old-fashioned rye bread

Yield: 1 large loaf.

Freezes well.

½ tsp. sugar

½ cup warm water (105°F to 115°F)

1 pkg. yeast (1 Tbsp.)

1¾ cups all-purpose flour (approximately)

1¼ cups rye flour

2 Tbsp. granulated or brown sugar

1½ tsp. salt

1 Tbsp. oil

⅔ cup lukewarm water

2 Tbsp. caraway seeds

2 Tbsp. cornmeal for baking pan

1 tsp. instant coffee dissolved in 1 Tbsp. boiling water

1 egg yolk beaten with 1 tsp. water

In a measuring cup, dissolve ½ tsp. sugar in ½ cup warm water. Sprinkle yeast over and let stand for 8 to 10 minutes, until foamy. Stir to dissolve.

STEEL BLADE: Process flours, 2 Tbsp. sugar and salt for 5 seconds. Pour dissolved yeast mixture over and process for 12 to 15 seconds. Add oil and lukewarm water; process dough 15 to 20 seconds longer. If processor begins to slow down, add up to ¼ cup all-purpose flour through feed tube.

Turn out onto well-floured surface. Dough will be somewhat sticky. Flour surface of dough lightly. Knead by hand for about 2 minutes, until smooth and elastic, adding just enough flour to prevent dough from sticking. Knead in caraway seeds.

Place dough in large greased bowl; turn dough over so all surfaces are lightly greased. Cover bowl and let rise until doubled, about 2 hours; punch down. If you have time, let dough rise a second time. Punch down once again.

To shape: Roll on lightly floured surface into 12 x 18-inch rectangle. Roll up jelly-roll style from the longer side. Seal ends by pressing down with edge of your hand. Place seam-side down on sprayed baking sheet that has been sprinkled with cornmeal. Cover and let rise until doubled, about 2 hours. Brush with coffee mixture, then with egg glaze.

Bake in preheated 375°F oven about 45 minutes, or until bread sounds hollow when tapped lightly. Cool completely.

variation:

- To make rye crescents, divide dough in half. Roll out each piece on a floured surface into a 12-inch circle; cut each circle into 8 wedges. Beginning at outer edge, roll up. Place on a sprayed baking sheet and curve into crescents. Cover and let rise until doubled. Brush with coffee mixture, then with beaten egg. Baking time will be 20 to 25 minutes. Makes 16 crescents.

pumpernickel bread

$1/2$ tsp. sugar

$1/2$ cup warm water (105°F to 115°F)

1 pkg. yeast (1 Tbsp.)

1 Tbsp. cocoa

$2/3$ cup boiling water

3 Tbsp. molasses

2 Tbsp. oil

$1^3/4$ cups all-purpose flour (approximately)

$1^1/2$ cups rye flour

$1^1/2$ tsp. salt

1 to 2 Tbsp. caraway seeds

2 Tbsp. cornmeal for baking pan

1 tsp. instant coffee dissolved in 1 Tbsp. boiling water

1 egg yolk beaten with 1 tsp. water

In measuring cup, dissolve ½ tsp. sugar in ½ cup warm water. Sprinkle yeast over and let stand for 8 to 10 minutes, until foamy. Stir to dissolve. Dissolve cocoa in boiling water. Add molasses and oil; stir well. Cool until lukewarm.

STEEL BLADE: Reserve ¼ cup all-purpose flour. Process remaining all-purpose flour, rye flour and salt for 5 seconds. Add dissolved yeast mixture and process for 12 to 15 seconds. Add cocoa mixture through feed tube while machine is running. As machine slows down, add reserved all-purpose flour through feed tube and process 10 seconds longer. Dough will be quite sticky.

Turn out onto well-floured surface. Flour surface of dough lightly. Knead by hand 2 to 3 minutes, until smooth and elastic, adding just enough flour to keep dough from sticking. Knead in caraway seeds.

Place dough in large greased bowl; turn dough over so all surfaces are lightly greased. Cover bowl and let rise in warm place until doubled in bulk, about 2 hours; punch down. If you have time, let dough rise a second time; punch down once again.

To shape: Shape into 1 large or 2 smaller balls. Place on sprayed baking sheet that has been sprinkled with cornmeal. Cover and let rise until doubled, about 2 hours. Brush with coffee mixture, then with egg glaze.

Bake in preheated 375°F oven about 45 minutes for a large loaf or 35 to 40 minutes for smaller loaves. Cool completely.

variation:

• To make rolls, divide dough into 12 pieces. Shape each piece into a ball and flatten slightly. Let rise until doubled, then glaze and bake as directed. Baking time will be 20 to 25 minutes.

confetti bread

What a wonderful
way to eat your
veggies! This
dough is also
excellent for
Focaccia (p. 144).

Yield: 1 loaf.
Freezes well.

1 tsp. sugar	$1/4$ red bell pepper ($1/4$ cup grated)
$3/4$ cup warm water (105°F to 115°F)	$31/4$ cups flour (approximately)
1 pkg. yeast (1 Tbsp.)	2 Tbsp. olive oil
1 carrot ($1/2$ cup grated)	1 tsp. salt
$1/2$ small zucchini ($1/2$ cup grated)	1 additional tsp. sugar
$1/4$ small red onion ($1/4$ cup grated)	$1/2$ tsp. dried thyme
	$1/2$ tsp. dried basil

In a measuring cup, dissolve 1 tsp. sugar in warm water. Sprinkle yeast over and let stand for 8 to 10 minutes, until foamy. Stir to dissolve.

GRATER: Grate vegetables, using medium pressure. Transfer to measuring cup. You need about 1½ cups of vegetables.

STEEL BLADE: Place flour, oil, salt, remaining 1 tsp. sugar, thyme and basil in processor. Process 10 seconds, until combined. Add dissolved yeast mixture through feed tube while machine is running. Process until dough gathers together around the blades. Add grated vegetables and let machine knead dough 30 to 40 seconds longer. If machine slows down because dough is too sticky, add a few tablespoons of flour through feed tube; if dough is too dry, add a few tablespoons of water.

Turn out onto a lightly floured surface. Knead by hand for 1 to 2 minutes, until smooth and elastic, adding just enough flour to prevent dough from sticking to your hands.

Place dough in large greased bowl, turning to grease all surfaces. Cover bowl with plastic wrap and let rise in warm place until doubled, about 1½ hours. Punch down. If you have time, let rise a second time; punch down once again.

To shape: On lightly floured surface, roll dough into 9 x 12-inch rectangle. Roll up like a jelly-roll from the shorter side. Seal ends by pressing down with edge of your hand. Place seam-side down in sprayed 9 x 5-inch loaf pan. Cover and let rise until doubled, about 1 hour.

Bake in preheated 425°F oven for 25 to 30 minutes, until golden brown. Bread should sound hollow when tapped with your fingertips. Remove from pan and let cool.

focaccia

This addictive Italian flatbread is also delicious using the dough for Confetti Bread (p. 143). Focaccia is wonderful with soups and salads, for sandwiches, or as an hors d'oeuvre.

Yield: 8 servings. Reheats and/or freezes well.

Dough

1 tsp. sugar
$1/2$ cup warm water (105°F to 115°F)
1 pkg. yeast (1 Tbsp.)
3 cups flour
1 tsp. salt
$1/2$ tsp. each of dried basil, dried thyme and dried rosemary
2 Tbsp. olive oil
$3/4$ cup lukewarm water

Topping

2 Tbsp. olive oil
2 or 3 cloves garlic, crushed
fresh or dried basil, thyme and rosemary to taste
Kosher (coarse) salt to taste

For dough: In measuring cup, dissolve 1 tsp. sugar in ½ cup warm water. Sprinkle yeast over and let stand 8 to 10 minutes, until foamy. Stir to dissolve.

STEEL BLADE: Place flour, salt, herbs and oil in processor. Process for 10 seconds, until combined. Add dissolved yeast and process 10 seconds. Add lukewarm water through feed tube while machine is running; process until dough gathers together and forms a mass around the blades. Let machine knead dough 30 to 40 seconds longer.

Turn out onto lightly floured surface and knead for 1 to 2 minutes, until smooth and elastic.

Place dough in large greased bowl, turning to grease all surfaces. Cover bowl with plastic wrap and let rise until doubled, 1 to 1½ hours. Punch down.

To shape: Transfer dough to sprayed baking sheet and pat into a large rectangle or 8 smaller ovals about ½ inch thick. Cover with a towel and let rise for 45 minutes, or until doubled.

For topping: Combine olive oil with garlic. Poke your fingers into surface of dough to give it a dimpled appearance. Brush top of dough with garlic oil. Sprinkle with desired herbs and salt.

Bake in preheated 375°F oven for 25 to 30 minutes, until crisp and golden.

variations:

• Top with sliced zucchini, red onions and roasted red pepper strips. Sautéed onions also make a delicious topping. Finish off with herbs and salt. If desired, top with ½ cup grated Parmesan. For hors d'oeuvres, cut baked Focaccia in 2-inch squares.

pita bread

Pita is also known as "pocket bread." This Middle Eastern fat-free bread is popular for falafel, sandwiches and wraps.

Yield: 16 pitas. Store in plastic bags. These will keep for a day or two at room temperature. Freezes well.

1 tsp. sugar	3$^{1}/_{4}$ cups flour
$^{1}/_{4}$ cup warm water (105°F to 115°F)	1 tsp. salt
1 pkg. yeast (1 Tbsp.)	1 cup lukewarm water

In measuring cup, dissolve 1 tsp. sugar in ¼ cup warm water. Sprinkle yeast over and let stand for 8 to 10 minutes, until foamy. Stir to dissolve.

STEEL BLADE: Place flour and salt in processor. Add dissolved yeast and process 8 to 10 seconds to mix. Pour lukewarm water through feed tube while machine is running; process until dough is well kneaded and forms a mass around the blades. Process 30 to 40 seconds longer.

Turn out onto lightly floured surface. Knead dough by hand for 2 minutes, until smooth and elastic.

To shape: Divide into 16 balls about 2 inches in diameter. Use a rolling pin to roll each ball to ¼-inch thickness. Cover with a towel and let rise for ½ hour. Roll once again and let rise ½ hour longer.

Preheat oven to 500°F. Place pitas on sprayed baking sheet and bake about 8 minutes, or until puffed and golden.

whole wheat pitas:
• Use 1¾ cups flour and 1½ cups whole wheat flour.

pita chips

Split each pita into 2 rounds. Brush with olive oil and minced garlic; sprinkle with oregano, basil and salt. Cut in wedges. Bake in preheated 400°F oven for 10 minutes, until crisp and golden. Serve with Hummous (p. 52) or your favorite dip.

croissants

These croissants
are light and
flaky. Well worth
the effort!

Yield: 18 croissants.
Freezes well. To thaw:
Place frozen croissants
on parchment-lined
baking sheet and heat
at 400°F for about
5 minutes.

¹/₂ tsp. sugar	2 Tbsp. butter
¹/₄ cup warm water (105°F to 115°F)	1 Tbsp. sugar
1 pkg. yeast (1 Tbsp.)	¹/₂ tsp. salt
1 cup milk	¹/₂ cup chilled butter, cut in chunks
2¹/₂ cups flour	1 egg yolk plus 2 tsp. water

In measuring cup, dissolve ½ tsp. sugar in warm water. Sprinkle yeast over and let stand for 8 to 10 minutes, until foamy. Stir to dissolve. Microwave milk until steaming, about 1½ minutes on HIGH; cool to lukewarm.

STEEL BLADE: Process flour with 2 Tbsp. butter, 1 Tbsp. sugar and salt for 10 seconds. Add dissolved yeast and process 5 or 6 seconds longer. Add milk through feed tube while machine is running; process until dough forms a mass around the blades. Process for 30 to 40 seconds longer.

Turn dough out onto lightly floured surface and knead by hand 1 to 2 minutes, until smooth and elastic.

Place dough in large greased bowl; turn dough over so all surfaces are lightly greased. Cover bowl with plastic wrap and let rise 1½ hours, or until doubled. Punch down. Refrigerate dough for ½ hour.

STEEL BLADE: Process ½ cup chilled butter until lump-free and smooth, about 45 seconds, scraping down sides of bowl as needed. Refrigerate butter while you roll out dough.

Rolling/Folding technique: On floured surface, roll dough into a rectangle about 9 x 15 inches. Working from the shorter side, spread lower ⅔ of dough with butter, leaving a ½-inch border around edges. Fold dough in three, as if you were folding a business letter. Rotate dough 90 degrees, so that it resembles a book you are going to open. Roll out once again into a large rectangle, adding flour as needed to prevent dough from sticking. Fold into three as before. You have now completed 2 "turns." Repeat twice more, turning dough a quarter turn (90 degrees) each time. You will have completed 4 "turns" in all. Place in a plastic bag and refrigerate at least 2 hours or overnight.

To shape: Roll dough on floured surface into a 12-inch square. Cut into 9 squares. Cut each square in half diagonally to make 18 triangles. Starting at the base of each triangle, roll up, stretching dough slightly. Shape into crescents. Place on parchment-lined baking sheet with the point of the triangle underneath.

Cover and let rise for about 1 hour at room temperature. Brush with egg glaze. Bake in preheated 425°F oven 12 to 15 minutes, until puffed and golden.

I can't believe it's broccoli bread!

None of my testers could guess the mystery ingredient! This is a wonderful way to use broccoli stems. If you don't have enough broccoli, add grated carrots. Use the florets in your favorite stir-fry.

Yield: 1 loaf. Freezes well.

1 1/2 cups flour (part whole wheat can be used)
1 1/2 tsp. ground cinnamon
1/2 tsp. baking powder
1/2 tsp. baking soda
pinch salt
2 or 3 thick broccoli stems, trimmed and peeled (1 cup grated)
1 cup brown sugar, packed
1 egg
1/4 cup canola oil
1/2 tsp. vanilla extract
1 tsp. orange zest
2 Tbsp. orange juice
1/2 to 3/4 cup fresh or dried cranberries
1/2 cup slivered almonds (optional)

STEEL BLADE: Process flour, cinnamon, baking powder, baking soda and salt for 5 to 10 seconds, until blended. Transfer to a medium bowl.

GRATER: Grate broccoli, using medium pressure. Measure 1 cup loosely packed and set aside.

STEEL BLADE: Process brown sugar, egg, oil, vanilla extract and orange zest until mixed, about 30 seconds. Add grated broccoli and process 1 minute longer, until well blended. Add flour mixture, orange juice, cranberries and almonds, if using. Process with quick on/off pulses, just until flour mixture disappears, scraping down bowl as necessary.

Spread batter in sprayed 9 x 5-inch loaf pan. Bake in preheated 350°F oven for 50 to 60 minutes, or until a wooden toothpick inserted in the center comes out clean.

orange corn bread

This recipe has traveled as far away as Israel, to rave reviews. Serve it warm or toasted with butter or preserves. Delicious!

Yield: 1 loaf.
Freezes well.

1 cup plus 3 Tbsp. flour
$1/2$ tsp. salt
4 tsp. baking powder
$3/4$ cup cornmeal
1 medium seedless orange (unpeeled)

$3^1/2$ Tbsp. sugar
$1/2$ cup margarine or butter, cut in chunks
1 egg
$1^1/4$ cups milk or soy milk
$3/4$ cup raisins (optional)

STEEL BLADE: Process flour, salt, baking powder and cornmeal until blended, about 5 seconds. Empty bowl.

Cut orange in quarters. Process on STEEL BLADE for 20 seconds. Add sugar and margarine or butter and process for 1 minute. Add egg and milk through feed tube while machine is running. Process for 3 seconds. Add dry ingredients. Process, using 3 or 4 quick on/off pulses, just until blended. If adding raisins, process 2 seconds longer.

Pour into sprayed 9 x 5-inch loaf pan or 8-inch square pan. Bake in preheated 375°F oven about 45 minutes, until cake tester comes out clean.

best banana bread

The large amount of baking soda and long baking time at a low temperature give this delicious banana bread its dark color.

Yield: 1 loaf.
Freezes well. If your processor has a large (14-cup) bowl, you can double the recipe.

3 medium very ripe bananas (the blacker the better)
1 cup sugar
3 tsp. baking soda
dash salt
2 eggs (or 1 egg plus 2 egg whites)

$1/4$ cup oil
$1^1/2$ cups flour
1 tsp. lemon juice plus milk to equal $1/2$ cup (or $1/2$ cup buttermilk)
2 Tbsp. ground flax seed or wheat germ (optional)

STEEL BLADE: Process bananas until puréed, 15 to 20 seconds. Measure 1 cup banana purée. Add sugar, baking soda and salt; process for 30 seconds. Add eggs and oil and process until blended, about 10 seconds. Pour flour over, then add sour milk or buttermilk. Process 8 to 10 seconds longer, until smooth. Blend in flax seed or wheat germ, if using.

Line 9 x 5-inch loaf pan with buttered parchment paper or aluminum foil. Pour in batter. Bake on middle rack in preheated 275°F oven about 2½ hours, or until loaf tests done.

banana muffins

Yield: About 18 muffins.

Freezes well.

1/2 cup margarine or butter,
   cut in chunks
2 eggs (or 1 egg plus 2 whites)
1 tsp. vanilla extract
1 1/4 cups sugar
1 medium banana

1 tsp. baking soda
3/4 cup buttermilk (or 2 tsp. lemon
   juice plus milk to make 3/4 cup)
1 tsp. baking powder
2 cups flour

STEEL BLADE: Process margarine or butter, eggs, vanilla extract and sugar for 2 minutes, scraping down bowl once or twice. Do not insert pusher in feed tube. Break banana into 2-inch pieces and add through feed tube while machine is running. Dissolve baking soda in buttermilk or sour milk. Add through feed tube while machine is running and process for 3 seconds. Add baking powder and flour; process with 3 or 4 quick on/off pulses, just until flour disappears.

Fill paper-lined muffin tins 2/3 full. Bake in preheated 400°F oven for 18 to 20 minutes.

mom's blueberry muffins

When you're in a blue mood, these will make you "berry" happy! Try using a combination of blueberries and raspberries.

Yield: About 2 dozen muffins.
Freezes well.

1/2 cup margarine or butter,
   cut in chunks
3/4 cup sugar
2 eggs
1 tsp. baking soda

1 Tbsp. white vinegar plus milk to
   equal 1 cup
2 tsp. baking powder
2 cups flour
1 1/2 cups fresh or frozen blueberries

STEEL BLADE: Process margarine or butter, sugar and eggs for 2 minutes, scraping down bowl once or twice. Do not insert pusher in feed tube. Dissolve baking soda in vinegar-milk mixture. Add through feed tube while machine is running and process for 3 seconds. Add baking powder and flour. Process with 3 or 4 quick on/off pulses, just until flour disappears. Carefully stir in berries with a rubber spatula.

Pour into paper-lined muffin tins. Bake in preheated 375°F oven for 25 to 30 minutes.

lighter variation:
• Reduce margarine to 1/3 cup. Use 1 egg plus 2 egg whites; use skim or 1% milk.

sugar-free bran muffins

These muffins
are moist, light
and delicious.

Yield: 1 dozen muffins.
Freezes well.

1 cup flour (part whole wheat,
    if desired)
1 tsp. baking soda
1 tsp. baking powder
$1/4$ tsp. salt
$1/3$ cup pitted dates (about 10)

sugar substitute to equal $1/2$ cup sugar
1 cup bran cereal
1 egg (or 2 egg whites)
2 Tbsp. canola oil
1 cup buttermilk (or 1 Tbsp. lemon juice
    plus skim milk to equal 1 cup)

STEEL BLADE: Place flour, baking soda, baking powder, salt, dates and sugar substitute in processor. Start with 3 or 4 quick on/off pulses, then process 6 to 8 seconds longer, until dates are coarsely chopped. Add remaining ingredients and process with 3 or 4 quick on/off pulses, just until mixed. Do not overprocess.

Spoon batter into sprayed muffin cups. Bake in preheated 400°F oven for 20 to 25 minutes, until nicely browned.

nutrition note:

- With sugar substitute, 1 muffin contains 109 calories, 25 grams carbohydrate, 3.1 grams fat and 2 grams fiber. If made with regular sugar, 1 muffin contains 127 calories.

variation:

- Raisins or dried cranberries may be substituted for dates. Processing time for dry ingredients will be about 5 seconds.

oatmeal raisin muffins

Yield: 12 muffins.
Freezes well.

1 cup flour (part whole wheat,
    if desired)
1 tsp. ground cinnamon
$1/4$ tsp. salt
1 tsp. baking powder
$1/2$ tsp. baking soda
1 cup quick-cooking oats

1 Tbsp. white vinegar plus milk to equal
    1 cup (or 1 cup buttermilk)
1 egg
$1/2$ cup sugar (granulated or brown)
$1/2$ cup oil
$3/4$ cup raisins

STEEL BLADE: Process flour, cinnamon, salt, baking powder and baking soda until blended, about 5 seconds. Transfer to large mixing bowl. Place rolled oats and sour milk or buttermilk in processor and let stand 2 or 3 minutes. Add egg, sugar and oil; process for 10 seconds. Add to flour mixture along with raisins. Stir with a wooden spoon just enough to moisten.

Spoon into paper-lined muffin tins. Bake in preheated 400°F oven for 18 to 20 minutes, until golden.

lighter variation:

- Substitute 2 egg whites for 1 egg. Use skim milk. Replace half the oil with unsweetened applesauce. Dried cranberries can replace raisins, if desired.

fudgy chocolate muffins

Rolled oats add fiber to these crusty-topped muffins, making them a guilt-free treat.

1/2 cup unsweetened applesauce	3/4 cup flour
1/2 cup quick-cooking oats	1/4 cup unsweetened cocoa
1 cup sugar	1/2 tsp. baking powder
1/4 cup margarine	1/2 tsp. baking soda
1 egg	3/4 cup chocolate chips
1 tsp. vanilla extract	

Yield: 12 muffins.
These freeze well.

In a small bowl, mix applesauce with oats. Set aside.

STEEL BLADE: Process sugar, margarine, egg and vanilla extract until well mixed, about 2 minutes, scraping down sides of bowl as needed. Add applesauce/oatmeal mixture and process just until blended. Add flour, cocoa, baking powder and baking soda. Process with 3 or 4 quick on/off pulses, just until combined. Do not overprocess. Stir in chocolate chips with a rubber spatula.

Spoon batter into sprayed muffin tins. Bake in preheated 375°F oven for 20 to 25 minutes.

variation:

- Add 2 tsp. instant espresso coffee powder and 1 tsp. cinnamon with dry ingredients. If desired, replace chocolate chips with butterscotch chips.

cakes and frostings

- You can whip up cakes in the food processor in about ⅓ the time it usually takes. They will be light and delicious, although they may be slightly smaller and not quite as light as those made with an electric mixer.
- All the cakes in this book can be made in a standard-sized (7-cup) processor. Check your manual for recommended quantities.
- A general guideline is to make cakes not exceeding 2 cups of flour. When converting a recipe, the total volume of ingredients should not exceed 6½ cups. Calculate each egg as ¼ cup liquid.
- Combine dry ingredients by processing for 5 to 10 seconds, until blended. Insert the pusher in the feed tube. Empty the mixture into another bowl. When creaming ingredients, do not insert the pusher, so that more air can be incorporated into the batter.

- Creaming Method (**Steel Blade**)
  - Cut chilled butter or margarine in chunks. Process with sugar, eggs and flavoring for about 2 minutes, until well mixed. (Or process butter and sugar for 45 seconds. Add eggs one at a time; process for 15 seconds after each addition. Add flavoring.)
  - Stop the machine once or twice to scrape down the sides of the bowl with a rubber spatula.
  - Add the liquids; process for 3 seconds. Add them either through the feed tube or directly into the processor bowl.

- Add the combined dry ingredients over the top of the batter and process with 3 or 4 quick on/off pulses. If necessary, scrape down the sides of the bowl once again.
- Process just until the flour mixture disappears. Do not overprocess, or your cakes will be tough and heavy.

- Spin the blade! To clean batter off the blade, empty most of the batter from the bowl. Put the bowl and blade back onto the base of the machine, replace the cover, then turn on the processor. Centrifugal force will spin your blade clean in seconds!
- Too much batter? If the amount of batter is too large for your processor, process all the ingredients except the flour and baking powder/soda. Then place all the ingredients in a large mixing bowl and stir with a wooden spoon for about 45 seconds, just until the batter is blended.

- Flour Power
  - The recipes in this book are made with all-purpose or whole wheat flour (either bleached or unbleached). To substitute cake flour for all-purpose flour, add 2 Tbsp. more per cup. To substitute all-purpose flour for cake flour, subtract 2 Tbsp. You can replace 1 cup all-purpose flour with ½ cup whole wheat flour and ½ cup all-purpose flour; the texture may be slightly heavier. You can also use 2 Tbsp. wheat germ or soy flour, ½ cup whole wheat flour, plus enough all-purpose flour to equal 1 cup.
  - To measure flour, use dry measuring cups, not a glass measuring cup. Stir the flour before measuring. Dip the cup into the flour and fill to overflowing. Level off with the straight edge of a knife. Never bang the cup on the counter or you will end up using too much flour, causing heavy or dry cakes, or cracks on the top.
- Baking powder, baking soda and cocoa should be stirred before measuring. Baking powder loses its strength after a year. To test if it is still good, add ½ tsp. baking powder to ½ cup hot water. If it fizzes, it's fine.

- How Sweet It Is
  - To measure brown sugar, pack it firmly into a measuring cup. Level with a straight-edge knife.
  - For 1 cup of brown sugar, you can use 1 cup granulated sugar plus 2 Tbsp. molasses.

- You can usually replace up to half the sugar in baked goods with sugar substitute (e.g., Splenda) with good results. Baked products may be lower in volume or slightly drier.

- Fat Facts
  - Butter and margarine are generally interchangeable. Use directly from refrigerator unless otherwise indicated. Diet margarine is not suitable for baking but is fine for streusel toppings.
  - Use the water method to measure butter or margarine. Fill a 2-cup glass measuring cup with 1 cup of cold water. To measure ½ cup butter, for example, add butter until the water level reaches 1½ cups. You will then have 1 cup of water and ½ cup butter. Spill out the water. (Or you can press butter or margarine into a nested measuring cup; press firmly so there are no air spaces underneath.)

- Prune Pureé
  - Combine 2 cups pitted prunes with 1 cup hot water in the processor; let it stand for 5 minutes. Process until smooth, about 1 minute. Scrape down the sides of the bowl as needed. Makes 2 cups of Prune Pureé. Refrigerate up to 3 months or freeze. (One tablespoon contains only 20 calories and is fat-free!)
  - Lighten up! To replace ½ cup fat in cakes, quick breads and muffins, use 3 Tbsp. tub margarine or canola oil plus ⅓ cup unsweetened applesauce or Prune Purée. For 1 cup fat, use ⅓ cup margarine or oil plus ⅔ cup applesauce or Prune Purée. Use applesauce in light-colored cakes and Prune Purée in dark-colored cakes.

- Dairy Replacements
  - For dairy-free baking, replace milk with water, apple or orange juice, coffee, soy milk, rice milk, or non-dairy creamer diluted with water.
  - Buttermilk/Sour Milk/Pareve Buttermilk: For 1 cup, measure 1 Tbsp. vinegar or lemon juice in a glass measuring cup. Add milk, soy milk or rice milk to equal 1 cup. Another substitute is ½ cup yogurt mixed with ½ cup milk.
  - Sour cream and yogurt are interchangeable in baking. When dissolving baking soda in yogurt, be sure to use a large enough container—the mixture will nearly double in volume.

- About Chocolate
  - One square (1 oz.) of unsweetened chocolate in baking can be replaced with 3 Tbsp. cocoa plus ½ Tbsp. canola oil. A great lower-fat alternative!
  - A 6-oz. package of chocolate chips contains 1 cup.
  - To melt chocolate in the microwave, microwave uncovered on MEDIUM (50%). For 1 to 2 ounces chocolate or 1 cup chocolate chips, allow 2 to 3 minutes, stirring every minute. For 8 to 16 ounces, allow 3 to 4 minutes. Stir after 2 minutes, then every minute.
  - Container must be dry and chocolate should not be covered. Otherwise it can seize (get thick and lumpy).
  - Chocolate Rescue: If chocolate seizes, add oil a teaspoon at a time; stir until smooth. Another remedy is to add an equal volume of hot liquid (cream, milk or coffee) plus a few drops of vanilla extract or liqueur—instant chocolate sauce!

- About Nuts and Dried Fruit
  - Soak raisins or other dried fruit (e.g., cranberries, apricots) in hot water for 3 to 4 minutes to make them plump and juicy. Drain and dry well.
  - To prevent nuts, raisins, dates or currants from sinking to the bottom of the batter, mix them with a little of the flour called for in the recipe before adding them to the batter. After the dry ingredients have been added to the batter, mix nuts or dried fruits in with on/off pulses.
  - Store nuts and coconut in the freezer for up to a year. There's no need to defrost them before you use them.
- When using packaged cake mixes, begin with the dry ingredients; add liquids through feed tube while machine is running. Process about 1½ minutes.
- For sponge and chiffon cakes, use an electric mixer. These cakes rely on egg whites for volume and a mixer will produce superior results.

- About Baking with Eggs
  - To replace 1 egg in baking, use 2 egg whites (or ¼ cup liquid egg whites), ¼ cup egg substitute, or use reduced-cholesterol eggs. Don't replace more than half the eggs in a recipe with just whites or the texture could be affected.
  - Vegans can replace each egg with ¼ cup mashed banana, tofu, low-fat

sour cream, yogurt or soy dairy product. Baked goods may be more dense and heavy.

- To replace 1 egg with flax seed, combine 1 Tbsp. ground flax seed with 3 Tbsp. water. Let stand until thick, 2 to 3 minutes. To grind flax seed, see Smart Chart (p. 18).

- I don't use the processor to whip egg whites for meringues. They will only increase four times in volume (instead of seven) and will not be as stiff. Use an electric mixer or a wire whisk for best results.

- For maximum volume, egg whites should be at room temperature before beating. To warm them quickly, place them in a bowl; immerse in another bowl filled with warm water. Stir to warm evenly. Egg whites will not whip to maximum volume if they contain any particles of egg yolk, or if bowl or beaters are greasy or moist. Use a stainless steel, glass or copper bowl; don't use plastic. Add ¼ tsp. cream of tartar or 1 tsp. lemon juice for every 4 whites for maximum volume. (Omit if using a copper bowl.) Add cream of tartar and flavoring when egg whites become frothy. Beat until stiff but not dry. To test if they are stiff enough, turn the bowl upside down; egg whites should not fall out!

- For meringues, begin adding sugar when whites form soft peaks. Add sugar 1 Tbsp. at a time, beating until you cannot feel sugar when you rub the meringue between your fingertips. It should look like marshmallow cream.

- When adding beaten egg whites into a batter, stir about ¼ of the whites into the batter to lighten it. Then add the remaining egg whites to the top of the batter. Using the edge of your spatula like a knife, gently cut down from the top center of the mixture to the bottom of the bowl. Pull the spatula across the bottom of the bowl towards you, until you reach the edge of the bowl, then up and out. Rotate the bowl ¼ turn after each cut-and-fold movement. This should take no more than a minute; don't be too thorough or the whites will deflate.

- Bake Someone Happy
  - Preheat the oven to the required temperature before placing the cake batter in the oven. Do not open the oven door for the first 15 minutes of baking.
  - Incorrect oven temperatures often cause poor results. If the temperature is too low, the cake may rise too much before it sets. If the temperature is too high, the top crust will set before the cake has

finished rising, causing it to crack. An oven thermometer is an excellent investment. If your temperature is incorrect, adjust it according to your thermometer.

- Lower the temperature by 25°F if using dark or glass baking pans.
- Spray cake pans with nonstick spray. Butter or margarine may cause sticking.
- Place cake pans on the center rack or in the lower third of the oven. Pans should not touch each other or the sides of the oven for proper heat circulation.

- Ready or Not?
  - When the cake is completely baked, it will shrink slightly from the sides of the pan and will feel firm to the touch. The top of the cake should spring back; a toothpick inserted in the center will come out dry.
  - Let cakes cool in the pan for a few minutes. Allow 5 minutes for layers, 10 minutes for square or rectangular cakes and 15 to 20 minutes for large cakes. If the cake is left in the pan too long, it may stick or be difficult to remove. If the cake is removed too soon, it may break when inverted.
  - Loosen the edges with a flexible spatula or knife and invert onto a rack.
- Frost cakes when they are completely cool. Dip a knife in hot water as often as necessary to help spread the frosting easily.
- Most frostings are easily made in the processor. Use the **Steel Blade** to process all ingredients until smooth and blended, usually 10 or 15 seconds. Scrape down the sides of the bowl with a rubber spatula as necessary.

- Freeze with Ease
  - Unfrosted cakes can be frozen for 4 to 6 months. Frosted cakes will keep for 2 to 3 months. It's best to freeze frosted cakes first, then wrap them.
  - It takes 1 to 3 hours to defrost a cake, depending on its size. Keep cakes wrapped while defrosting to prevent them from drying out.
  - Cakes become stale more quickly if they have been frozen.
  - If necessary, cakes can be frozen a second time, but they will be drier.
  - Whipped cream cakes freeze very well. Defrost them overnight in the refrigerator, not at room temperature. Keep chilled.

baking faults	Cracked or peaked surface	Oven too hot; too much flour; batter overmixed; not enough liquid; cake batter not spread right into corners.
	Sunken	Too much sugar, fat or baking powder; underbaked; opening oven door too soon; not enough eggs or flour.
	Poor volume	Not enough baking powder; batter overmixed; uneven oven temperature (too hot at top); too much fat or liquid; ingredients too cold or too warm.
	Too pale	Too little sugar; underbaked.
	Too brown	Overbaked; oven temperature too high; too much sugar.
	Tunnels and holes inside	Batter overmixed after flour is added; too much flour; too much baking powder; undercreaming fat and sugar.
	Heavy, rubbery layer on bottom	Too much liquid; batter undermixed.
	Dry	Insufficient fat or sugar; overbaked; too much flour or not enough liquid; cake not covered when completely cooled.
	Tough	Overmixed; overbaked; insufficient fat.
	Compact and heavy	Too much sugar, liquid, fat or flour.
	Cake breaks when removed from pan	Undergreasing of pan; removed from pan too soon. A good guide is 10 minutes for small cakes, 15 to 20 minutes for large cakes. Sponge and chiffon cakes should cool inverted for at least 1 hour. (Do not grease pan.)

Cake sticks to pan	Undergreasing of pan; butter or margarine used to grease pan; cake left in pan too long.
Uneven height	Oven temperature not even; batter spread unevenly in pan.

cake pans, baking temperatures and times

Use:	**Instead of:**
9-inch square pan 350°F for 40 to 45 minutes	7 x 11-inch pan 350°F for 40 to 50 minutes
Two 8-inch round layer pans 350°F for 25 to 30 minutes	7 x 11-inch or 9-inch square pan 350°F for 40 to 50 minutes
Two 9-inch round layer pans 350°F for 30 to 35 minutes	9 x 13-inch pan 350°F for 40 to 50 minutes
9 x 5-inch loaf pan 350°F for 40 to 50 minutes	8-inch square pan 350°F for 35 to 40 minutes
Two 9 x 5-inch loaf pans 350°F for 40 to 50 minutes	9 x 13-inch pan 350°F for 40 to 50 minutes
Two 9 x 5-inch loaf pans 350°F for 40 to 50 minutes	12-cup fluted tube pan 325°F for 50 to 60 minutes
9 x 13-inch pan 350°F for 40 to 50 minutes	12-cup fluted tube pan 325°F for 50 to 60 minutes

cupcakes Any cake batter may be baked in muffin tins. Line cups with paper liners and fill them 2/3 full. Bake at 400°F for 18 to 20 minutes. (Note: When baking cupcakes or muffins, fill empty muffin cups 1/3 full with water to prevent the pan from discoloring or burning.)

Pan	**Yield**
8-inch square or 9 x 5-inch loaf pan	12 to 14 cupcakes
9-inch square or 7 x 11-inch pan	18 to 20 cupcakes
12-cup fluted tube or 9 x 13-inch pan	24 to 30 cupcakes

apple lover's cake

An all-time family
favorite! This is a
winner. It's also
delicious with
raspberries.

Yield: 9 servings.
Delicious warm or at
room temperature.
May be frozen.

14 to 16 apples, peeled,
   quartered and cored
$1/3$ to $1/2$ cup sugar (or to taste)
2 tsp. ground cinnamon
$1/2$ cup additional sugar
$1/2$ cup canola oil
$1/2$ cup unsweetened
   applesauce

1 tsp. vanilla extract (or 1 Tbsp. brandy)
2 eggs (or 1 egg plus 2 egg whites)
1 cup flour (half whole wheat flour
   can be used)
1 tsp. baking powder
$1/4$ tsp. salt

Preheat oven to 350°F.

SLICER: Slice apples, using medium pressure. Place in sprayed 9 x 13-inch glass baking dish, filling it nearly to the top. (Apples will shrink during baking.) Sprinkle with ⅓ to ½ cup sugar and cinnamon and mix well; spread evenly in pan.

STEEL BLADE: Process remaining ½ cup sugar, oil, applesauce, vanilla extract and eggs for 1 minute, until well blended. Add flour, baking powder and salt; process with 3 or 4 quick on/offs, until blended. Pour batter evenly over apples. Bake about 1 hour, or until golden.

note:
• For a small family, make half the recipe in a 7 x 11-inch baking dish and bake 45 to 50 minutes.

blueberry crumble cake

$2 1/4$ cups flour
$1 1/4$ cups sugar
$3/4$ cup butter or margarine,
   cut in chunks
1 tsp. baking soda

1 cup sour cream or yogurt
1 tsp. baking powder
2 eggs
$1 1/2$ cups fresh blueberries

Preheat oven to 375°F.

STEEL BLADE: Process flour, sugar and butter or margarine until fine crumbs are formed, 12 to 15 seconds. Remove 1 cup of crumb mixture from processor and set aside. Dissolve baking soda in sour cream or yogurt. Add to processor along with baking powder and eggs. Process for 6 to 8 seconds, just until blended, scraping down sides of bowl with a rubber spatula as necessary. Do not overprocess. Stir in blueberries by hand.

Spread batter evenly in sprayed 9-inch square baking pan. Sprinkle with reserved crumb mixture. Bake for 40 to 45 minutes, until done.

pareve chocolate cake

cakes and frostings

Big, moist, dark and delicious, this dairy-free cake is a family favorite all over the world.

Yield: 12 servings.
Freezes well.

$2/3$ cup cocoa
$2^1/_4$ cups flour
2 cups sugar
$1^1/_2$ tsp. baking powder
$1^1/_2$ tsp. baking soda
$1/_2$ tsp. salt

$1^1/_2$ tsp. instant coffee powder
$1^1/_2$ cups orange juice or water
3 eggs (or 2 eggs plus 2 egg whites)
$1^1/_4$ cups canola oil
Pareve Chocolate Ganache (p. 322)
  (optional)

Preheat oven to 350°F.

STEEL BLADE: Combine cocoa, flour, sugar, baking powder, baking soda, salt and coffee powder in processor. Process until blended, about 10 seconds. Add orange juice or water and eggs. Start processor and add oil through feed tube while machine is running. Process batter for 45 seconds. Do not insert pusher in feed tube and do not overprocess.

Pour batter into sprayed 12-cup fluted tube pan. Bake for 55 to 60 minutes, until cake tests done. Cool for 20 minutes before removing cake from pan. Place on serving platter. When completely cooled, drizzle with Ganache if desired.

note:
- This amount of batter may be too large for some processors. For a smaller version, use ½ cup cocoa, 2 cups flour, 1½ cups sugar, 1 tsp. baking powder, 1 tsp. baking soda, dash salt, 1 tsp. instant coffee, 1¼ cups orange juice, water or milk, 3 eggs and ¾ cup oil. Bake at 325°F for 55 to 60 minutes. Makes 10 servings.

high skor chocolate cake

Bake batter in 4 sprayed 9-inch layer pans at 350°F about 25 minutes. Whip 2 cups non-dairy topping or whipping cream with an electric mixer until nearly stiff. Beat in $1/_4$ cup icing sugar and 1 Tbsp. chocolate liqueur. Fold in 1 cup toffee bits. Fill and frost cooled layers. Sprinkle with additional toffee bits. Refrigerate. Serves 12 to 15.

best coffee cake

The name says
it all!

Yield: 9 servings.
Freezes well.

Topping	Batter
$3/4$ cup pecans or almonds	6 Tbsp. butter or margarine
$1/2$ cup brown sugar, packed	1 cup granulated sugar
2 tsp. ground cinnamon	2 eggs
1 Tbsp. cocoa	1 tsp. vanilla extract
1 cup chocolate chips	1 tsp. baking soda
	1 cup sour cream or yogurt
	$1 1/3$ cups flour
	$1 1/2$ tsp. baking powder

Preheat oven to 350°F. Process all ingredients on the STEEL BLADE.

For topping: Process nuts, brown sugar, cinnamon and cocoa with 6 to 8 quick on/off pulses, until nuts are coarsely chopped. Transfer to small bowl. Stir in chocolate chips. Wipe processor bowl clean with paper towels.

For batter: Process butter or margarine, sugar, eggs and vanilla extract for 2 minutes, scraping down sides of bowl as needed. Do not insert pusher in feed tube. Dissolve baking soda in sour cream or yogurt. Add to batter and process for 3 seconds. Add flour and baking powder. Process with 4 quick on/off pulses, just until flour disappears. Do not overprocess. Scrape down bowl if necessary.

Pour half the batter into sprayed 9-inch square baking pan. Sprinkle with half the topping. Repeat with remaining batter and topping. Bake for 40 to 45 minutes, until cake tests done.

cakes and frostings

marbled streusel coffee cake

cakes and frostings

This is a favorite of my nephew Marshall Matias.

Yield: 12 to 15 servings.
Freezes well.

Topping

1 cup walnuts or pecans
$1/2$ cup coconut (optional)
$1/2$ cup brown sugar, packed
2 tsp. ground cinnamon
2 Tbsp. cocoa

Batter

$3/4$ cup margarine or butter
$1 1/2$ cups granulated sugar
3 eggs (or 2 eggs plus 2 egg whites)
2 tsp. vanilla extract
3 cups flour
4 tsp. vinegar plus milk or soy milk to make $1 1/2$ cups
$1 1/2$ tsp. baking soda
$1 1/2$ tsp. baking powder
$1/4$ tsp. salt
1 square (1 oz.) semi-sweet chocolate, melted and cooled

Preheat oven to 350°F. Process all ingredients on the STEEL BLADE.

For topping: Chop nuts coarsely, using several quick on/off pulses. Remove ½ cup nuts and set aside. Add remaining topping ingredients to processor. Process for a few seconds to mix. Empty bowl and wipe with paper towels.

For batter: Process margarine or butter, sugar, eggs and vanilla extract for 2 minutes. Do not insert pusher in feed tube. Add half the flour and process with 2 or 3 on/off pulses, until nearly blended. Add vinegar/milk mixture, remaining flour, baking soda, baking powder and salt. Process with several quick on/offs, just until blended. Do not overprocess. Mix in reserved nuts with 1 or 2 quick on/offs.

Pour half the batter into sprayed 12-cup fluted tube pan. Drizzle half the melted chocolate over batter and cut through with a knife. Sprinkle with ¾ of the topping. Add remaining batter and drizzle with remaining chocolate. Cut through second layer of batter with a knife. Sprinkle with remaining topping.

Bake for 55 to 60 minutes. Let cool in pan for 15 minutes. Invert cake onto a plate, then turn cake over so that nut mixture is on top.

lighter variation:

• For batter, combine equal parts of margarine and unsweetened applesauce to make ¾ cup. Use skim milk; omit semi-sweet chocolate. For topping, combine ½ cup sugar, 2 tsp. cinnamon and ½ cup chopped nuts.

chocolate melt-away coffee cake

For topping, use $3/4$ cup pecans, $1/2$ cup packed brown sugar and 8 oz. chilled semi-sweet chocolate, cut in chunks. Process on the STEEL BLADE, using several quick on/off pulses, until coarsely chopped. Prepare batter for Marbled Streusel Coffee Cake. Assemble and bake as directed.

toffee coffee cake

My helpers loved this addictive cake so much, they barely left any for taste-testing.

Yield: 12 servings.
Freezes well.

Topping
$3/4$ cup pecans
$1/4$ cup brown sugar, lightly packed
1 cup toffee bits (or 4 Skor bars [1.4-oz each], broken up)

Batter
$1/2$ cup margarine or butter, cut in chunks
1 cup granulated sugar
2 eggs
$1 1/2$ tsp. vanilla extract
1 tsp. baking soda
1 cup yogurt or sour cream (light or regular)
$1 3/4$ cups flour
1 tsp. baking powder
$1/4$ tsp. salt

Preheat oven to 350°F. Process all ingredients on the STEEL BLADE.

For topping: Coarsely chop nuts, brown sugar and toffee bits, using 10 to 12 on/off pulses. (If using Skor bars, processing time will take slightly longer.) Remove from bowl and reserve. Wipe out bowl with paper towels.

For batter: Process margarine or butter, sugar, eggs and vanilla extract for 2 minutes, until well mixed. Do not insert pusher in feed tube. Add baking soda to yogurt or sour cream; stir to dissolve. Add to processor and process 5 seconds. Add flour, baking powder and salt. Process with 4 or 5 quick on/off pulses, just until flour disappears. Do not overprocess.

Spread half the batter in sprayed 12-cup fluted tube pan. Sprinkle with half the topping. Add remaining batter, then sprinkle with remaining topping. Bake for 50 to 55 minutes, until cake tests done. Cool in pan for 20 minutes. Loosen edges with a flexible spatula, invert cake onto a platter, then invert it onto another platter so the topping is on top. Let cool—if you can control yourself!

cinnamon marble cake

I love anything made with cinnamon! This cake contains no baking powder; baking soda is the leavening agent. It is delicious frosted with Cinnamon Frosting (p. 172).

Yield: 9 servings.
Freezes well.

$1/2$ cup margarine or butter, cut in chunks
$1 1/4$ cups sugar
3 eggs (or 2 eggs plus 2 egg whites)
$3/4$ cup yogurt

2 cups flour
1 tsp. baking soda
$1/4$ cup brandy or rum
1 Tbsp. ground cinnamon
2 Tbsp. sugar

Preheat oven to 350°F.

STEEL BLADE: Process margarine or butter with 1¼ cups sugar and eggs for 2 minutes. Do not insert pusher in feed tube. Add yogurt and process for 3 seconds. Add flour, baking soda and brandy or rum. Process with 4 quick on/off pulses, just until blended. Do not overprocess. Scrape down bowl if necessary.

Pour into sprayed 9-inch square baking pan. Combine cinnamon and 2 Tbsp. sugar. Sprinkle over cake. Cut through with a knife to give a marbled effect. Smooth out surface of cake with a rubber spatula. Bake for 45 minutes, until cake tests done.

lighter variation:

• Reduce margarine to ¼ cup and add ¼ cup unsweetened applesauce. Do not frost cake.

marble marvel cake

Chocolate syrup added to the batter makes this marble cake fudgy and delicious. Ice it with your favorite chocolate frosting, or glaze with Chocolate Glaze (p. 170).

Yield: 12 servings.
Freezes well.

$3/4$ cup margarine or butter, cut in chunks
$1 1/2$ cups sugar
3 eggs (or 2 eggs plus 2 egg whites)
$1 1/2$ tsp. vanilla extract

$3/4$ cup milk or orange juice
$2 1/2$ cups flour
2 tsp. baking powder
$1/4$ tsp. salt
$1/2$ cup chocolate syrup
$1/4$ tsp. baking soda

Preheat oven to 325°F.

STEEL BLADE: Process margarine or butter, sugar, eggs and vanilla extract for 2 minutes, scraping down bowl once or twice. Do not insert pusher in feed tube. Add milk or juice through feed tube while machine is running. Process for 3 or 4 seconds. Add flour, baking powder and salt. Process with 4 or 5 quick on/off pulses, scraping down bowl once or twice, just until mixed. Do not overprocess.

Pour ⅔ of batter into sprayed 12-cup fluted tube pan. Add chocolate syrup and baking soda to remaining batter. Process for a few seconds, just until blended. Scrape down bowl as necessary. Pour chocolate batter over white batter. Cut through batters in a swirl design with a spatula or fork.

Bake for 60 to 70 minutes, until cake tests done. Cool for 20 minutes before removing from pan.

zesty orange loaf

This tastes even better the next day!

Yield: 1 loaf (10 servings). Freezes well.

1 Tbsp. grated orange zest	$1/2$ cup applesauce
$1^3/_4$ cups flour	$1/_4$ cup fresh orange juice
$1^1/_2$ tsp. baking powder	$1/2$ cup yogurt
$1/2$ tsp. baking soda	
2 eggs (or 1 egg plus 2 egg whites)	**Orange Syrup**
	$1/_4$ cup fresh orange juice
$3/_4$ cup sugar	$1/_4$ cup sugar
$1/_4$ cup margarine	

Preheat oven to 350°F.

STEEL BLADE: Process orange zest, flour, baking powder and baking soda for 10 seconds, until mixed. Empty bowl.

Process eggs, ¾ cup sugar, margarine and applesauce until light, about 2 minutes. Do not insert pusher in feed tube. Add orange juice and yogurt. Process for 3 seconds to blend. Add dry ingredients and process with quick on/off pulses, just until flour disappears. Do not overprocess.

Spread batter in sprayed 9 x 5-inch loaf pan. Bake for 40 to 45 minutes. Loaf will crack slightly down the center.

For syrup: Combine orange juice with sugar and heat until steaming hot; stir well. Poke holes all over top of loaf with wooden skewer. Slowly drizzle hot syrup all over loaf, letting it soak up the liquid. Remove from pan when cooled.

zucchini spice cake

I once had a student whose children hated her cooking. When she made this cake, her son asked, "What are the green flecks?" She replied "Pistachio nuts." He exclaimed, "If you made it, it's probably mold!" Believe it or not, he loved the cake!

Yield: 12 to 15 servings. Freezes well.

2 cups flour
2 tsp. baking soda
1 tsp. baking powder
$1/2$ tsp. salt
1 Tbsp. ground cinnamon
$1/4$ tsp. allspice (optional)
1 cup walnuts
2 medium zucchini (2 cups grated)

3 eggs (or 2 eggs plus 2 egg whites)
2 cups sugar (or $1 1/2$ cups brown sugar, packed)
1 cup oil
2 tsp. vanilla extract
1 cup raisins or chocolate chips
Cream Cheese Frosting (p. 172)

Preheat oven to 350°F.

STEEL BLADE: Process flour, baking soda, baking powder, salt, cinnamon and allspice for about 10 seconds to blend. Empty into large mixing bowl. Process nuts until chopped, about 6 seconds. Empty into a small bowl.

GRATER: Grate unpeeled zucchini, using medium pressure. Measure out 2 cups loosely packed.

STEEL BLADE: Process eggs with sugar for 1 minute. Do not insert pusher in feed tube. While machine is running, add oil and vanilla extract through feed tube. Process for about 45 seconds. Add zucchini and process for 10 seconds. Remove cover and add dry ingredients. Process with 3 or 4 quick on/off pulses, just until flour disappears. Sprinkle nuts and raisins or chocolate chips over batter. Mix in with quick on/off pulses. (See note.)

Pour batter into sprayed 9 x 13-inch pan or 12-cup fluted tube pan. Bake for 55 to 60 minutes, until cake tests done. Cool 20 minutes before removing cake from pan. Frost oblong cake with Cream Cheese Frosting. Also delicious without frosting.

note:

- Batter will almost fill bowl of standard-size processor, but will not overflow. If amount of batter is too much for your processor, reverse procedure and add zucchini mixture to dry ingredients in mixing bowl. Mix with a wooden spoon until blended, about 45 seconds. Stir in nuts and raisins or chocolate chips.

carrot cake   Replace zucchini with 4 medium carrots (or 3 carrots plus 1 apple, peeled and cored). If desired, add 10-oz. can of well-drained crushed pineapple to batter with nuts and raisins.

dark rich fruitcake

This is a variation of the fruitcake my mother made for my wedding. Fruitcake will last for several years if properly stored. Sometimes it lasts even longer than the marriage!

Yield: 8 lbs. fruitcake or 3 loaves. Freezes well.

1 lb. sultana raisins
1 lb. dried cranberries
1 lb. candied mixed fruits
1 lb. shelled nuts (almonds, pecans, walnuts, etc. or a combination)
1 lb. candied cherries
3^1/$_2$ cups flour
1 tsp. baking powder
^{1}/$_2$ tsp. baking soda
2 Tbsp. cocoa

2 tsp. ground cinnamon
1 tsp. each nutmeg and ground cloves
1 seedless orange, quartered (unpeeled)
1 cup margarine, cut in chunks
1^1/$_2$ cups sugar
6 eggs
^{1}/$_2$ cup grape or apple jelly
^{1}/$_4$ cup brandy
^{1}/$_2$ cup corn syrup (optional)
^{1}/$_4$ cup water (optional)

Preheat oven to 275°F.

Pour boiling water over raisins and cranberries to cover completely. Let stand for 5 minutes. Drain well; pat dry. Place in a very large mixing bowl. Add candied mixed fruits.

STEEL BLADE: Chop nuts in batches of 1 to 2 cups at a time. Use on/off pulses, until coarsely chopped. Add to mixing bowl. Coarsely chop cherries with ¼ cup flour in 2 batches, using quick on/off pulses. Add to mixing bowl with an additional 1 cup flour. Mix well.

Process remaining flour, baking powder, baking soda, cocoa, cinnamon, nutmeg and cloves for 10 seconds. Add to mixing bowl. Process orange until fine, about 20 seconds. Add to mixing bowl.

Process margarine, sugar and eggs for 2 minutes, until well blended. Do not insert pusher in feed tube. Add jelly and process 10 seconds to blend. Add brandy and process 2 or 3 seconds longer. Add to mixing bowl.

Stir with a wooden spoon until well mixed. Batter will be very heavy. Line three 9 x 5-inch loaf pans with well-greased parchment paper or aluminum foil. Fill ¾ full. Bake for about 3 hours, until done. Cool in pans for ½ hour. Remove from pans; cool completely.

For a shiny glaze, combine corn syrup and water in a saucepan. Bring to a boil, remove from heat and cool to lukewarm. Pour over cooled fruitcakes.

For long-term storage, wrap fruitcakes in brandy-soaked cheesecloth, then in foil. Store in a cool place to ripen. If cheesecloth is remoistened occasionally, fruitcakes will keep at least 2 or 3 years.

note:
• For gift-giving, bake fruitcakes in small tinfoil pans about 2 hours.

chocolate ganache

This dark and shiny glaze is true decadence! It's fabulous on cakes, tortes and brownies.

Yield: Enough glaze for a large fluted cake or 9-inch pan of brownies.

cakes and frostings

3/4 cup whipping cream (35%)   2 tsp. almond, coffee or orange liqueur
8 oz. chilled semi-sweet or bitter-
    sweet chocolate, cut in chunks

Microwave whipping cream uncovered on HIGH for 1½ minutes, until almost boiling.

STEEL BLADE: Process chocolate with several on/off pulses, then let machine run until chocolate is finely ground, about 30 seconds. Pour hot cream through feed tube while machine is running. Process until chocolate is melted. Blend in liqueur.

Cover and refrigerate for 30 minutes, until cooled and slightly thickened. Drizzle over your favorite cake or torte or pour over brownies. Refrigerate after glazing.

pareve chocolate ganache

For Pareve Chocolate Ganache, replace whipping cream with 3/4 cup boiling water plus 2 Tbsp. dairy-free margarine.

For Mocha Ganache, use 1/2 cup non-dairy topping plus 1/4 cup brewed coffee.

chocolate glaze

Yield: About 3/4 cup.
Do not freeze.

1 1/2 cups icing sugar   1 square (1 oz.) unsweetened chocolate,
2 Tbsp. milk or water   melted and cooled

STEEL BLADE: Combine all ingredients and process for 6 to 8 seconds to blend, scraping down sides of bowl once or twice. Drizzle over your favorite cake. Excellent on Marble Marvel Cake (p. 166).

chocolate frosting

Yield: For a 9-inch square cake. Double the recipe for a large cake. Freezes well.

1 square (1 oz.) unsweetened chocolate, melted and cooled
1/4 cup soft margarine or butter
1 1/2 cups icing sugar

2 to 3 Tbsp. cream, milk, sour cream or boiling water
1/2 tsp. vanilla extract

STEEL BLADE: Process all ingredients until smooth and blended, about 10 seconds. Scrape down sides of bowl as necessary.

variations:
- For Rocky Road Frosting, mix ½ cup chopped nuts and 1 cup miniature or cut-up marshmallows into frosting.
- For Chocolate Mint Frosting, substitute ½ tsp. peppermint extract for vanilla extract.

chocolate cocoa frosting

Yield: For a 9-inch square cake. Freezes well.

1 cup icing sugar
2 Tbsp. soft margarine or butter
2 Tbsp. cocoa

2 Tbsp. milk, soy milk or hot water
1/2 tsp. vanilla extract
pinch salt

STEEL BLADE: Process all ingredients until smooth and blended, about 10 seconds. Scrape down sides of bowl as necessary.

note:
- Recipe may be doubled for a large cake.

one-two-three mint frosting

Place chocolate mint patties on the top of a chocolate cake or brownies immediately upon removal from the oven. As the patties melt, spread them evenly with a spatula.

cakes and frostings

171

chocolate fudge frosting

Yield: For two 9-inch
layers, or a
9 x 13-inch cake.
Freezes well.

1 cup chocolate chips	3 cups icing sugar
3 Tbsp. butter or margarine	$1/2$ cup milk (scant)
dash salt	1 tsp. vanilla extract

Melt chocolate chips with butter or margarine on low heat (or microwave on MEDIUM for 2 to 3 minutes, stirring every minute). Let cool.

STEEL BLADE: Combine all ingredients in processor, using slightly less than ½ cup milk. Process until smooth and blended, about 15 seconds. If frosting seems too thick, add a few more drops of milk. If frosting is too loose, add a tablespoon or two more of icing sugar.

note:
• Frosting will thicken somewhat upon standing.

cinnamon frosting

Yield: For a 9-inch
square cake. To frost a
9 x 13-inch cake,
make 1$1/2$ times
the recipe.
Freezes well.

1 cup icing sugar	2 Tbsp. sour cream
2 Tbsp. soft butter or margarine	$1/2$ tsp. ground cinnamon
$1/2$ tsp. vanilla extract	

STEEL BLADE: Process all ingredients until smooth, about 10 seconds. Scrape down sides of bowl as necessary.

cream cheese frosting

Yield: For a
9 x 13-inch cake or
two 9-inch layers.
Freezes well.

$1/4$ cup soft butter or margarine	2 cups icing sugar
$1/2$ cup softened cream cheese	$1/4$ tsp. salt

STEEL BLADE: Process all ingredients until smooth, about 10 seconds.

cakes and frostings

desserts and tortes

- Whipping cream (35% cream) will turn to butter if it is warmer than 35°F when being whipped. To avoid this, chill whipping cream (and even the **Steel Blade** and work bowl) in the freezer for a few minutes before whipping. Whipped cream continues to stiffen as you work with it, so underwhip it slightly. Processor whipped cream is excellent as a garnish. However, it only increases 1½ times in volume and is firmer than cream that is whipped with an electric mixer, which doubles in volume.
- Dessert topping can be whipped in the processor, but will also not double in volume. See Smart Chart, Whipping Cream (p. 34) for method. Non-dairy topping needs to be whipped with an electric mixer.
- **Almost Whipping Cream:** Process 1 cup curd cottage cheese or ricotta cheese (low-fat or regular) on the **Steel Blade** for 2 to 3 minutes, until silky smooth. Add 2 Tbsp. icing or granulated sugar (to taste) and ¼ tsp. vanilla extract or orange liqueur. Chill; serve with fresh berries or cut-up fruit.
- Blended Tofu (p. 33) can replace uncooked eggs in mousses or is delicious in smoothies.
- Keep frozen fruit handy for sherbets, smoothies or fruit purées. Your processor will whip them up in moments!
- **Strawberry or Raspberry Purée:** Thaw two 10-oz. packages of frozen strawberries or raspberries; drain, reserving juice. (Or use 2 cups of fresh, ripe berries.) Purée briefly on the **Steel Blade**. Raspberries should be strained to remove seeds. If necessary, thin with some of the reserved juices. Sweeten with 2 to 3 Tbsp. sugar or honey. Serve chilled.

- For fruit coulis or purée, cut peeled and pitted fruit in chunks (e.g., peaches, nectarines, mangoes, apricots). Process on the **Steel Blade** until smooth. Add a few drops of lemon juice to prevent discoloration. Sweeten with honey or sugar. Serve chilled. Canned, drained fruits also make delicious purées.
- **Superfine/Fruit Sugar:** Process granulated sugar for 1 to 2 minutes on the **Steel Blade**. Ideal for meringues!
- Cookies or wafers broken into chunks, then processed on the **Steel Blade** until fine, are ideal for cookie crumb crusts. See Smart Chart, Crumbs (p. 23) for yields.
- Process nuts on the **Steel Blade** with quick on/off pulses (see Smart Chart, Nuts, p. 28). You can also "chop" nuts with the **Grater**, using medium pressure.
- Grind cookie crumbs (and nuts) for cheesecake in your processor, then process with remaining crust ingredients. Wipe out the processor bowl with paper towels. It will take less than a minute to whip up your cheesecake!
- To prevent cheesecake from cracking, place a pie plate half-filled with water on the bottom rack of the oven. Place the cheesecake on the middle rack and bake as directed in your recipe.
- Chop chocolate for mousses, sauces and desserts on the **Steel Blade** or grate on the **Grater** (see Smart Chart, Chocolate, p. 22). For melted chocolate, pour hot liquid called for in your recipe through feed tube while machine is running; chopped chocolate will melt instantly! See also About Chocolate (p. 156) in the Cakes and Frostings chapter.
- **Chocolate Curls:** Temperature is the key. If the chocolate is cold, you will get flakes or small curls. For larger curls, the surface of the chocolate should be slightly warm. Place it briefly under a desk lamp or quickly pass a blowdryer across the surface. Do not melt the chocolate. Then take long strokes along the flat side of the chocolate with a sharp knife, vegetable peeler, melon baller or spoon. Lift the curls carefully with a metal spatula or toothpick.

easy cheesecake

I've been making this recipe for years, with rave reviews! You can substitute chocolate or vanilla wafers in the crust.

Crust

18 single graham wafers (about 1 1/2 cups crumbs)

6 Tbsp. soft butter or margarine, cut in small chunks

2 Tbsp. sugar (granulated or brown)

1/2 tsp. ground cinnamon

Filling

4 cups (2 lbs.) cream cheese, cut in chunks (half cottage cheese may be used)

1 1/2 cups sugar

4 eggs (or 2 eggs plus 4 egg whites)

1 Tbsp. vanilla extract (or 2 Tbsp. lemon juice)

topping of your choice (see below)

Yield: 12 servings. If frozen, crust won't be as crisp. For best results, add topping when cheesecake has thawed.

Preheat oven to 350°F.

For crust: Break wafers into chunks. Process on STEEL BLADE until coarse crumbs are formed. Add remaining crust ingredients and process until blended, 5 or 6 seconds. Press into sprayed 10-inch springform pan. Wipe bowl and blade with paper towels.

For filling: Process cheese with sugar until blended, about 15 seconds. Add eggs and vanilla extract. Process until smooth and creamy, 20 to 30 seconds longer. Pour over crust.

Place a pie plate half-filled with water on lowest rack of oven. Place cheesecake on middle rack. Bake for 40 to 45 minutes. When done, edges will be set but center will jiggle slightly. Turn off heat and let cheesecake cool in oven with door partly open for about 1 hour. It will firm up during this time. Refrigerate. Add desired topping and chill for 3 to 4 hours before serving. (Can be made a day or two ahead.)

cheesecake toppings

- **Canned Pie Filling:** Spoon a 19-oz. can of cherry, blueberry or pineapple pie filling evenly over cheesecake.
- **Mandarin Orange Topping:** Drain three 10-oz. cans mandarin oranges. Pat dry. Arrange in an attractive design over cooled cheesecake. Microwave 1/2 cup apricot preserves on HIGH for 45 seconds, until melted. Gently brush glaze over fruit.
- **Fresh Strawberry Topping:** Hull 2 pints of strawberries; cut in half lengthwise. Arrange cut-side down in an attractive design over cooled cheesecake. Microwave 1/2 cup apricot preserves on HIGH for 45 seconds, until melted. Gently brush glaze over fruit.

desserts and tortes

Prepare cheesecake filling as directed. Omit crust. Place vanilla wafers in paper-lined muffin tins. Top with cheesecake mixture. Bake in preheated 350°F oven for 10 to 12 minutes, until set. When cooled, top each cheesecake with a spoonful of thick jam or a large strawberry. Makes 24.

chocolate cheesecake

desserts and tortes

This delicious cheesecake is extremely rich, so serve very small portions.

Yield: 12 to 15 servings. May be frozen. Thaw overnight in refrigerator.

8-oz. pkg. chocolate wafers (about 1³/₄ cups crumbs)
¹/₂ cup butter or margarine, melted
¹/₂ tsp. ground cinnamon
2 Tbsp. granulated or brown sugar
2 cups chocolate chips

2 cups (1 lb.) cream cheese, cut in chunks
³/₄ cup granulated sugar
4 eggs
¹/₂ cup sour cream
¹/₂ cup chilled whipping cream
1 Tbsp. icing sugar
chocolate curls (p. 174), for garnish

Preheat oven to 350°F.

STEEL BLADE: Break wafers in chunks. Drop through feed tube while machine is running; process until fine crumbs are formed. Add butter or margarine, cinnamon and the 2 Tbsp. sugar; process a few seconds longer to blend. Press into sprayed 9-inch springform pan, reserving ⅓ cup crumb mixture for topping. Wash and dry bowl and blade.

Melt chocolate chips (2 to 3 minutes on MEDIUM in the microwave), stirring once or twice.

STEEL BLADE: Process cheese with the ¾ cup sugar for 30 seconds. Do not insert pusher in feed tube. Add eggs and process until well blended, scraping down sides of bowl as necessary. Add melted chocolate and sour cream; process about 20 seconds longer.

Pour chocolate mixture over crust and sprinkle with reserved crumbs. Place a pie plate half-filled with water on bottom rack of oven. Place cheesecake on middle rack. Bake for 50 to 55 minutes. When done, edges of cake will be set, but center will be somewhat soft. Turn off oven and let cake cool inside for ½ hour with the door partly open. When completely cooled, place cheesecake on a serving plate. Remove sides of pan.

Place a thick book under back of processor base so that machine is tipped forward. Do not insert pusher in feed tube. Whip cream on the STEEL BLADE until thick, 35 to 40 seconds. Add icing sugar and process a few seconds longer, until stiff. Pipe rosettes of whipped cream around edges of cheesecake. Garnish with chocolate curls. Refrigerate until serving time.

dreamy creamy chocolate cheesecake

This scrumptious unbaked cheese-cake is a breeze to prepare!

Yield: 12 servings. May be frozen. Thaw overnight in refrigerator.

1 square (1 oz.) chilled semi-sweet chocolate, for garnish
8-oz. pkg. chocolate wafers
$1/2$ cup melted butter or margarine
2 envelopes dessert topping mix
1 cup cold milk
2 cups (1 lb.) cream cheese, cut in chunks (light or regular)

2 Tbsp. coffee or chocolate liqueur
$2/3$ cup sugar
2 cups chocolate chips, melted
1 cup chilled whipping cream (or 1 envelope dessert topping plus $1/2$ cup cold milk)

GRATER: Grate chocolate, using firm pressure. Set aside.

STEEL BLADE: Break wafers in chunks. Drop wafers through feed tube while machine is running. Process until fine crumbs are formed. Add butter or margarine and process a few seconds longer to blend. Press into ungreased 10-inch spring-form pan. Bake in preheated 350°F oven for 7 to 8 minutes. Cool. Wash and dry bowl and blade; replace blade in bowl.

Place a thick book under back of processor base so machine is tipped forward. Do not insert pusher in feed tube. Process dessert topping with milk for 2 minutes, until stiff. Remove book from under machine. Add chunks of cream cheese through feed tube while machine is running. Process until smooth. Add liqueur, sugar and melted chocolate. Process until smooth and light, about 2 minutes. Scrape down sides of bowl as necessary. Pour mixture over crust. Wash bowl and blade.

Tip processor forward once again, using a thick book underneath the base. Process whipping cream until stiff, 35 to 40 seconds (2 minutes for dessert topping). Pipe rosettes of whipped cream around edges of cake; sprinkle with reserved grated chocolate. Refrigerate for 6 to 8 hours, or overnight.

note:
- Recipe may be halved, if desired, using a 9-inch pie plate. Decrease crumbs to $1\frac{1}{4}$ cups and butter to $\frac{1}{3}$ cup. Do not decrease whipping cream for topping.

desserts and tortes

basic torte layers

Yield: 5 to 6 layers. May be prepared in advance and frozen until needed.

1 cup butter, cut in chunks
¹/₂ cup sugar
2 eggs

1 tsp. baking powder
2 cups flour

Preheat oven to 350°F.

STEEL BLADE: Process butter, sugar and eggs until well blended, about 1 minute. Add baking powder and flour. Process just until mixed, using on/off pulses. Do not overprocess.

Divide dough into 5 or 6 equal portions. Roll out each piece into an 8-inch circle. Place on inverted 8-inch layer pans. (Greasing is not necessary.) Bake until light brown, 10 to 12 minutes. Remove from pans immediately and let cool. Fill and assemble as directed in any torte recipe (pp. 178–180).

cinnamon torte

Yield: 10 servings. Do not freeze.

Basic Torte Layers (above)
3 cups chilled whipping cream
¹/₃ cup icing sugar
1 tsp. ground cinnamon

¹/₂ tsp. vanilla extract
chocolate curls (p. 174), for garnish
pecan halves, for garnish

Prepare Basic Torte Layers as directed, adding 1½ Tbsp. cinnamon to batter along with dry ingredients.

Cream may be whipped with either an electric mixer or processor, using the STEEL BLADE. (Electric mixer will yield a larger volume.) Place a thick book under back of processor base so machine is tipped forward. Do not insert pusher in feed tube. Pour cream through feed tube while machine is running. Whip until texture of sour cream, 30 to 40 seconds. Add sugar, cinnamon and vanilla extract. Process about 10 seconds longer, or until cream is stiff. Do not overprocess.

Spread whipped cream between torte layers, ending with cream. Garnish with chocolate curls and pecans.

sour cream torte

Yield: 10 servings.
Do not freeze.

Basic Torte Layers (p. 178)
1 1/2 cups walnuts (or your favorite nuts)

1 1/2 cups sour cream
1 tsp. vanilla extract
1/2 cup icing sugar (or to taste)
additional icing sugar, for garnish

Prepare Basic Torte Layers as directed.

STEEL BLADE: Process nuts until finely chopped, 15 to 20 seconds; do not overprocess. Add sour cream, vanilla extract and ½ cup icing sugar. Process a few seconds longer to mix. Spread filling between torte layers. Refrigerate at least 24 hours before serving. Sprinkle generously with sifted icing sugar at serving time.

napoleon torte

Yield: 10 servings.
Do not freeze.

Basic Torte Layers (p. 178)
4 3/4-oz. pkg. (6 servings) vanilla pudding (not instant)
2 1/3 cups milk

1 cup chilled whipping cream (or 1 envelope dessert topping plus 1/2 cup cold milk)
icing sugar, for garnish

Prepare Basic Torte Layers as directed.

Cook pudding according to package directions, using 2⅓ cups milk. Cover surface of cooked pudding with waxed paper; refrigerate until completely cold.

STEEL BLADE: Place a thick book under processor base so machine is tipped forward. Do not insert pusher in feed tube. Process whipping cream until stiff, about 45 seconds (2 minutes for dessert topping). Add chilled pudding and process until smooth, about 20 seconds.

Spread cream filling between layers. Sprinkle top of torte with icing sugar. Refrigerate for at least 24 hours before serving. Cut with very sharp knife.

fruit variation:

• Arrange sliced bananas (sprinkled with lemon juice to prevent darkening) between layers along with pudding mixture. Other fruits may be substituted (e.g., peaches, mandarin oranges, mangoes, kiwis, strawberries).

desserts and tortes

chocolate fantasy torte

Decadent and delicious! If you have concerns about using raw eggs, refer to Egg Safety, below, for other alternatives.

Yield: 12 servings.
Do not freeze.

1 cup pecans
3 squares (3 oz.) unsweetened chocolate
1 1/4 cups chocolate or vanilla wafer crumbs (see Smart Chart, p. 23)
1/4 cup melted butter or margarine

2 Tbsp. granulated sugar
1/2 cup chilled butter, cut in chunks
1 1/2 cups icing sugar
3 eggs
1 1/2 cups chilled whipping cream
1/2 cup maple syrup
4 cups cut-up or mini marshmallows
chocolate curls (p. 174), for garnish

STEEL BLADE: Chop pecans coarsely, using several quick on/off pulses. Empty bowl and set aside. Microwave chocolate on MEDIUM for 2 to 3 minutes, until melted, stirring every minute. (Chopping chocolate first on the STEEL BLADE until fine will make it melt more quickly.)

Process crumbs with 1/4 cup melted butter or margarine and granulated sugar until blended, about 8 seconds. Press mixture into sprayed 10-inch springform pan. Bake in preheated 375°F oven for 7 to 8 minutes. Wash and dry bowl and blade.

Process 1/2 cup chilled butter with icing sugar and eggs for 45 seconds, until mixed. Do not insert pusher in feed tube. Add melted chocolate and process until blended, about 20 seconds. Scrape down sides of bowl as necessary. Pour mixture over crust. Place in freezer while preparing topping.

Use an electric mixer for maximum volume. Whip cream with maple syrup until thick. Fold in marshmallows and pecans. Spread over chilled chocolate layer. Garnish with chocolate curls. Refrigerate overnight.

egg safety

To avoid possible salmonella bacteria, there are several alternatives to using uncooked eggs in recipes. You can substitute pasteurized eggs in the shell. Alternately, use pasteurized egg substitute or Blended Tofu (p. 33), using 1/4 cup for each egg you replace.

For updated information on egg safety, check out www.aeb.org/safety.

heavenly chocolate trifle

This company dessert is worth every calorie! See Egg Safety (p. 180) for alternatives to uncooked eggs.

1 square (1 oz.) chilled semi-
   sweet chocolate, for garnish
2 cups chocolate chips
2 envelopes dessert topping mix
1 cup cold milk
4 eggs (or 1 cup Blended Tofu,
   p. 33

$1/_4$ cup sugar
1 large angel-food cake, cut in
   1-inch chunks
$1^1/_2$ cups chilled whipping cream
3 Tbsp. icing sugar
3-oz. pkg. toasted slivered almonds,
   for garnish (see below)

Yield: 12 to 16 servings.
Do not freeze.

GRATER: Grate semi-sweet chocolate, using firm pressure. Set aside. Microwave chocolate chips on MEDIUM for 2 to 3 minutes, until melted, stirring every minute. Let cool. Using an electric mixer, whip dessert topping with milk until stiff.

STEEL BLADE: Process eggs with sugar for 30 seconds, until well mixed. Add melted chocolate and process a few seconds longer, until blended. Scrape down sides of bowl as necessary. Add whipped dessert topping and process 10 to 15 seconds longer.

Place half the cake in 3-quart glass serving bowl. Top with half the chocolate mixture. Repeat with remaining cake and chocolate.

Use an electric mixer to whip cream. (If you use the processor, you will have less volume.) When nearly stiff, add icing sugar and whip until stiff. Top trifle with whipped cream. Garnish with reserved grated chocolate and toasted almonds. Chill for several hours or overnight before serving.

toasting almonds

Bake almonds at 300°F for a few minutes, until golden, or microwave, uncovered, on HIGH for 2 minutes. Almonds will continue to darken after you remove them from the oven or microwave. Cool before using.

lemon trifle

A delightful and refreshing dessert.

Yield: 12 servings.
Do not freeze.

1 pkg. lemon pie filling
$2^1/_4$ cups chilled whipping
  cream
$^1/_4$ cup sugar

1 sponge or angel cake, cut in
  1-inch squares
2 cups fresh blueberries
10-oz. can mandarin oranges, well drained

Prepare pie filling according to package directions. Cool completely.

STEEL BLADE: Place a thick book underneath processor base so machine is tipped forward. Do not insert pusher in feed tube. Whip cream until it's the texture of sour cream, about 35 seconds. Add sugar and process a few seconds longer, until stiff. Set aside half the whipped cream for garnish. Add cooled lemon mixture to remaining whipped cream and process with several quick on/off pulses to blend, scraping down bowl as necessary.

Arrange half the cake in 3-quart glass bowl. Add half the blueberries, then top with half the lemon cream. Repeat with remaining cake, blueberries and lemon cream. Garnish with reserved whipped cream. Arrange mandarin oranges in attractive design on top of trifle. Refrigerate for 4 to 6 hours, or overnight.

light 'n' lemony cheese dessert

Yield: 6 to 8 servings.
Do not freeze.

3-oz. pkg. lemon gelatin
  (4-serving size) (regular or
  sugar-free)
1 cup boiling water
$1^1/_3$ cups creamed cottage cheese

1 envelope dessert topping mix
$^1/_2$ cup cold skim milk
$^3/_4$ cup crushed pineapple, well drained
8 whole strawberries, for garnish

Dissolve gelatin in boiling water. Chill until partially set (the consistency of unbeaten egg whites).

STEEL BLADE: Process cheese until smooth and creamy, 1 to 2 minutes. Add gelatin; process 30 seconds longer, until blended. Scrape down sides of bowl as necessary.

For maximum volume, use an electric mixer to whip dessert topping with milk. Beat until stiff. Add to lemon/cheese mixture. Process until blended, about 20 seconds. Add crushed pineapple and process with quick on/off pulses.

Pour into parfait dishes. Garnish each serving with a strawberry. Refrigerate 3 to 4 hours or overnight.

variation:
• Pour mixture into baked 9-inch graham wafer crust. If desired, substitute different flavors of gelatin and fruit.

blueberry streusel dessert

Delicious served warm with ice cream or frozen yogurt. Substitute your favorite berries in season. Sliced peaches, nectarines or plums can replace part of the berries.

Yield: 8 servings.
Can be frozen.

3 cups fresh or frozen blueberries
1/2 cup granulated sugar
1/3 cup water
2 Tbsp. cornstarch

2 Tbsp. orange juice
1 cup flour
1/2 cup icing sugar or brown sugar
1/4 cup margarine, cut in chunks
1/2 tsp. ground cinnamon

Preheat oven to 350°F.

Combine blueberries, granulated sugar and water in 2-quart microwavable bowl. Microwave, uncovered, on HIGH for 8 to 10 minutes, or until bubbling, stirring once or twice. Dissolve cornstarch in orange juice; stir into blueberry mixture. Microwave 1 to 2 minutes longer, until thick and shiny. Pour into sprayed deep 9-inch pie plate or 10-inch ceramic quiche dish.

STEEL BLADE: Process remaining ingredients for 10 seconds, until crumbly. Sprinkle streusel topping over hot blueberry mixture. Bake for 30 minutes, or until golden.

english plum pudding with brandy hard sauce

Make this 2 to 3 weeks ahead so it can mellow.

Yield: 6 to 8 servings.
Freezes well.

4 or 5 slices white bread (2 cups fresh bread crumbs)
1/2 cup almonds, walnuts or pecans
1 cup sultana raisins
1 cup mixed candied peel
1/2 cup flour
3/4 cup brown sugar, packed
1 tsp. ground cinnamon
1/4 tsp. nutmeg

pinch ground cloves
1/2 cup candied cherries
1 apple, peeled, cored and cut in chunks
2 eggs
1/2 cup orange juice (part brandy may be used)
1 Tbsp. lemon juice
1/3 cup oil
Brandy Hard Sauce

STEEL BLADE: Tear bread in chunks. Process until fine crumbs are formed, about 20 seconds. Transfer to large mixing bowl. Chop nuts coarsely, using 6 to 8 on/off pulses. Add to bowl along with raisins and candied peel. Process flour, brown sugar, cinnamon, nutmeg, cloves and cherries with 3 or 4 quick on/off pulses, until cherries are coarsely chopped. Add to bowl and mix well. Process apple until fine, about 15 seconds. Add to bowl. Process eggs, orange and lemon juice and oil for 5 seconds. Add to bowl and mix well.

Spread evenly in lightly sprayed 6-cup casserole. Cover with a double layer of greased aluminum foil and tie securely with string. Place on rack in steamer or

Dutch oven. Add enough boiling water to come halfway up sides of bowl. Cover pot tightly and simmer for 6 hours. Add boiling water as needed to maintain water level.

Remove pudding from steamer and cool 15 to 20 minutes. Loosen edges with a spatula and unmold. Cool completely; wrap in foil and refrigerate or freeze. (May also be wrapped in cheesecloth moistened with brandy, then wrapped tightly with foil.)

To serve: Thaw if frozen. Return pudding to greased bowl; cover tightly with foil. Steam 1½ to 2 hours. Serve with the sauce.

brandy hard sauce

Yield: 1⅓ cups.
Freezes well.

1 Tbsp. lemon or orange zest
1½ cups icing sugar
½ cup butter, cut in chunks

3 Tbsp. brandy (or 1 Tbsp. brandy
   and 2 Tbsp. milk)
1 tsp. vanilla extract
½ tsp. nutmeg (optional)

STEEL BLADE: Process all ingredients until smooth, about 20 seconds. Pour over steamed pudding.

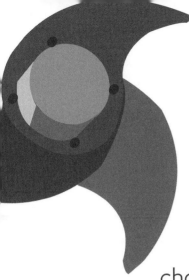

chocolates, cookies and squares

- With the help of your processor and the quick tips and techniques in this book, you can whip up easy and delicious chocolate treats, cookies and squares in a fraction of the time!
- Use the **Steel Blade** to mix up your cookie dough, make crumb mixtures, chop dried fruits or mince citrus zest. Chop or grate nuts and chocolate with the **Steel Blade** or **Grater**. Refer to the Smart Chart (p. 28, 22) for basic techniques. Many baking tips for cakes (pp. 153–160) and desserts (pp. 173–174) also apply.
- As a general guideline, cookie recipes using 2 to 2½ cups of flour can be made in a standard-sized processor. A large processor will handle up to twice the amount.
- If a recipe calls for chopped ingredients (e.g., nuts, chocolate, orange zest), chop them first while the processor bowl is clean and dry, then set them aside until needed.
- Next, prepare the cookie dough. This usually takes 2 or 3 minutes. Add chopped nuts, chocolate chips, etc., using quick on/off pulses to prevent overprocessing. Some recipes call for mixing them in with a spatula or wooden spoon.
- To process sticky fruits (e.g., dates, prunes, raisins, candied fruits), freeze them for 10 minutes. Then add some of the flour called for in the recipe (about 2 to 4 Tbsp.) and process with quick on/off pulses, until the desired texture is reached. This helps prevent fruit from sticking to the blade.

- To chop nuts, use on/off pulses, until the desired texture is reached (see Smart Chart, p. 28). To prevent overprocessing and creating nut butter, add some of the flour or sugar called for in the recipe to the nuts before processing (up to ½ cup for each cup of nuts).

- Chill chocolate before processing. Otherwise, the heat from the speed of the blades may melt the chocolate. Chocolate can be chopped or ground on the **Steel Blade**, or grated on the **Grater**. See Smart Chart (p. 22) and About Chocolate (p. 156) in the Cakes and Frostings chapter.

- Batter up! Process butter or margarine with sugar on the **Steel Blade** until well-creamed, 1 to 2 minutes. Eggs are either processed with butter and sugar or added through the feed tube. Blend in flour and dry ingredients with quick on/off pulses, just until blended. In some recipes, dough is processed just until it forms a ball.

- Butter and margarine are interchangeable in most recipes. Don't bake with light margarine; it contains too much water.

- If dough is too soft, refrigerate until firm enough to handle. Work with small amounts at a time. Keep the rest refrigerated.

- Size does count! For even baking, cookies should be uniform in size. A small cookie scoop works perfectly! Leave 1 to 2 inches between cookies as some doughs spread during baking.

- For best results, use shiny, heavy-quality aluminum cookie sheets. Dark pans absorb too much heat and the bottoms of the cookies may burn. You can insulate light-weight pans by lining them with heavy-duty foil, or by placing one pan on top of another.

- To grease or not to grease? I used to grease and flour my pans. Now I use nonstick spray or line pans with parchment or foil. Greasing or spraying is not necessary if cookies are high in fat (e.g., shortbread).

- Not enough cookie sheets? While the first batch of cookies is in the oven, place the next batch on parchment or foil. When the first batch is baked, slide the parchment or foil (and cookies) off the pan. Cool the pan slightly, then replace with the next batch. (Lining pans with foil or parchment also saves on clean-ups.)

- Cookies can spread or flatten if placed on hot cookie sheets, so cool pans between batches.

- Preheat oven for best results. Make sure your oven temperature is accurate. An oven thermometer is helpful.

- Position is everything! Bake cookies on the middle rack of your oven. If baking 2 pans at once, place racks so they divide the oven evenly into thirds. For even browning, switch pans (top to bottom and front to back) for the last few minutes of baking.

- Use a timer for accurate results. Check a few minutes before the end of baking time to prevent overbaking.
- Ready or not? When checking for doneness, open and close the door quickly so the oven won't lose too much heat. Some cookies will still be soft when ready, but will firm up after a few minutes. If the bottoms are too brown, remove the cookies from the pan immediately to prevent continued baking.
- Let cookies cool on pans for a few minutes, then transfer to cooling racks.
- To prevent sticking, always cool cookies before transferring them to your cookie jar. If sprinkling cookies with icing sugar, cool them first so the sugar doesn't melt.
- Dip tip! Microwave 4 oz. semi-sweet or white chocolate on MEDIUM (50%) for 3 to 4 minutes, stirring every minute, until melted. Stir in 2 tsp. oil. Dip cookies halfway into melted chocolate. Place on waxed paper to dry.
- Chocolate meltdown! When melting chocolate, the bowl and mixing spoon must be completely dry to prevent chocolate from seizing (lumping and clumping). If this happens, see Chocolate Rescue (p. 156) in the Cakes and Frostings chapter.
- Sweetened condensed milk: It's so easy to make your own. (See recipe on p. 188.) Sweetened condensed milk and evaporated milk are **not** interchangeable in recipes.
- Unbaked cookies can be frozen for several months. Shape, then freeze. Transfer to freezer containers when frozen. No need to defrost them before baking! Take out as many as you need and bake, increasing cooking time slightly.
- Cookies and squares freeze well. They take about 15 minutes to defrost, depending on size.
- That's the way the cookie crumbles! Process leftover or broken cookies on the **Steel Blade** until fine. Use to make cookie crumb crusts for squares and desserts.
- Substitute granola for half the graham wafer crumbs in cookies and squares for an interesting taste and texture.
- The bar scene! Bars and squares are a great timesaver and use only one pan. Cool bar cookies in the pan, then cut with a sharp knife. For entertaining or gift-giving, cut into small squares and place in pretty paper baking cups.
- Reduce oven temperature by 25°F when baking in glass pans.

fast fudge

So quick and easy!
Great for gifts.

Yield: 1¹/₂ lbs. or
25 squares.
Freezes well.

**1 cup walnuts, almonds, pecans
   or cashews
2 cups chocolate chips
2 squares (2 oz.) unsweetened
   chocolate**

**1 Tbsp. margarine or butter
14-oz. can sweetened condensed
   milk (see below)
1 tsp. vanilla extract**

STEEL BLADE: Process nuts with quick on/off pulses, until coarsely chopped.
Set aside.

Combine chocolate chips, chocolate, margarine or butter and milk in 2-quart
microwavable bowl. Microwave on HIGH for 2 minutes; stir well. Microwave
1 minute longer, until melted. Mixture should be smooth and shiny. Stir in nuts
and vanilla extract.

Spread mixture evenly in sprayed 8-inch square pan and chill until firm. Cut
into squares. Serve in small paper cups.

variations:

• Stir 2 cups cut-up marshmallows into fudge along with chopped nuts.
• Drop mixture by small spoonfuls into pretty paper baking cups.

make your own
sweetened
condensed milk

Combine 6 Tbsp. butter, 1 cup plus 2 Tbsp. sugar, ¹/₂ cup water and
1¹/₂ cups instant skim milk powder in 3-quart microwavable bowl. Mix
well. Microwave on HIGH for 5 to 6 minutes, until boiling and thickened.
Stir well 2 or 3 times during cooking. Mixture will thicken upon standing.
Let cool. Store in refrigerator for 2 to 3 weeks. Makes equivalent of a
14-oz. can of sweetened condensed milk.

easy rum balls

This is a great
way to use up
stale cake.

Yield: 5 dozen.
Delicious right from
the freezer!

2 cups almonds or hazelnuts
4 cups stale chocolate or white
   cake, cut in chunks
2 cups icing sugar
3 Tbsp. cocoa

$1/4$ cup margarine or butter
$1/4$ cup milk
2 Tbsp. rum (or chocolate, orange
   or almond liqueur)

STEEL BLADE: Process nuts until finely ground, about 30 seconds. Empty bowl. Process cake until finely ground, about 30 seconds. Measure 4 cups. Process icing sugar with cocoa, margarine or butter, milk and rum until blended, 15 to 20 seconds. Add cake crumbs and ½ cup of the ground nuts; process until well mixed.

Roll mixture into 1-inch balls. Roll in reserved nuts. Place on foil-lined cookie sheets and refrigerate or freeze until firm. Serve in paper cups.

variation:

• For Passover "Yum" Balls, replace rum with Passover chocolate liqueur or wine; use stale Passover sponge cake. For a pareve version, replace milk with non-dairy creamer.

chocolate rogelach

I usually double
this recipe be-
cause they disap-
pear so quickly.
The variations are
equally delicious.

Yield: 2 dozen.
Freezes well.

Cream Cheese Pastry (p. 208)
   or Flaky Ginger Ale Pastry
   (p. 207)
$1/4$ cup sugar (granulated or
   brown)

$1/2$ tsp. ground cinnamon
$1/3$ cup chocolate chips
$1/3$ cup walnuts or almonds
   icing sugar (optional)

Preheat oven to 375°F.

Prepare dough as directed. Divide into 2 balls. (Ginger Ale Pastry should be chilled first.) Flour dough lightly. Roll out one portion of dough on a lightly floured surface into a circle about ⅛ inch thick.

STEEL BLADE: Process sugar, cinnamon, chocolate chips and nuts until finely chopped, 25 to 30 seconds.

Sprinkle dough with ¼ cup of filling. Cut with a sharp knife or pastry wheel into 12 wedges. Roll up from the outside edge towards the center. Place on ungreased foil-lined cookie sheets. Repeat with remaining dough and filling. Bake for 18 to 20 minutes, until lightly browned. If desired, dust with icing sugar when cooled.

chocolate chip cookies

These are my granddaughter Lauren Sprackman's absolutely favorite cookies! I've added a new variation with reduced flour and a lower baking temperature that makes a softer, chewier, melt-in-your mouth cookie.

Yield: 6 to 8 dozen, depending on size. Freezes well.

$1/2$ to 1 cup pecans (optional)
1 cup margarine or butter, cut in chunks
$3/4$ cup granulated sugar
$3/4$ cup brown sugar, packed
2 eggs
1 tsp. vanilla extract or 1 Tbsp. coffee liqueur

$2^1/4$ cups flour
1 tsp. baking soda
$1/2$ tsp. salt
2 cups chocolate chips (or 1 cup white chocolate chips and 1 cup semi-sweet chocolate chips)

Preheat oven to 375°F.

STEEL BLADE: Process nuts, if using, until coarsely chopped, 8 to 10 seconds. Empty bowl. Process margarine or butter, sugars, eggs and vanilla extract or liqueur for 1 minute. Add flour, baking soda and salt, and process with several quick on/off pulses, just until blended. Do not overprocess. Stir in chips and nuts with a rubber spatula.

Drop by small spoonfuls onto parchment or foil-lined cookie sheets. Bake for 10 to 12 minutes, until lightly browned.

variations:
- For a soft, chewy cookie, reduce flour to 2 cups and omit nuts. If desired, replace chocolate chips with chocolate chunks. Lower the baking temperature to 350°F. Bake for 10 minutes, until edges are golden. Let cool for 10 minutes before removing from pans.
- Omit nuts and chocolate chips. Drop batter by small spoonfuls onto cookie sheets. Press five M & M chocolate candies into each cookie. Bake at 350°F for 10 minutes.

chef's tip:
- For that just-baked taste, microwave 2 or 3 cookies for 10 seconds on HIGH. Perfect with a glass of milk.

butterscotch toffee dreams

These easy, elegant shortbread cookies taste like a dream.

1 cup butter or margarine, cut in chunks
$^1/_2$ cup brown sugar, packed
$^1/_2$ cup granulated sugar

1$^1/_2$ cups flour
$^1/_2$ cup cornstarch
$^3/_4$ cup toffee bits
$^1/_2$ cup butterscotch chips

Yield: 5 dozen.
Freezes well.

Preheat oven to 350°F.

STEEL BLADE: Process butter or margarine and sugars until well creamed, about 1 minute. Add flour and cornstarch. Process with several on/off pulses, just until blended. Do not overprocess. Sprinkle toffee bits and butterscotch chips over batter. Stir in with a wooden spoon.

Shape dough into 1-inch balls (a small cookie scoop works well). Place on parchment-lined cookie sheets. Bake for 12 to 15 minutes, until edges are golden. Cool slightly before removing from pan.

sesame crescents

Yield: About 3$^1/_2$ dozen cookies.
Freezes well.

$^1/_2$ cup butter or margarine, cut in chunks
$^1/_2$ cup brown sugar, packed
1 egg plus 1 egg yolk
1 tsp. vanilla extract

1$^1/_2$ cups flour
$^1/_4$ tsp. baking soda
$^1/_2$ cup sesame seeds (approximately)
3 Tbsp. sugar

Preheat oven to 375°F.

STEEL BLADE: Process butter or margarine, brown sugar, egg, egg yolk and vanilla extract for 2 minutes. Add flour and baking soda and process just until dough is mixed and begins to gather in a ball around the blades. Do not overprocess.

Use 1 tsp. of dough for each cookie; shape into crescents. Roll in a mixture of sesame seeds and sugar. Place on parchment-lined cookie sheets. Bake for 10 minutes, until golden.

variation:
• Replace sesame seeds with chopped nuts.

cinnamon twists

My grandmother and mother made these cookies for my sister Rhonda and me when we were children and now we make them for our children.

Yield: 4 to 5 dozen. Freezes well, if you can put them away quickly enough!

1/2 cup sugar	3/4 cup oil
1 Tbsp. ground cinnamon	2 tsp. baking powder
3 eggs	3 cups flour
1 cup granulated or brown	
sugar, lightly packed	

Preheat oven to 375°F.

STEEL BLADE: Process 1/2 cup sugar and cinnamon with several quick on/off pulses, then let machine run until well mixed. Empty mixture into a small bowl.

Process eggs, 1 cup sugar and oil until blended, about 5 seconds. Add baking powder and flour. Process with several on/off pulses, just until flour disappears. Do not overprocess.

Using about 1 Tbsp. dough for each cookie, roll between your palms to form a pencil-shaped roll. Shape into twists, crescents, rings, the letter "S," or any initial you wish. Kids love to make their own designs. Roll in cinnamon-sugar mixture.

Place on sprayed foil-lined cookie sheets. Bake for 12 to 15 minutes, until nicely browned. (Baking time depends on size of cookies, which can vary if the children are assisting you.)

lighter variation:
• Reduce oil to 1/2 cup. Use 2 eggs plus 2 egg whites.

sesame nothings

It only takes 2 minutes to mix up this batter in the processor, compared to 20 minutes with an electric mixer. They're excellent for diabetics as they can be made sugar-free.

3 eggs	1/2 cup oil
2 Tbsp. sugar (or sugar substitute	1 cup flour
to equal 2 Tbsp. sugar)	3/4 cup sesame seeds
dash salt	2 additional Tbsp. sugar

Preheat oven to 500°F.

STEEL BLADE: Process eggs with 2 Tbsp. sugar and salt for 30 to 60 seconds, until light. While machine is running, pour oil through feed tube in a steady stream. Process 1 minute longer. Add flour by heaping spoonfuls through feed tube while machine is running. Process 30 to 40 seconds longer. (Processor may shut off automatically after about 40 seconds because batter is very sticky. If you have an inexpensive processor, don't let machine shut itself off or you may require a service call!)

Yield: About 40 cook-
ies. Each cookie con-
tains about 40 calories
if made with sugar
substitute, 43 calories
if made with sugar.
Freezes well.

Combine sesame seeds with 2 Tbsp. sugar on a flat plate. Take a scant teaspoon of dough and use another spoon to push it off into sesame seed mixture. Roll dough in sesame seeds. Stretch dough to about 3 inches in length, then twist it to make a long, twisted finger shape. Roll again in sesame seeds. Place on sprayed foil-lined cookie sheets, leaving 3 inches between cookies for expansion.

Reduce heat to 400°F. Place cookies on middle rack of oven and bake for 7 to 8 minutes. Reduce heat to 300°F and bake 10 to 12 minutes longer. Turn off heat and leave cookies in oven 10 minutes longer to dry.

variations:

- Replace sesame seeds with poppy seeds.
- Instead of shaping batter into fingers, drop from a teaspoon onto sprayed cookie sheets, leaving about 3 inches between cookies. If desired, sprinkle lightly with sugar before baking.

basic oil dough (pareve)

1 medium seedless orange (thin-skinned)	$1/2$ cup oil
2 eggs	2 tsp. baking powder
$3/4$ cup sugar	$2^3/4$ cups flour (approximately)

STEEL BLADE: Cut orange in quarters but do not peel. Process until fine, about 25 seconds. Add eggs, sugar and oil. Process for 10 seconds. Add baking powder and flour. Process with several on/off pulses, just until flour is blended into dough. Do not overprocess. Dough will be fairly sticky. Remove from bowl with a rubber spatula onto a lightly floured surface. Use as directed.

chocolate variation:

- For Chocolate Oil Dough, increase sugar to 1 cup. Reduce flour to 2½ cups and add ½ cup cocoa.

french unbaked cake

Good any time, but especially in the summertime when you don't want to turn on the oven.

Yield: About 25 squares. Freezes well.

1/2 cup walnuts	1/4 cup butter or margarine
1 egg	1/2 tsp. vanilla extract
1/4 cup brown sugar, lightly packed	16 double graham wafers
2 Tbsp. cocoa	Chocolate Cocoa Frosting (p. 171)

STEEL BLADE: Chop nuts with several quick on/off pulses. Empty bowl. Process egg, brown sugar and cocoa for a few seconds, until mixed. Melt butter in a heavy-bottomed saucepan. Add chocolate mixture to saucepan. Cook on medium heat, stirring constantly, just until thickened, like custard. Do not boil or mixture will curdle. Stir in vanilla extract.

Break up wafers into chunks about the size of corn flakes. Place in a large mixing bowl. Add half the nuts. Pour chocolate mixture over wafers and mix with a wooden spoon until wafers are well coated. Spread evenly in a sprayed 8-inch square glass baking dish.

Spread frosting over chocolate/wafer mixture and swirl with a knife. (You can double the recipe for a thicker layer of frosting.) Sprinkle with reserved nuts and refrigerate. Cut into squares.

nanaimo crunch bars

These delicious squares are sure to be a favorite with your family! No baking required.

Yield: 2 dozen. Freezes well, but cut into squares before freezing.

Base
1/2 cup butter or margarine
1/4 cup granulated sugar
1/3 cup cocoa
1 egg
1 tsp. vanilla extract
1/2 cup walnuts or pecans
1 1/2 cups granola cereal or graham wafer crumbs
1 cup coconut

Filling
1/4 cup soft butter or margarine
2 Tbsp. vanilla pudding powder or custard powder
3 Tbsp. milk
2 cups icing sugar

Glaze
4 squares (4 oz.) semi-sweet chocolate
1 Tbsp. butter or margarine

For base: In a large microwavable bowl, microwave butter or margarine on HIGH until melted, about 1 minute. Blend in sugar, cocoa, egg and vanilla extract. Microwave uncovered for 1 minute, stirring after 30 seconds. Mixture will resemble custard. Chop nuts on the STEEL BLADE with 6 or 8 quick on/off pulses. Add nuts, granola or graham wafer crumbs and coconut to microwaved mixture; stir well. Press evenly into a sprayed 9-inch square pan.

For filling: Process all filling ingredients until well mixed, 15 to 20 seconds. Scrape down sides of bowl as needed. Spread filling evenly over base. Chill for 15 minutes.

For glaze: Microwave chocolate and butter or margarine on MEDIUM for 2 to 3 minutes, until melted, stirring after each minute. Let cool for 10 minutes. Pour glaze over filling. Tilt pan back and forth so that glaze coats evenly. Chill. Cut into squares.

almond crisp bars

Warning—these may become habit-forming!

Yield: About 25 squares. Freezes well.

$1/2$ cup butter or margarine, cut in chunks	1 egg yolk
$1/4$ cup granulated sugar	$1/2$ cup flour
$1/4$ cup brown sugar, lightly packed	$1/2$ cup rolled oats or granola
$1/2$ tsp. vanilla or almond extract	$3/4$ cup chocolate chips
	1 Tbsp. additional butter
	$1/4$ cup almonds

Preheat oven to 350°F.

STEEL BLADE: Process the ½ cup butter or margarine with sugars, vanilla or almond extract and egg yolk for 45 seconds. Add flour and process for 5 seconds to mix. Add oats or granola and process with several quick on/off pulses to mix.

Spread mixture with rubber spatula in sprayed 8-inch square baking pan. Bake for 25 minutes, until golden. Melt chocolate chips with the 1 Tbsp. butter (about 2 minutes on MEDIUM in the microwave). Stir well; spread over base.

Process almonds until fine, about 15 seconds. Sprinkle over chocolate. Cut into squares while still warm.

note:
• Recipe may be doubled and baked in sprayed 10 x 15-inch jelly roll pan. Increase baking time slightly.

marbled cheesecake brownies

Cheesecake and brownies are combined in one luscious recipe!

Yield: 48 squares. Freezes for up to 2 months if well wrapped and well hidden!

Cheesecake Batter
1 cup (8 oz.) cream cheese
   (regular or light)
$1/3$ cup granulated sugar
1 egg
$1/2$ tsp. vanilla extract

Brownie Batter
1 cup butter or margarine, melted
$3/4$ cup cocoa
1 cup granulated sugar
1 cup brown sugar, lightly packed
3 eggs
1 tsp. vanilla extract
1 cup flour
$1/2$ tsp. baking powder
$1/8$ tsp. salt

Preheat oven to 350°F.

For cheesecake batter: Process cream cheese with sugar on the STEEL BLADE until blended, about 20 seconds. Add egg and vanilla extract; process until smooth and creamy, about 30 seconds longer. Scrape down sides of bowl as needed. Transfer mixture to a 2-cup measuring cup. (No need to wash the bowl or blade.)

For brownie batter: Process butter or margarine, cocoa, sugars, eggs and vanilla extract until well mixed, about 1 minute. Scrape down sides of bowl. Add flour, baking powder and salt; process with quick on/off pulses, just until blended. Do not overprocess.

Pour half the brownie batter into sprayed 9 x 13-inch baking pan. Drizzle half the cheesecake batter over brownie batter. Repeat layers. With a knife, cut through batters in a swirl design to make a marbled effect.

Bake for 30 minutes. When done, a toothpick inserted into the center will come out clean. Cool completely. Cut into squares and refrigerate.

polka dot brownies Omit cheesecake batter. Prepare brownie batter, adding 1 cup white chocolate or peanut butter chips. Bake as directed. Frost cooled brownies with your favorite chocolate frosting. Top with additional "chips" to make polka dots.

by cracky bars

These luscious three-layered squares from the late 1950s come from my friend Roz Brown's recipe collection.

$^1/_2$ cup walnuts or pecans
1 cup sugar
$^3/_4$ cup butter or margarine, cut in chunks
2 eggs
1 tsp. vanilla extract
$^1/_3$ cup milk

$1^1/_2$ cups flour
$^1/_4$ tsp. baking soda
1 square (1 oz.) unsweetened chocolate, melted
15 to 18 single graham wafers
1 cup chocolate chips

Yield: About 3 dozen. Freezes well.

Preheat oven to 350°F.

STEEL BLADE: Process nuts until chopped, 6 to 8 seconds. Empty bowl. Process sugar, butter or margarine, eggs and vanilla extract for 1 minute. Add milk through feed tube while machine is running. Process 3 seconds. Add flour and baking soda. Process with 3 or 4 quick on/off pulses, just until blended. Do not overprocess.

Remove half the batter and set aside. Add melted chocolate and nuts to batter in processor. Process with quick on/off pulses, just until blended, scraping down sides of bowl as needed. Do not overprocess.

Spread chocolate-nut batter evenly in sprayed 9 x 13-inch baking pan. Arrange wafers over batter to cover. Mix chocolate chips into remaining batter and spread evenly over wafers. Bake for 30 to 35 minutes, until a cake tester comes out dry. When cool, cut into squares.

chocolate chip nut chews

Yield: 25 squares. Freezes well.

Base
$^1/_2$ cup butter or margarine, cut in chunks
$^1/_2$ cup sugar (granulated or brown)
1 cup flour
1 cup chocolate chips

Topping
1 cup walnuts, pecans or peanuts
1 cup brown sugar, packed
2 eggs
$^1/_2$ tsp. vanilla extract
2 Tbsp. flour
$^1/_2$ tsp. baking powder
$^1/_2$ cup coconut

Preheat oven to 350°F.

For base: Process butter or margarine, sugar and flour on the STEEL BLADE for 20 seconds, until blended. Press into lightly sprayed 8-inch square pan. Bake for 15 minutes. Remove from oven and sprinkle with chocolate chips.

For topping: Process nuts until coarsely chopped, 6 to 8 seconds. Empty bowl. Process brown sugar, eggs and vanilla extract for 30 seconds. Add remaining ingredients and mix in with 2 or 3 quick on/off pulses. Spread over chocolate chips. Bake about 25 minutes longer. When cool, cut into squares.

crumbly jam squares

Yield: 25 squares.

Freezes well.

4 oz. Cheddar cheese (1 cup grated)	1 1/2 cups flour
1/2 cup butter or margarine, cut in chunks	3 Tbsp. sugar
	1 tsp. baking powder
	1 cup apricot jam or orange marmalade

Preheat oven to 350°F.

STEEL BLADE: Cut cheese into chunks. Process until fine, about 15 seconds. Add butter or margarine and process 30 seconds longer, scraping down sides of bowl as needed. Add flour, sugar and baking powder. Process 10 to 15 seconds longer, until crumbly.

Press half the mixture into ungreased 8-inch square pan. Spread with jam. Sprinkle remaining crumbs over top. Bake for about 30 minutes. When cool, cut into squares.

halfway squares

They're half gone before you look around!

Yield: 25 squares.

Do not freeze.

1/3 cup butter, cut in chunks	3/4 tsp. baking powder
1 egg, separated	1/2 tsp. vanilla extract
1/4 cup granulated sugar	3/4 cup chocolate chips
1/4 cup brown sugar, packed	1/2 cup additional brown sugar, packed
1 cup flour	

Preheat oven to 375°F.

For base: Process butter, egg yolk and ¼ cup granulated and brown sugars on the STEEL BLADE for 45 seconds, until blended. Add flour, baking powder and vanilla extract. Process with several on/off pulses, until mixed. Press into sprayed 8-inch square pan. Sprinkle with chocolate chips.

Using an electric mixer or whisk, beat egg white until soft peaks form. Gradually add ½ cup brown sugar and beat until stiff. Carefully spread meringue over chocolate layer. Bake for about 25 minutes. When cool, cut into squares.

heavenly squares

Yield: About
25 squares.
Freezes well.

Base

$1/2$ cup walnuts

$1/4$ cup brown sugar, lightly
    packed

$3/4$ cup flour

6 Tbsp. butter or margarine,
    cut in chunks

Topping

1 cup pitted dates

5 Tbsp. flour, divided

$1/4$ cup maraschino cherries, well drained

2 eggs

1 cup brown sugar, lightly packed

$1/2$ tsp. baking powder

$1 1/4$ cups coconut

$1/2$ cup chocolate chips

Preheat oven to 350°F.

For base: Process base ingredients with quick on/off pulses, until crumbly. Press into lightly sprayed 8-inch square pan. Bake for 15 minutes. Remove from oven.

For topping: Process dates with 2 Tbsp. of the flour until coarsely chopped, 6 to 8 seconds. Empty bowl. Pat cherries dry with paper towels. Process cherries with 1 Tbsp. of the flour, using 2 quick on/off pulses. Add to dates. Process eggs, brown sugar, baking powder and remaining 2 Tbsp. flour until well blended, about 30 seconds. Add dates, cherries, coconut and chocolate chips. Mix in with several quick on/off pulses. Scrape down sides of bowl as needed.

Spread mixture over base. Bake 25 to 30 minutes longer, until golden. Cut into squares while warm.

hello dolly squares

My daughter Jodi
adores these!

Yield: About 4 dozen.
Freezes well.

$1/2$ cup walnuts, almonds
    or pecans

$1 1/4$ cups graham wafer crumbs
    (or 15 single graham wafers)

$1/2$ cup butter or margarine

$1 1/2$ cups chocolate chips

$1/2$ cup raisins (optional)

$1 1/2$ cups coconut

14-oz. can sweetened condensed milk
    (see p. 188)

Preheat oven to 350°F.

STEEL BLADE: Process nuts until coarsely chopped, 6 to 8 seconds. Empty bowl. If using graham wafers, break in chunks. Process to make fine crumbs, 25 to 35 seconds.

Place butter or margarine in 9 x 13-inch baking pan and place in oven to melt.

Mix in crumbs; spread evenly in pan. Sprinkle with chocolate chips, raisins, coconut and nuts. Drizzle condensed milk evenly over top. Bake for 25 to 30 minutes, until golden. Cool and cut into squares.

variations:

- Substitute 1½ cups granola or any leftover cookies for graham wafer crumbs.
- Combine melted butter with graham wafer crumbs; spread evenly in pan. Sprinkle with 1 cup chocolate chips, 1 cup Skor bar pieces and 1 cup slivered almonds or chopped pecans. If desired, add ½ cup glazed cherries, halved. Drizzle condensed milk over mixture. Bake as directed.

lemon squares

This is a favorite of Elaine Kaplan, who worked tire-lessly by my side to guide the creation of this cookbook.

Yield: About 48 squares. Freezes well.

Base
1 cup butter or margarine, cut in chunks
2 cups flour
$1/2$ cup sugar

Topping
4 eggs
$1/4$ to $1/3$ cup lemon juice (preferably fresh)
2 cups sugar
$1/4$ cup flour
1 tsp. baking powder

Preheat oven to 350°F.

For base: Process base ingredients on the STEEL BLADE until crumbly, about 20 seconds. Press into sprayed 9 x 13-inch baking pan. Bake for 18 to 20 minutes, until golden.

For topping: Process topping ingredients until blended, about 10 seconds. Pour over base. Bake 25 to 30 minutes longer, until golden. Cut into squares when cool.

pies and pastries

- Making pastry dough is as easy as pie! For the best results when making pastry, measure accurately and use cold ingredients. Freeze butter or shortening in advance and use ice-cold water.
- Cut shortening and/or butter into 1-inch pieces and place in the processor bowl. Add flour and salt. Process on the **Steel Blade** with several quick on/off pulses, until the mixture resembles coarse oatmeal.
- Add cold water through the feed tube in a thin stream while the machine is running. In 12 to 15 seconds, the dough will begin to gather around the blades. Do not overprocess or the dough will be tough.
- If the dough is too dry, add extra liquid a few drops at a time. Use on/off pulses, just until the dough begins to hold together.
- If the dough is too sticky, remove it from the processor and gently knead in a little more flour. Do not overhandle.
- Shape the dough into 1 or 2 round discs (like a large, thick hamburger).

- Roll It Right!
  - Chill the dough before rolling for easier handling. Wrap well and refrigerate for at least ½ hour or place it in the freezer for 15 minutes.
  - A floured surface prevents the dough from sticking. The less flour used, the flakier the pastry.
  - A lightly floured pastry cloth and stockinette rolling pin cover make rolling dough easy. Anchor the pastry cloth by tucking it under your pastry board.

- Rolling dough on parchment or waxed paper is an excellent alternative. Wet the countertop so the paper won't slip.
- Roll dough equally in all directions, like the spokes of a wheel. This helps keep the pastry round. Take your time! Use light strokes and a lifting motion. Flour the rolling pin or stockinette cover from time to time to prevent sticking.
- If the dough begins to stick, lift it up carefully with a floured spatula and add a little more flour.
- Roll the pastry into a large circle about 2 inches larger than your pie plate when inverted. Mend cracks as they form.
- Fold the dough in half carefully, then in half again to make a pie-shaped wedge. Transfer to an ungreased pie plate, placing the point at the center of the plate. Unfold carefully. Do not stretch the dough or it will shrink during baking.

- Easy Doughs It!
  - For a single prebaked 9-inch pie shell, roll out the dough and place it in the pie plate. Trim the edge, leaving a ½-inch overhang. Fold the edge under to form a rim. Flute the edge, then press firmly against the pie plate. Prick the bottom of the pastry all over with a fork. Chill for ½ hour before baking; this prevents the crust from shrinking. Bake at 425°F for about 10 minutes, until golden.
  - For a partially-baked pie shell, prepare the pastry shell as above, then line it with aluminum foil. Weigh the foil down with dried beans or uncooked rice. Bake at 400°F for 10 minutes. Remove the foil and beans. (Careful—don't spill the beans!) Bake 5 minutes longer.
  - For two-crust pie, roll out the bottom crust and place it in the pan. Trim the overhanging edges. Fill as desired. Roll out the top crust and fold it in half. Place the top crust over the filling and unfold it carefully. Trim the top pastry, leaving a 1-inch overhang around the rim. Fold the edge of the top crust under the bottom crust (not under the pan). Press the edges together to seal, using one of the methods below. Cut several slits in the top crust to release steam while the pie is baking. (Don't cut the slits if you're freezing the unbaked pie.)
  - Fork edge: Dip the tines of a fork in flour, then press firmly to make a decorative edge.
  - Spoon edge: Press the rounded tip of a teaspoon into the edge to form a scalloped design.

- Ruffled edge: Place your thumb and index finger about ½ inch apart along the rim of the pie plate, pointing towards the center. With the index finger of the opposite hand, pull the pastry gently towards the center. Repeat every inch or so, forming a rounded, ruffled edge.
- Save the scraps of dough. Roll them out and cut out shapes with tiny cookie cutters. Brush the bottoms of the cut-outs with water and arrange them attractively on top of the pie.
- For a shiny top, brush the crust with milk before baking. For a glazed top, brush with beaten egg. For a sugary top, brush with water, then sprinkle with sugar.
- To make a lattice top, use a sharp knife or pastry wheel to cut dough into twelve ½-inch strips. (Use a ruler to keep the strips straight.) Carefully lay half the strips 1 inch apart across the top of the filled pie. Arrange the remaining strips at right angles. (To create a woven effect, lift every other strip as you arrange the strips at right angles.) Trim the ends even with the edge of the pie. Press the ends of the strips into the rim of the crust. Fold the bottom pastry over the lattice-work. Seal and flute.
- If the edges of the pie start to brown too quickly, cover the edge with strips of foil.

- Pan-tastic!
  - Glass or aluminum pie plates are best for baking pies. Disposable foil pans are handy for freezing.
  - A 9-inch pie plate holds 4 cups of filling and serves 8 people. An 8-inch pie plate holds 3 cups of filling and serves 6 people. You can replace a 9-inch pie plate with a 10-inch or 11-inch quiche pan.
  - When using a quiche pan with a fluted or rippled sharp edge, roll your rolling pin over the edge. The excess pastry will automatically be cut away!
  - To grease or not to grease? Pastry is high in fat, so don't grease the pie plate. For cookie crumb crusts, spray the pie plate first with non-stick spray to prevent sticking.
  - To prevent spill-overs in your oven, place a foil-lined baking sheet under fruit or custard-type pies before baking.

- Freeze with Ease
  - Fruit pies freeze well, but don't freeze those with a custard base.
  - Don't freeze pies in glass pie plates. They may crack from extreme temperature changes when baking or reheating.
  - Disposable foil pie plates are great for freezing. However, pies baked in foil do not brown evenly. To offset this, bake them on a heavy-quality baking sheet.
  - Unbaked pastry can be frozen for 1 to 2 months. Baked pie shells can be frozen for 2 to 4 months. Baked pies can be frozen for about 3 months. Wrap them well.
  - To defrost baked pies, place the frozen pie in a 425°F oven for 20 to 25 minutes. To prevent overbrowning, cover loosely with foil. To defrost in the microwave, transfer the frozen pie to a microwavable glass pie plate. Microwave on MEDIUM (50%) for 8 to 12 minutes. Let stand for 5 to 10 minutes to complete thawing.
  - To bake a frozen unbaked pie, bake at 450°F for 15 minutes. Cut slits in the top crust, reduce the heat to 375°F and bake 45 minutes longer.

pastry problems	Dough dry and hard to work with	Insufficient liquid; dough is too cold; dough was not shaped into round disc and flattened before chilling and rolling.
	Baked pastry is hard	Too much water; overmixing; excess flour on pastry board; dough overhandled.
	Baked pastry is tough	Insufficient shortening; overmixing shortening and flour; dough overhandled; oven temperature too low.
	Too pale	Oven temperature too low; underbaked.
	Too dark	Oven temperature too high; overbaked.
	Soggy lower crust	Pastry overhandled; too much filling; filling too moist; pastry not put in oven soon enough; pie baked too high up in oven; oven temperature too low. (To help prevent a soggy pie shell, brush with unbeaten egg white before adding filling.)
	Crust thick and doughy	Insufficient fat; too much water; water not cold enough; pastry rolled too thick; oven temperature too low.
	Crust shrinks while baking	Pastry rolled too thin or not chilled before baking; pastry overhandled or stretched when fitted in pan; too much water; oven temperature too low.
	Baked pie shell has bumps and does not lie flat in pan	Pastry not pricked enough; oven temperature too low.
	Apple pie has large air space under top crust of pie	Apples not packed tightly into shell; apples sliced too thick; apples not mounded high enough in center.

standard butter pastry

A simple, delicious dough that's perfect for any pie!

$1/_4$ lb. frozen butter	2 cups flour
($1/_2$ cup/1 stick)	$1/_2$ tsp. salt
$1/_4$ cup frozen shortening	$1/_2$ cup ice water

Yield: Two 9-inch crusts
or 12 medium
tart shells.
Freezes well.

STEEL BLADE: Cut butter and shortening into 6 or 8 pieces; place in processor. Add flour and salt. Turn machine on and off quickly 4 or 5 times (2 or 3 seconds each time), until mixture looks like coarse oatmeal. Add water in slow stream through feed tube while machine is running. Process just until dough begins to gather around the blades, 10 to 12 seconds once all the liquid is added. Do not overprocess.

Remove dough from machine, press into a ball and divide in 2 equal pieces. (Dough should look like a large, thick burger.) Wrap in plastic wrap. Chill in refrigerator for at least ½ hour (or in freezer for 15 minutes) while you prepare filling.

Roll out dough on lightly floured surface (or use a pastry cloth and rolling pin stockinette cover). Use a light, lifting motion. Roll equally in all directions, making sure to keep dough circular and mending cracks as they form. Roll about 2 inches larger than pie plate, about ⅛ inch thick. Use as directed.

note:
• Dough may be refrigerated for 3 or 4 days. For easier rolling, let dough stand at room temperature for a few minutes to soften slightly.

pareve pie crust (basic pastry)

This easy, versatile pastry contains no dairy or meat products.

$2/_3$ cup frozen shortening,	1 tsp. vinegar
cut in chunks	scant $1/_2$ cup ice water or orange juice
2 cups flour	(about $3 1/_2$ oz.)
$1/_2$ tsp. salt	

Yield: Two 9-inch
pie crusts.
Freezes well.

STEEL BLADE: Place shortening, flour and salt in processor. Process with 5 or 6 quick on/off pulses, stopping to check texture, until mixture begins to look like coarse oatmeal. Add vinegar. With machine running, add liquid in a steady stream through feed tube just until dough begins to gather around the blades, about 10 seconds after all the liquid is added. Do not overprocess.

Remove dough from machine, press into a ball and divide in 2 equal pieces. (Dough should look like a large, thick burger.) Wrap in plastic wrap. Chill dough in refrigerator for at least 1 hour before rolling out. (May be made 2 or 3 days in advance.)

Roll out dough on lightly floured surface (or use a pastry cloth and rolling pin stockinette cover). Use a light, lifting motion. Roll equally in all directions, making sure to keep dough circular and mending cracks as they form. Roll about 2 inches larger than pie plate, about ⅛ inch thick. Use as directed.

variation:
• Use 1 egg plus enough ice water to equal a scant ½ cup. This crisp, golden pastry is ideal for turnovers or pies.

flaky ginger ale pastry

Versatile, easy and dairy-free! Use stick margarine, not soft tub margarine. Otherwise, the dough will be difficult to roll out. Excellent for Tuna Strudel (p. 75).

1 cup plus 1 Tbsp. flour
½ cup frozen margarine, cut in 6 or 8 pieces

$^1/_4$ cup ginger ale or soda water
1 $^1/_2$ tsp. vinegar or lemon juice

STEEL BLADE: Process flour and margarine with 4 or 5 on/off pulses (2 to 3 seconds each time), until mixture looks like coarse oatmeal. Add liquids through feed tube while machine is running. Process just until dough begins to gather in a mass around the blades, 8 to 10 seconds. Do not overprocess.

Remove dough from machine, divide into 2 balls and wrap in plastic wrap. Chill in the refrigerator at least 1 hour or overnight. The colder the dough, the easier it is to roll. Roll out on lightly floured surface (or on a pastry cloth, using a rolling pin stockinette cover for easier rolling). Use as directed.

Dough may be frozen baked or unbaked. Recipe may be doubled.

cream cheese pastry

pies and pastries

Quick and easy!

$1/2$ cup butter or margarine,
cut in chunks
$1/2$ cup cream cheese or
cottage cheese

1 cup flour
2 Tbsp. sugar (optional)

STEEL BLADE: Combine all ingredients in processor. Process until dough forms a ball on the blades, 18 to 20 seconds. Chilling is not necessary. Roll out on lightly floured surface (or on a pastry cloth, using a rolling pin stockinette cover for easier rolling).

Use as directed. Freezes well. Recipe may be doubled.

chocolate cream cheese pastry

1 cup cream cheese,
cut in chunks
1 cup butter or margarine,
cut in chunks

6 Tbsp. sugar
2 cups flour
$1/4$ cup cocoa

STEEL BLADE: Combine all ingredients in processor. Process until dough forms a ball on the blades, 18 to 20 seconds. Divide dough into 4 balls, wrap in plastic wrap and refrigerate for ½ hour for easier rolling. Roll out on lightly floured surface (or on a pastry cloth, using a rolling pin stockinette cover for easier rolling).

Use as directed. Freezes well.

ruby-red rhubarb pie

Rhubarb roots and
leaves are poison-
ous, so be sure to
trim the stalks
carefully and wash
them well.

Yield: 8 servings.
Freezes well.

Standard Butter Pastry (p. 206)
  or any pastry for a 2-crust pie
2 Tbsp. bread crumbs
4 cups sliced rhubarb

1 1/4 cups sugar (or to taste)
1/3 cup flour
1 Tbsp. butter or margarine

Preheat oven to 425°F.

Prepare pastry and chill as directed. Roll out one portion into large circle and transfer to ungreased 9-inch pie plate. Trim off overhanging edges. Sprinkle with crumbs.

SLICER: Cut rhubarb to fit feed tube. Slice, using firm pressure. Measure 4 cups. Mix with sugar and flour. Fill pastry shell with rhubarb filling; dot with butter or margarine. Roll out remaining pastry and place over filling. Trim away edges, leaving ½-inch border all around. Tuck top crust under bottom crust. Flute edges. Cut several slits in crust and sprinkle lightly with sugar.

Bake for 40 to 50 minutes, until golden.

variations:

- Substitute 2 to 3 cups sliced strawberries for half the rhubarb.
- Replace rhubarb with 4 cups pitted cherries. If using canned drained cherries, baking time will be 35 to 45 minutes.

fresh strawberry flan

Very berry good!

Yield: 8 servings.
Best served
the same day.
Do not freeze.

Standard Butter Pastry,
  1/2 recipe (p. 206)
1 pkg. vanilla pudding (not instant)

1/2 cup red currant jelly or apricot jam
1 pint strawberries, hulled and cut in
  half lengthwise

Preheat oven to 400°F.

Prepare pastry as directed. Roll out chilled pastry on floured pastry cloth into 12-inch circle. Transfer to 11-inch flan pan with removable bottom. Roll the rolling pin over edges of pan to cut away excess dough. Line pastry with aluminum foil; fill with uncooked rice or beans to weigh down pastry.

Bake for 10 minutes. Remove foil and rice or beans. Bake 5 minutes longer, until golden. Cool completely.

Prepare pastry cream or pudding according to directions. Place a piece of waxed paper directly on surface to prevent skin from forming; cool completely. (May be prepared in advance up to this point.)

Heat jelly or jam on low heat until melted (or microwave on HIGH for 45 seconds). Brush bottom of pie shell lightly with jelly. Allow to set for 5 minutes, then add pastry cream. Do not fill more than ½ inch thick. Arrange berries attractively over pastry cream. Brush with remaining jelly. (If using apricot jam, first press it through a sieve.) Refrigerate flan for 2 to 3 hours before serving.

variation:

- Use a colorful combination of fresh or canned fruits arranged in an attractive design (e.g., sliced kiwis, apricots, seedless grapes, berries, mandarin oranges). If using canned fruits, drain well and pat dry.

pumpkin pie

A Thanksgiving tradition that's good any time of year! If using fresh pumpkin purée, drain it well.

Standard Butter Pastry, ½ recipe (p. 206)	½ tsp. ground ginger
1½ cups canned or fresh Pumpkin Purée (p. 59)	¼ tsp. each nutmeg and ground cloves
¾ cup brown sugar, packed	dash salt
2 eggs	1¼ cups whipping cream
1¼ tsp. ground cinnamon	¼ cup orange liqueur
	12 pecan halves, for garnish

Yield: 8 servings. Serve with lightly sweetened whipped cream. Can be frozen up to a month.

Preheat oven to 425°F.

Prepare pastry as directed. Roll out chilled dough on floured pastry cloth about 2 inches larger than pie plate. Carefully transfer to deep 9-inch pie plate. Trim off overhanging edges, leaving about ½ inch excess. Turn edges under and make a decorative fluted edge.

STEEL BLADE: Process pumpkin, brown sugar, eggs, spices and salt for 30 seconds, until blended. Scrape down sides of bowl as necessary. Pour whipping cream and liqueur through feed tube while machine is running; process a few seconds longer to blend. Pour filling into unbaked pie shell.

Bake for 15 minutes, then reduce heat to 325°F and bake 40 to 45 minutes longer. When done, knife inserted into center of pie will come out clean.

Place 8 pecans in a circular design around edge of warm pie and press lightly into filling. Arrange remaining 4 pecans in a smaller circle.

pareve (non-dairy) variation:

- Use Pareve Pie Crust (p. 206). Replace whipping cream with non-dairy creamer.

pecan pie

They'll go nuts over this!

Yield: 8 servings.
May be frozen.

9-inch unbaked pie shell	1 tsp. vanilla or rum extract
1 cup sugar	$1/2$ tsp. salt
4 eggs	$1 1/2$ cups pecans
1 cup dark corn syrup	

Preheat oven to 350°F.

Prepare your favorite pastry and place in ungreased 9-inch pie plate.

STEEL BLADE: Process sugar, eggs, corn syrup, vanilla or rum extract and salt for 8 to 10 seconds, until blended. Add pecans and mix in with 1 or 2 very quick on/off pulses. Pour filling into pie shell.

Bake for 55 to 60 minutes, or until knife inserted in center of pie comes out clean.

chef's tip:

• To catch spillovers, place a foil-lined cookie sheet under the pie before baking it.

choc' full of pecan pie

Easy as pie.

Yield: 8 servings.
May be frozen.

9-inch unbaked pie shell	$1 1/2$ cups pecans
2 squares (2 oz.) unsweetened chocolate	3 eggs
2 Tbsp. butter or margarine	$1 1/4$ cups sugar

Preheat oven to 375°F.

Prepare your favorite pastry and place in ungreased 9-inch pie plate. Melt chocolate and butter or margarine (2 to 3 minutes on MEDIUM [50%] in the microwave). Let cool.

STEEL BLADE: Process pecans with 5 or 6 quick on/off pulses, until coarsely chopped. Empty bowl and set aside. Process eggs and sugar for 5 seconds. Add melted chocolate mixture and process 8 to 10 seconds longer, until blended. Add nuts with 1 or 2 very quick on/off pulses. Pour mixture into unbaked pie shell.

Bake for 35 to 45 minutes, just until set. Pie will firm up when cooled.

fudge ribbon baked alaska pie

Yield: 8 servings.

9-inch baked pie shell
peppermint candy
  ($1/2$ cup crushed)
$3/4$ cup sugar
$1/2$ cup evaporated milk
  (not condensed milk)

1 cup chocolate chips
1 tsp. vanilla extract
1 quart vanilla ice cream, slightly softened
3 egg whites
$1/4$ tsp. cream of tartar
6 Tbsp. sugar (see Chef's Tips, below)

Prepare pie crust, bake and cool completely.

STEEL BLADE: Drop peppermint stick candy through feed tube while machine is running. Process until crushed. Set aside.

Combine the ¾ cup sugar and evaporated milk in saucepan. Simmer until sugar is dissolved, stirring occasionally.

Process chocolate chips until finely chopped, about 30 seconds. Pour hot milk mixture and vanilla extract through feed tube while machine is running; process until chocolate is melted and mixture is blended. Cool chocolate sauce completely.

Reserve 2 Tbsp. candy for garnish and stir remainder into ice cream. Press half of ice cream into pie shell. Cover with half of cooled chocolate sauce. Repeat with remaining ice cream and sauce. Wrap well and freeze until firm.

Preheat oven to 475°F about 15 minutes before serving. Using an electric mixer, beat egg whites with cream of tartar until soft peaks form. Gradually beat in the 6 Tbsp. sugar. Continue beating until whites are stiff and no sugar can be felt when you rub the meringue between your fingertips. Spread meringue over frozen filling, sealing edges well. Swirl meringue to make decorative peaks. Place on baking sheet and bake for 3 to 5 minutes, until golden. Sprinkle reserved candy over meringue. Serve immediately.

variation:

• Omit peppermint candy. Substitute your favorite flavor of ice cream.

chef's tips:

• To prevent meringue from weeping, process the 6 Tbsp. sugar on the STEEL BLADE until fine, about 1 to 2 minutes, before beating it into the egg whites.
• Dip knife into water before cutting pie to prevent meringue from sticking to knife. Repeat as needed.

index

Recipes which are suitable for Passover, or that have a Passover variation, are marked with an asterisk*.

index

index

index

index

index

index

Savor the Good Life®

Cuisinart countertop appliances are designed to be versatile and easy to use. They reduce the time you spend on the mundane tasks of food preparation, allowing you the freedom to be more creative in the kitchen. Look for the latest Cuisinart collection of innovative products.

Grind & Brew Thermal™
10-Cup Automatic Coffeemaker

Brew Central™
12-Cup Programmable Coffeemaker

Supreme™ Commercial Quality
Ice Cream Maker

4-Cup Rice Cooker

Electric Fondue Set

Grind Central™
Coffee Grinder

Cuisinart®
SAVOR THE GOOD LIFE®

www.cuisinart.com